IANN ROBERT ADAMS AMY ADLER JOHN AHEARN CRAIGIE AITCHISON LAYLAH
VID ARMSTRONG RICHARD ARTSC  SHKIN KUTLUG ATAMAN
A STEPHAN BALKENHOL FIONA BARNEY TINA BARNEY
LITZ LOTHAR BAUMGARTEN PETE HILLA BECHER ROBERT
ASHLEY BICKERTON RICHARD BILLINGHAM NAYLAND BLAKE PETER BLAKE
SKY LOUISE BOURGEOIS ELLEN BROOKS CECILY BROWN GRISHA BRUSKIN
JEAN-MARC BUSTAMANTE SOPHIE CALLE PETER CAMPUS JAMES CASEBERE
OHN CHAMBERLAIN MICHAEL RAY CHARLES SARAH CHARLESWORTH SANDRO
JEANNE-CLAUDE ANNE CHU CHUCK CLOSE WILLIE COLE HANNAH COLLINS
MICHAEL CRAIG-MARTIN MARTIN CREED GREGORY CREWDSON RUSSELL
CY DAVIDSON KARIN DAVIE RICHARD DEACON TACITA DEAN WIM DELVOYE
IEKE DIJKSTRA MARK DION PETER DOIG LEONARDO DREW MARLENE DUMAS
N MITCH EPSTEIN INKA ESSENHIGH RICHARD ESTES TONY FEHER RACHEL
DAVID WEISS SYLVIE FLEURY TOM FRIEDMAN KATHARINA FRITSCH MAUREEN
RGE BRUCE GILDEN LIAM GILLICK JIM GOLDBERG NAN GOLDIN LEON GOLUB
NEY GRAHAM JOANNE GREENBAUM TIMOTHY GREENFIELD-SANDERS TOLAND
HARD HAMILTON CHRIS HAMMERLEIN JANE HAMMOND MONA HATOUM JOSÉ
HIRSCHHORN NICKY HOBERMAN JIM HODGES HOWARD HODGKIN CANDIDA
INES JIM ISERMANN BILL JENSEN CHRIS JOHANSON JOAN JONAS BRAD
KURT KAUPER MIKE KELLEY MARY KELLY WILLIAM KENTRIDGE ANSELM
KUSAMA ROBERT KUSHNER JIM LAMBIE LIZ LARNER JONATHAN LASKER
EVINTHAL GLENN LIGON DONALD LIPSKI SHARON LOCKHART RICHARD LONG
RT MANGOLD SYLVIA PLIMACK MANGOLD SALLY MANN CHRISTIAN MARCLAY
MCELHENY BARRY MCGEE ANNETTE MESSAGER JOEL MEYEROWITZ DUANE
A TRACEY MOFFATT DONALD MOFFETT MARIKO MORI YASUMASA MORIMURA
MULLICAN VIK MUNIZ TAKASHI MURAKAMI ELIZABETH MURRAY YOSHITOMO
H NOLAND DANIEL OATES MANUEL OCAMPO MARCEL ODENBACH ALBERT
TORRES TOM OTTERNESS TONY OURSLER BILL OWENS ROXY PAINE MIMMO

PALADINO   PANAMARENKO   CORNELIA PARKER   MARTIN PARR   RICHARD
PATTERSON   A.R. PENCK   SIMON PERITON   RAYMOND PETTIBON   RICHARD
PETTIBONE   ELIZABETH PEYTON   PAUL PFEIFFER   RICHARD PHILLIPS   PIERRE
ET GILLES   JACK PIERSON   ADRIAN PIPER   LARI PITTMAN   JAUME PLENSA
KEN PRICE   STEPHEN PRINA   RICHARD PRINCE   MARC QUINN   FIONA RAE
MICHAEL RAEDECKER   ARNULF RAINER   MEL RAMOS   NEO RAUCH   ROBERT
RAUSCHENBERG   DAVID REED   PAULA REGO   TOBIAS REHBERGER   JAMES RIELLY
BRIDGET RILEY   PIPILOTTI RIST   DOROTHEA ROCKBURNE   ALEXIS ROCKMAN
UGO RONDININE   JAMES ROSENQUIST   SUSAN ROTHENBERG   MICHAL ROVNER
NANCY RUBINS   THOMAS RUFF   ALLEN RUPPERSBERG   EDWARD RUSCHA
LISA RUYTER   TOM SACHS   SAM SAMORE   JÖRG SASSE   JENNY SAVILLE   KENNY
SCHARF   SEAN SCULLY   RICHARD SERRA   ANDRES SERRANO   JOEL SHAPIRO
JIM SHAW   CINDY SHERMAN   STEPHEN SHORE   JOSÉ MARÍA SICILIA   JAMES
SIENA   SANTIAGO SIERRA   AMY SILLMAN   LAURIE SIMMONS   SANDY SKOGLUND
ANDREAS SLOMINSKI   KIKI SMITH   RAY SMITH   ROY STAAB   DOUG & MIKE STARN
GEORGINA STARR   PAT STEIR   JOEL STERNFELD   JESSICA STOCKHOLDER
THOMAS STRUTH   JOCK STURGES   HIROSHI SUGIMOTO   DO-HO SUH   DONALD
SULTAN   LARRY SULTAN   PHILIP TAAFFE   ANTONI TÀPIES   JUERGEN TELLER
ROBERT THERRIEN   WOLFGANG TILLMANS   FRED TOMASELLI   ARTHUR TRESS
ROSEMARIE TROCKEL   TUNGA   SPENCER TUNICK   LUC TUYMANS   KEITH
TYSON   NICOLA TYSON   IKÉ UDÉ   JUAN USLÉ   JEFFREY VALLANCE   GUS
VAN SANT   BILL VIOLA   CHARLINE VON HEYL   CATHERINE WAGNER   KARA
WALKER   JOHN WATERS   GILLIAN WEARING   MARNIE WEBER   CARRIE MAE
WEEMS   WILLIAM WEGMAN   LAWRENCE WEINER   JAMES WELLING   JOHN
WESLEY   TOM WESSELMANN   FRANZ WEST   PAE WHITE   RACHEL WHITEREAD
T.J. WILCOX   SUE WILLIAMS   FRED WILSON   JANE & LOUISE WILSON   TERRY
WINTERS   JOEL-PETER WITKIN   CHRISTOPHER WOOL   RICHARD WRIGHT
ERWIN WURM   B. WURTZ   KAREN YASINSKY   LISA YUSKAVAGE   ANDREA ZITTEL

No. 1

FIRST WORKS by 362 ARTISTS

Edited by Francesca Richer & Matthew Rosenzweig

d·a·p

Gerhard Richter
Table (Tisch)
1962
Oil on canvas
35¹/₂ x 44¹/₂ inches
(90.2 x 113 cm)

Barnett Newman
Onement I
1948
Oil on canvas
27¹/₄ x 16¹/₄ inches
(69.2 x 41.3 cm)

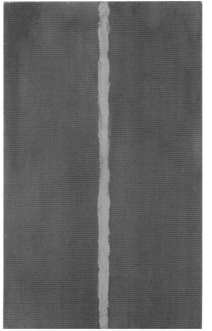

Several years ago, we attended a lecture on Gerhard Richter at The Museum of Modern Art in New York. Robert Storr, then the curator of the museum's Department of Painting and Sculpture, was showing slides of the works that were to be included in Richter's 2002 retrospective. Richter had chosen *Table* (Tisch), 1962, to be the first piece in both the show and in the accompanying catalogue raisonné; although he had been painting for a couple of years when he made it, Richter considered it his first work, the painting in which he recognized himself for the first time. Storr mentioned that Barnett Newman viewed his own painting *Onement I* in a similar way, as his personal artistic breakthrough and the true beginning of all that followed. We found the idea of an artist looking at his or her method by way of the "first work" intriguing, and wondered what other artists would choose as their "number one." An investigation into the origins of art-making, it sounded like a good subject for a visual book.

We drafted a call for entries and sent it out to a handful of artists we had worked with before, on books or in magazines. With positive responses and lots of interest in the idea, we expanded our list and sent out several more rounds. In a matter of months we had boxes of entries from all over the world, with new packages arriving every day.

Our invitation had been intentionally open-ended, so that each artist could bring his or her own meaning to the project—a personal interpretation of the "first work." The results were vast and varied. Some artists sent pieces from their childhoods, or works they found embarassing yet somehow still pertinent; others chose more recent or well-known works. Many, it turned out, like Richter and Newman, had a piece they already considered their "number one," the marker of a turning point that affected subsequent works. The common thread was how welcoming all were of the chance to look back and reflect, and how often what they came up with seemed to surprise even themselves.

These generous submissions gave us a chance to view, from a new angle, the artists' ways of thinking—their inspirations, their occasional frustrations, and their breakthroughs. Together, they form an incredible document of the creative process. We hope you enjoy them as much as we did.

—FRANCESCA RICHER AND MATTHEW ROSENZWEIG

Magdalena Abakanowicz

80 Backs 1983 burlap and resin. Installation view near Calgary, Canada I created headless crowds. I wanted to confront man with himself, with his solitude in multitude. It happened that I lived in times when the population of the planet increased threefold, when millions were killed in wars, nations were and are manipulated by leaders. Theories and philosophies justified the extermination of entire tribes and races. Crowds behave like a brainless organism and act like a brainless organism, worshipping on command and hating on command. I saw crowds trampling themselves.

I suspect that inside the human skull, instincts and emotions overpower the intellect without us being aware of it. Growing aggressiveness has changed our reality. Terrorists and suicide bombers develop from despair in the face of military might. Innocence does not protect anyone.

I visualize my fears, building the fence of my immobile crowds between my reality and the existing one. I bewitch the phenomenon of the crowd. I change it into the bridge between all creations of nature.

In the '70s, I began to cast human bodies in burlap. No commissions, no collectors, no galleries. Burlap was like an image of the world under Soviet domination. Headless, often handless, and shell-like—this was enough to say what I wanted. The number of figures was growing year after year. With time, I also made them in bronze, aluminum, and iron. The entire population of standing, walking, and seated figures—the Crowds, the Flocks, and the others—are enough to fill a public square. There might be over fifteen hundred, but they have never been seen together.

One can find them in groups of 30, 50, 80, 95, 112, 250, in museums and collections in different parts of the world. They constitute a sign of lasting anxiety; a warning.

I do not make editions. Every figure is an individuality.

There is another aspect of quantity: the law of nature, which also concerns us.

A crowd of people or birds, insects or leaves, is a mysterious assemblage of variants of a certain prototype. A riddle of nature's abhorrence of exact repetition or inability to produce it. Just as the human hand cannot repeat its own gesture, I invoke this disturbing law, switching my own immobile herds into that rhythm.

GRAIN OF SAND

I immerse myself in the crowd like a grain of sand in the friable sands. I am fading among the anonymity of glances, movements, smells, in the common absorption of air, in the common pulsation of juices under the skin. I become a cell of this boundless organism of the crowd, like others already integrated and deprived of expression. Destroying each other, we regenerate. Through hate and love, we stimulate each other.

b. Falenty, Poland, 1930. Lives and works in Warsaw, Poland.

Marina Abramović

Rhythm 10 (above) 1973 performance, Museo d'Arte Contemporanea, Villa Borghese, Rome

Rhythm 10 (top right) 1973 black-and-white photograph with letterpress text panel, edition of 16, 3 APs, 29³/₄ x 39¹/₂ inches (75.6 x 100 cm) framed

The first version of this performance involving twenty knives was presented at a festival in Edinburgh in 1973. In those days, I approached the statements in a simple manner, to be viewed like a music score, to act out the works by instruction. I never explained more than that.

PREPARATION

I lay a sheet of white paper on the floor. I lay twenty knives of different shapes and sizes on the floor. I place two cassette recorders with microphones on the floor.

PERFORMANCE

I switch on the first cassette recorder. I take the knife and plunge it, as fast as I can, into the flesh between the outstretched fingers of my left hand. After each cut, I change to a different knife. Once all the knives (all the rhythms) have been used, I rewind the tape. I listen to the recording of the first performance. I concentrate. I repeat the first part of the performance. I pick up the knives in the same sequence, adhere to the same rhythm, and cut myself in the same places. In this performance, the mistakes of the past and those of the present are synchronous. I rewind the same tape and listen to the dual rhythm of the knives. I leave.

b. Belgrade, Yugoslavia, 1946. Lives and works in Amsterdam, The Netherlands.

Proposal for Autry Park, Houston 1990 concrete, steel, light, water, grass, and trees, 40 x 200 x 416 feet (12.2 x 61 x 126.8 m)

Because I have to believe (at least for the time being) in what I'm doing *now* and not what I did *then*; because I'm an architect, I hope, and not an artist; because "Vito Acconci is dead, long live Acconci Studio," my choice is a park we proposed in 1990 for Houston.

A plot of land is pivoted, at its center, so that one half rises above ground and one half falls below; the pivoted plane is divided and then each division is subdivided, further and further, each smaller space pivoting in a different division; you walk through the space as if in a maze, finding the entrance to each division.

Acconci Studio started in 1988. For its first few years, and for the years before that when I did some public spaces myself, the projects *added* to a site: They replicated elements of the site, they installed conventions within the site. The Houston project brought us down to zero, leveled us to the ground. Rather than build something *on* the site, we built *with* the site. It was "only" landscape architecture; but we *built* the landscape, we built *by means of* the landscape. From there we could go on to build up and down and across and through; we had found a place, we had a ground to stand on, we had made a footing for ourselves, we could go on to do architecture.

Franz Ackermann

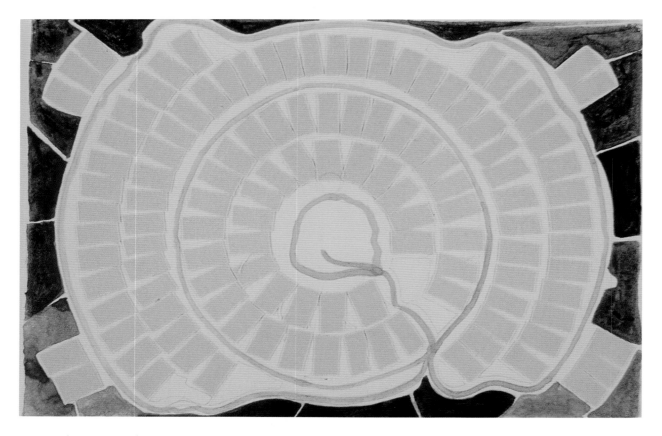

Untitled (Mental Map) 1994 mixed media on paper, 5¹/₈ x 7¹/₂ inches (13 x 19 cm) Marc and Allan Gould, where are you now? During my abidance in Hong Kong, I shared the same dormitory with Marc and Allan Gould. These two street guitar players from Scotland gave me an elementary education in how to move, where to eat, and where to drink without money. While standing on a street corner and not paying attention for a second, I lost them. They disappeared and I've missed them to this day.

b. Neumarkt St. Veit, Germany, 1963. Lives and works in Berlin, Germany.

Colorado Springs 1968–1972 silver gelatin print, 6 x 6 inches (15.2 x 15.2 cm) My intention was to record the newly fractured landscape of Colorado Springs. Unexpectedly the picture also suggested wholeness. This paradox set me to exploring.

b. Orange, NJ, USA, 1937. Lives and works in Astoria, OR, USA.

Amy Adler

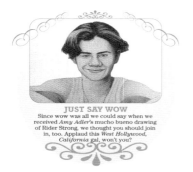

JUST SAY WOW

Since wow was all we could say when we received *Amy Adler's* mucho bueno drawing of Rider Strong, we thought you should join in, too. Applaud this *West Hollywood, California* gal, won't you?

BOP 1995 *BOP* magazine I made a drawing of this young actor from *BOP* magazine and sent it back to the magazine's "P.S. I Love You" section. This section is where love sick admirers can send their drawings of their beloved idols (the instructions are to send reproductions only, no originals please). Eight months later I was in Ralph's supermarket looking in the magazine and there was my drawing!

b. New York, NY, USA, 1966. Lives and works in Los Angeles, CA, USA.

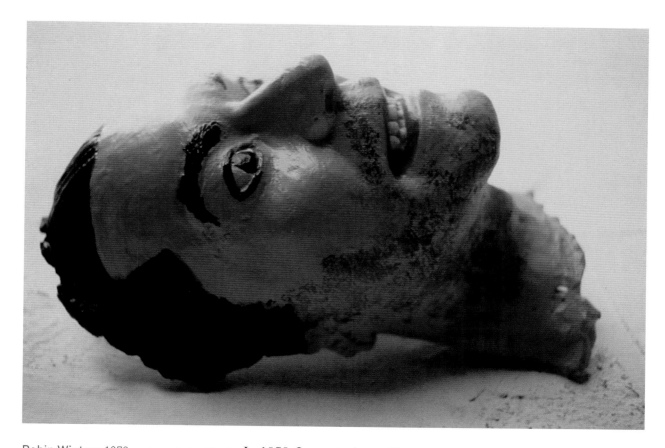

Robin Winters 1979 acrylic on plaster, life-size In 1978, I was staying at Patty Astor's East 10th Street apartment. I was planning to make a monster movie and I found a book on makeup. I was practicing face-casting with friends. Tom Otterness had shown me face-casts of indigenous peoples from the Museum of Natural History. Robin Winters was organizing a Colab theme show he called "The Dog Show." I made two casts of him, which were presented as *A dog and his master.* The "master cast" was painted like a "scary-manic" Robin. Later that month my brother Charlie suggested I try casting at Stefan Eins's Fashion Moda place in the Bronx. I went there almost every day for most of 1979. We called the project *The South Bronx Hall of Fame.*

b. Binghampton, NY, USA, 1951. Lives and works in New York, NY, USA. 11

Craigie Aitchison

Crucifixion and Angels 1960 oil on canvas, 44 x 34 inches (112 x 86.5 cm) In 1955, I went for the first time to Italy, and it wasn't until I traveled by car between Siena and Rome that I learned about dark color. I was completely struck by the dark raw umber fields and the white oxen and the white birds circling around tractors against the dark, things that I hadn't seen before.

As a result, I discovered what I should probably have known anyway, that dark could be beautiful. So, when I came back home in 1956, I painted a dark purple landscape, followed by a bright one of butterflies in a landscape. Then, in 1960, I painted *Crucifixion and Angels*, completely as a result of that trip to Italy and seeing for the first time what dark pictures could be.

Then, in 1961 I painted my first black person. I paint some white people, but mostly black, I think as a result of going there, of seeing the color.

You can see how the bright color stands out when contrasted with darkness. Basically, I learned that black was beautiful.

b. Edinburgh, Scotland, 1926. Lives and works in London, England.

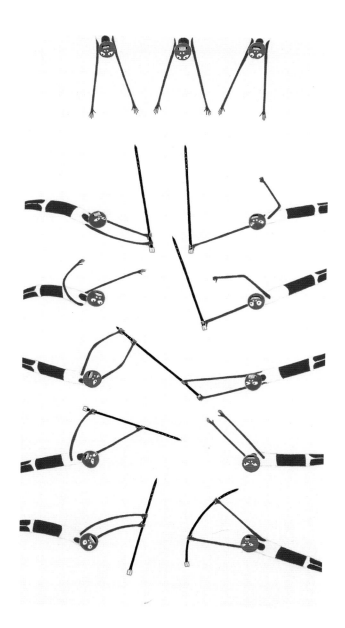

The Sinking of 3 Blueheads 1996

gouache on paper, 8 x 16 inches (20.3 x 40.6 cm)

This painting is part of a series called "Attack of the Blueheads." What makes it significant is that it marked the first time I started to understand the power of working in a series, which I have done since that time. While working on the *The Sinking of 3 Blueheads*, I knew that I wanted to see additional companion pieces (eventually there were six in this series) and that I was very interested in the way that narratives could be expanded and reconfigured in multiples.

Ghada Amer

Au Supermarche 1992 embroidery and acrylic on canvas, 39 x 53 inches (100 x 135 cm) *Au Supermarche* represents one of the first paintings I made where I felt that I had successfully accomplished the idea I had of painting with thread. I had been experimenting with thread as my medium, using it as my paint and I feel that is one of the first times that I was really satisfied with the outcome and knew that this was a medium I wanted and needed to explore in greater depth.

b. Cairo, Egypt, 1963. Lives and works in New York, NY, USA.

Joe Andoe

Untitled (Palm) 1987 oil on canvas, 20 x 24 inches (50.8 x 61 cm) Around the fall of 1986 I shed a skin, so to speak; some things became clear, and others fell away. I had come from Oklahoma to New York six years before and now I was moving into a studio on Broadway in a building full of small studios.

There I met a young artist who was born and bred in Manhattan, and he mirrored me back as a redneck. It felt the same as my first time in Europe and seeing what being American was.

One day he introduced me to his thoughts on morals and what a limiting and silly ideal they were and how he would do anything to further his career. And he did anything. Shocked but politely I told him I wouldn't do anything. His response was quick and he said, "that's because you are a fucked-up Christian."

Bingo.

That's it, that's exactly what I am, I thought. (It was always in the background culturally but I had never thought about it until then.) I went about recalling what I could remember of it and painted it.

My whole world pivoted on that moment and my sails popped out and the boat took off.

Genuine content that I could elaborate on with authenticity. (Personally anyway.)

This painting was about Mary and Jesus and Joseph and the flight to Egypt when they were hungry and Joseph could not reach the dates on the palm tree, so the angels bent it down.

Janine Antoni

Wean 1989–90 plaster and sheetrock, dimensions variable I consider *Wean* to be a pivotal piece for me because it mapped out a territory that I have been exploring ever since. This territory begins with the body and traces its evolution within the culture. The work consists of six concave impressions in a wall. From left to right, the first is my breast, the second is my nipple, then there are three latex nipples used for baby bottles, and the last is the store packaging that contained the three latex nipples. I chose the title *Wean* because I am interested in the stages of separation from the mother. The moment between the real nipple and the latex nipple is the crux of the piece. All of the objects that I deal with in my art share some characteristics with the latex nipple. They mediate our intimate interaction with our bodies, at times even replacing the body; but most importantly, they locate the body within the culture. I am not only interested in the stages of separation from the mother, but also in the stages of separation that we go through with our own bodies as we are weaned.

b. Freeport, Bahamas, 1964. Lives and works in New York, NY, USA.

Polly Apfelbaum

The Dwarves Without Snow White 1992 synthetic crushed stretch velvet, dye, cardboard boxes; Each box 27 x 16 x 3 inches (68 x 40.6 x 7.6 cm); overall 27 x 131 x 3 inches (68.6 x 332.7 x 7.6 cm) *The Dwarves Without Snow White* was first shown in 1992 in a group show titled "There Is a Light That Never Goes Out," after a song by the Smiths, curated by Terry R. Myers at the Amy Lipton Gallery in SoHo. The show was reviewed in the *New York Times* under the heading "Abstraction: A Trend That May Be Coming Back." I found that quite amusing. The piece was later included in a one-person show at the same gallery called "The Blot On My Bonnet."

Before this, I had shown prefabricated wood cutouts that worked with the space of the floor, with repetition and seriality in a way that is quite close to how I am working now. But in the end I decided that material (the synthetic crushed stretch velvet) and process (staining) were probably the decisive elements. They opened up a whole new area of formal investigation for me.

So, in that sense, this is the first of piece in a new body of work that deals with the material, formal and conceptual issues that I am still working with and thinking about today. I had moved the work away from fabricated and found objects. I limited my materials and introduced more painterly and color concerns: chance/order, flow, pop-abstraction-narrative. The piece is made up of eight closed cardboard garment boxes with synthetic velvet dye spills folded on top.

Finally, the title is also important, as continues to be the case today. I think of the titles as a chance to introduce narrative and concept into the work, to slant the meaning and interpretations. In this case, I thought of messy random spills as the emotions—the dwarves and Snow White

representing purity. I included a box for Snow White just in case she got her act together.

b. Philadelphia, PA, 1955. Lives and works in New York, NY, USA.

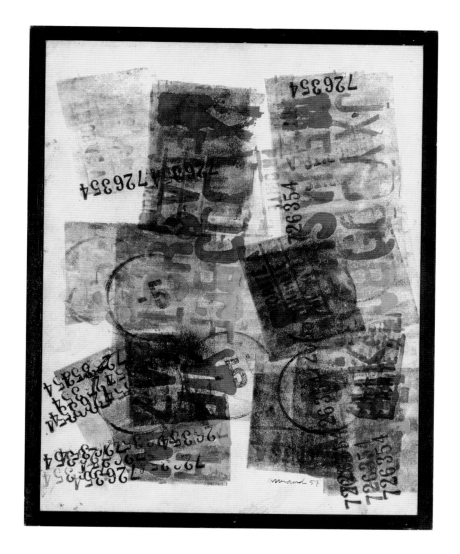

Priorité A 1957 rubber-stamped ink traces on paper; colors: green, red, black; 12³/₅ x 9³/₅ inches (32 x 24.5 cm) It is through the influence of Kurt Schwitters, whose work I saw in Paris in 1955, that I got the notion to use rubber stamps to make works of art.

David Armstrong

Bruce, Cambridge, 1974 gelatin silver print, 12¹/₈ x 18⁵/₈ inches (31.8 x 40.3 cm) I've
always liked dealing in my work with the things that are available to me,
be it light, people, or places. Kind of a wanting-what-you-have thing,
I guess. I am still ambivalent about the medium of photography: It has
the potential to be so powerful and so seldom achieves that. The incre-
mental nature of the process also drives me nuts. Whatever the medium
after a point it's all about you anyway. Once the elements are there,
I can try and make a picture. As time goes by, the pictures will show me
where to go and, if I'm lucky, something I may have never seen before.
If I had to soundbite what the content of the work is, I'd have to go
with "unfulfilled longing." Unapologetically romantic and currently
terribly out of fashion. It's still all light and shadows and a piece of
paper—who knows, right?

b. Boston, MA, USA, 1954. Lives and works in New York, NY, USA.

Portrait Zero 1961 wood, 45 x 27 x 6 inches (114.3 x 68.6 x 15.2 cm) This work has its origin in a story heard on the radio about a kid whose compulsive behavior was upsetting his father. The compulsive behavior was assembling pieces of scrap plywood (stacked in the garage) by nailing one on top of another, and yet another on top of that, etc. This reminded me of Cubist collages made by Braque and Picasso around the 1900s in Paris. I repeated the kid's experiment/obsession. It was the two-dimensional sneaking its way into the third dimension. This ultimately enabled/invited a co-presence of image and object.

b. Washington, DC, USA, 1923. Lives and works in New York, NY, USA.

Michael Ashkin

For Months He Lived Between the Billboards (later renamed No. 2) 1993
wood, metal, dirt, glue, paint, and HO-scale (1:87) models, 52 x 41 x 34 inches (132.1 x 104.1 x 86.4 cm)

The making of this piece followed a period of experimentation in sculpture. In the year prior I had created a number of full-scale enclosed structures designed for outdoor settings. These structures explored the possibility of creating spaces insulated from external power—spaces where the subject could assert some autonomy. However, none of these pieces gave me satisfaction. The pieces failed because they approached subjective space in an overly unmediated manner.

To work through ideas more quickly, I began making preliminary structures in miniature scale. At some point it occurred to me that if I considered the maquette as a self-sufficient medium, the scale change itself could add new layers of experiential complexity. Furthermore, if I were to use store-bought railroad-model components (in other words, mechanically produced miniature objects referring to full-scale, real-world commodities), the search for autonomous subjective space would take place not in a private, mythical world but within the constraints of the industrialized world.

For Months He Lived Between the Billboards takes place experientially in two spaces. The first is the narrative space within the miniature itself. In this space, the authorities have arrived at a billboard site where someone has built a small shelter between the two signs. The second is the space of the viewer's reality. Here, the sculptural presence of the model is not mitigated since it makes no attempt to deny the material of its own construction (crude table, rough edges). Thus a dialectical relation is established between both scales. The viewer may establish an empathetic relationship with the figure trapped between the billboards but remains equally in the exhibition space. If anything, the viewer's perspective is more akin to that of the authorities—perhaps that of a more privileged authority circling above in a helicopter.

b. Morristown, NJ, USA, 1955. Lives and works in Brooklyn, NY, USA.

Kutlug Ataman

kutlug ataman's semiha b. unplugged 1997 eight DVDs, single-screen projection with variable dimensions; edition of five This is the first frame of my first video.

I started working in the art world largely because of my experience with the film industry. In film, waiting for funding can be very frustrating, so while I was sitting around with my video camera waiting for the money for my second, and last, feature—a cult film about Turkish transvestites called *Lola + Bilidikid* (1998)—I had the idea for *kutlug ataman's semiha b. unplugged*, 1997. I started to shoot the first Turkish opera singer, Semiha Berksoy, who was then ninety-four years old. She had been left behind as opera evolved in Turkey during the twentieth century. What's fascinating is how this caused her to begin constantly changing her identity, rewriting and reinventing herself, constantly fighting to stay on stage though she wasn't wanted anymore. For me, this is a metaphor for death. Also, in Turkey, which is a very structured society, to have her discuss her own personal history was, for me, a way to mirror Turkish life and make fun of its artificiality.

The Semiha piece was also a way to reopen a critical discussion that was interrupted during the '70s, when Hollywood became so dominant and, perhaps, when *Cahiers du Cinéma* became more like *Daily Variety*. I wanted to engage the whole '60s discussion of objectivity in documentary and to make the point that it's impossible to make an objective film. By making *semiha b. unplugged* almost eight hours long—it's about an entire life, after all—I wanted the audience to have to return to this piece again and again without ever being able to see the whole thing, and to be forced to make their own Semiha out of the fragments that they do see.

b. Istanbul, Turkey, 1961. Lives and works in Buenos Aires, Argentina; London, England; and Istanbul, Turkey.

Frank Auerbach

b. Berlin, Germany, 1931. Lives and works in London, England.

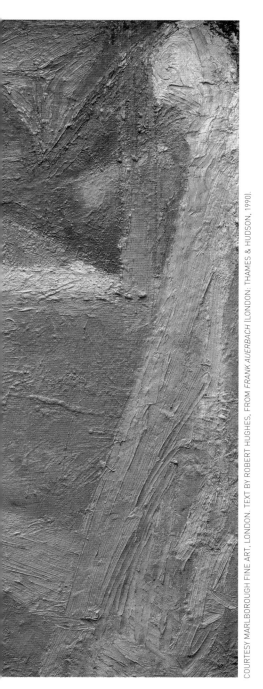

Summer Building Site, 1952 oil on board, 30 x 42 inches (76.2 x 196.7 cm) Frank Auerbach was able to finish a small painting he had been stalled on for weeks, and whose completion seemed to mark (however unassumingly) the beginning of his life as an artist. The subject was a building site in the Earl's Court Road. Auerbach had been there many times to make notes of its elements: the deep diagonal cut of the excavations, the small labouring figures and especially—by the instinctive stroke that lays open a peep, no more, at work to come—the triangular ladders and emphatic horizontal-vertical scaffolding that would predict the pictorial construction of his later paintings. He wanted prismatic color, a space defined entirely by color: "Making space with color was very much in the air then, and I took it in as an idea before I could really articulate it—at least it was more interesting than making an illustrative grid and covering that with some sort of color. I was very interested in [the color of] Ivon Hitchens." Today the grid of *Summer Building Site, 1952*, does look fairly illustrative, but its chrome yellow diagonals and the little red figures of bricklayer and hodman looked promisingly raw at the time and already, the impasto with which the vertical columns and the legs of ladders that lock the center of the painting together are rendered, there is a premonition (no more than that) of the thick surfaces to come. "Not until the very end did I get the courage to make some things bigger and others smaller than they were, to get the expression of the whole thing . . . When I had done it I recognized somehow that I had cut through my habits, I had made some shapes that seemed to conjure up a coherent plastic fact: I had done my own painting. I didn't know whether I would ever be able to do it again, but at least I knew what it felt like." —ROBERT HUGHES

Donald Baechler

Schwarzwald 1981–82 acrylic and fabric collage on canvas dropcloth, 105 x 152 inches (226.7 x 386.1 cm) In February 1981, after fourteen months on duty, I lost my job as the guard at Walter De Maria's *New York Earth Room*. I found a temporary job in Joe Glasco's studio, where I worked for a month while his regular assistant was on sabbatical.

My job had two main parts: to roll joints for Joe while he painted on scraps of canvas, and to glue his paintings together with gallons of Elmer's glue.

At night I'd go home and glue my own paintings together. *Schwarzwald* was painted during this period. Variations of this working method have persisted in my studio to this day.

b. Hartford, CT, USA, 1956. Lives and works in New York, and Columbia County, NY, USA.

SEMI-CLOSE-UP OF GIRL BY GERANIUM
(SOFT VIEW)

FINISHES WATERING IT – EXAMINES PLANT TO
SEE IF IT HAS ANY SIGNS OF GROWTH, FINDS
SLIGHT EVIDENCE – SMILES – ONE PART IS SAG-
GING – SHE RUNS FINGERS ALONG IT – RAISES
HAND OVER PLANT TO ENCOURAGE IT TO GROW.

Semi-close-up of Girl by Geranium (Soft View) 1966–68 acrylic on canvas, 68 x 56¹⁄₂ inches (172.7 x 143.5 cm) I did this at a time when I was doing works with text and photo on canvas and a lot of serial sequential photography as well. The lines are lifted from a script for D. W. Griffith's movie *Intolerance*. I guess I came across the script because I was doing a lot of movies and video at the time and looking at a lot of scripts. I liked the idea that it's not a frozen moment but it occurs in a very brief interval of time. It's almost like the description of a Futurist painting, but a Futurist painting of it would be very dynamic with a lot of bravado, and this is very simple. You could compare it to Giacomo Balla's *Dynamism of a Dog on a Leash*, which is a pretty simple thing too. I liked it because it's just a very simple gesture, but in my mind very beautiful.

Miroslaw Balka

The Jester Stanczyk Has Gone Nuts 1984 plaster, steel, textile, 59 x 40 x 50 inches (149.9 x 101.6 x 127 cm); Sculpture lost in 1985 I made this sculpture when I was a fourth-year student at Academy of Fine Arts in Warsaw.

Why number one?

I was making this sculpture based on the model dressed by my teacher in the costume of a jester. The jester was a kind of important figure in Polish history, and served as a wise adviser to the Polish king. Very often this figure was a popular subject for Polish artists. So from the beginning it was a rather normal task. But as I started to work on this sculpture, I got the feeling that certain aspects of the process were becoming clear. I gave the sculpture the features of my face hidden under the hood, and at the last moment I changed the sexuality of this figure by adding the element of female sexuality. This gesture was something more for me. I found at that moment, some other levels opened up. I felt a kind of freedom. And although the sculpture held many traces of my teacher, through some decisions the old frame was broken. The sculpture was made in clay, later cast in plaster, and after summer break it disappeared. Probably destroyed, as during the final show it was the subject of indignation. That's my number one.

b. Warsaw, Poland, 1958. Lives and works in Warsaw.

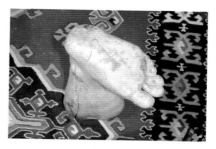

No Title 1971–76 photos taken in the artist's room in Kassel, Germany I was already interested in art by the age of twelve or thirteen. Maybe because my elder brother was studying fine art at the academy in our hometown of Kassel, I started to do 'artworks' of all kinds and from different materials. I was influenced by American Pop art and admired Documenta 5 in 1972, which I visited every day in the summer. Because my brother had a job in the show, I had the benefit of free entry! For myself, I worked mostly on sculptures (wood-carved: head, foot, hand) and assemblages, but also on painting and lots of drawings. My room was like a museum—I decorated all the walls, and, as you see in these photos, there was no place without something.

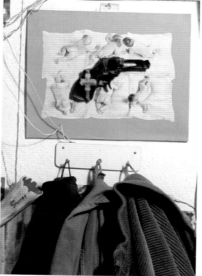

b. Fritzlar, Germany, 1957. Lives and works in Karlsruhe, Germany and Meisenthal, France.

Fiona Banner

IN 1996 I SPENT A WEEK IN A CINEMA, WATCHING ALL THESE FILMS, ON MY OWN — SOME TIMES TWO A DAY, THOUGH I'D ALREADY SEEN THEM BEFORE INDEPENDENTLY — SEEING THEM TOGETHER THEY ALL MERGED INTO ONE SEDUCTIVE, MYTHICAL, PORNOGRAPHIC HEROIC IMAGE OR STORY

THE NAM
by
fiona banner

it has been described as unreadable

The Nam is a 1000 page all text flick book. It is a compilation of total descriptions of well known Vietnam films, Full Metal Jacket, The Deer Hunter, Apocalypse Now!, Born on the Fourth of July, Hamburger Hill and Platoon. The films apparently never begin or end, but are described in their entirety, spliced together to make a gutting 11 hour supermovie.

Banner describes the films as if she is there, not influencing the plot, but always on set running alongside the action. The Nam is a constantly present, seamless account of the films. You might say that this book is the ultimate unedited text, a world in which *nothing is prioritised, but everything*. As you begin to know, you only see what you see.

'.....read at a stretch, Banner's simple, clear prose is hypnotic, and as exhausting as sitting through a Vietnam all-nighter. The text cascades in front of our eyes, melding and merging, and we read Banner's commentary as she's watching...'
Adrian Searle, Visual Arts, *The Guardian*, 22 April 1997.

Published in April 1997 by Frith Street Books with assistance from the Arts Council of England. The Nam is a 1000 page, 280,000 word paperback. Available from Frith Street Gallery, London at £35.00 and all leading bookshops in the UK and abroad.

I REALISED LATER, THAT EVERYTHING I HAD PREVIOUSLY KNOWN ABOUT VIETNAM WAS INFORMED BY THESE MOVIES. THE NAM WAS AN EXPLORATION OF MY OWN IGNORANCE

The Nam 1997 1,000-page all text flick book

Drawing Restraint 1 1987 performance documentation In *Drawing Restraint 1*, two mild inclines were constructed on either end of the studio. An elastic line from the floor was strapped to my thighs. As my body moved up the incline, resistance increased. Drawings were generated at the top of the slope and along the walls.

I made a number of Drawing Restraint pieces after the first one that all proposed that resistance is a prerequisite to creativity. The first Drawing Restraints were quite literally a restraint, self-imposed onto the act of drawing. With each succeeding piece, the project became more and more narrative, and my body became, increasingly, a character.

b. San Francisco, CA, USA, 1967. Lives and works in New York, NY, USA.

Tina Barney

Ada's Hammock 1982 chromogenic color print, 48 x 60 inches (121.9 x 152.4 cm) When I began making photographs, I found myself unconsciously and desperately trying to hold on to something precious. I wanted to make every living inch of life so as not to miss one detail: that crisp green-and-white New England landscape with the ubiquitous shingled houses, the porches, the green grass, and the weeping willows; the golf courses and the green-and-pink Lilly Pulitzer dresses that were the style of the times. And, with a stubbornness that I was born with, I demanded that you take notice—and never forget.

b. New York, NY, USA, 1945. Lives and works in Watch Hill, RI and New York, NY, USA.

Burt Barr

The Pool 1993 VIdeo projection still, 8 x 9 inches (20.32 x 22.9 cm) *The Pool*, a video work, begins with a man (Klaus Kertess) surveying the grounds of his summer home, deciding whether or not to take a swim. Nearby, and inching along the pool's edge is a woman (Dorothy Lichtenstein), who is seemingly oblivious to his presence. He takes the plunge, dives into the pool—much as I took the plunge leaving their narrative, as well as my own, behind. He swims from one end of the pool to the other, the water steadily receding until there's no more water in which to swim. It's a work of visual perception: the man swimming back and forth, from wall to wall, the eye traveling left to right, then down with the dropping water. It was a transitional work for me—the first fifteen minutes narrative, the latter fifteen, installation—a moving on to purely pictorial areas.

The Pool was shot in black and white. They became the only two colors I ever needed, a statement that I carried and held on to for many years, almost all of my works subscribing to that tenet.

It was my first one-person show in the art world, taking place at the Paula Cooper Gallery on Wooster Street in New York City, in 1993.

b. Lewiston, ME, USA, 1943. Lives and works in New York, NY, USA.

Judith Barry

PastPresentFutureTense 1977 three-projection performance/ installation, two tons of sand The year was 1977. I was hanging out in the performance/punk scene, commuting between the San Francisco Art Institute and the University of California, Berkeley, trying to figure out what it was that I should do with the rest of my life. It was the heyday of performance art—of Vito Acconci, Chris Burden, Yvonne Rainer, Lynda Benglis, Meredith Monk, and many, many others. Everyone was a performance artist and I wanted to be one, too. Every night it seemed that there were performances, all over. For me this was very exciting. It was also the heyday of alternative spaces. There were many in San Francisco. I began to approach various spaces with ideas for performances. Kathy O'Dell, the performance art historian, was working at 80 Langton Street (now called New Langton Arts). I proposed a performance to her and it was accepted. Below is the unedited description of that performance. I decided not to edit or change it for this context as I want to give the flavor of that time. I did that performance only once, but after it was over, I left the work in the space for a week as a performance installation. The slide projectors and slide track ran continuously and you could see the residue of my body in the three-foot sand mound that covered the floor around the hammock. Only about 75 people saw the performance. And it was much harder to dismantle than it was to put it up. But it gave me confidence and pleasure so I continued.

PastPresentFutureTense is a multidimensional performance environment created for 80 Langton Street, San Francisco on September 10, 1977. It is my model for the unconscious, a triptych of simultaneous events separated by time, a metaphor built into a metaphor and turned in on itself, predicated on the idea that the present is created out of the past in predicting the future and utilizing the synthesis as the primordial form belonging to consciousness.

The action occurs in a pre-constructed environment deliberately suggestive of other places, conjuring other associations. For example, the room where the piece takes place is covered in black mulch paper. It is shiny, hot, an inferno, an S&M den. At the back of the room there are three windows that are actually three rear-screen slide projections which continuously dissolve. The room seems like a stage, a train station, a waiting room, a rain-slicked night. It undulates. The piece begins with the slides which start slowly. Each window has a fragment of a story. Gradually the slides begin to go faster and faster—too fast to read and make sense of. At about two minutes into the performance, suddenly, a woman's voice. It is a beautiful voice. She seems to be reading the fragments, and when she reads, they make sense. All this time I have been in the space constructing a series of objects-images out of a piece of wire mesh—a dress, a dwelling, a moebius strip, a cape, a stair. After about 10 minutes the slides finish their first cycle and begin again and the woman continues reading, making yet another story out of these many fragments—all these other women's stories. By now I have made the mesh into a hammock and am swinging gently in the space. The voice becomes a whisper. It is a quiet time in the performance. The only audible sound is the sound track which consists of sand being poured into a bucket, marbles rolling across the floor and hitting other marbles or dropping into water and sand, pouring and pouring.

Suddenly buckets shoot out along the steel

b. Columbus, OH, USA, 1954. Lives and works in New York, NY and Berlin, Germany.

pulley system which until this time has been invisible. Slowly sand begins to fall on me, blowing through the air. As the last of the buckets finishes, a sliver opens in the ceiling, and several thousand pounds of sand pour down in a ribbon, totally covering me, like rain. When the sand pour finishes, the performance is over. I get up.

Robert Barry

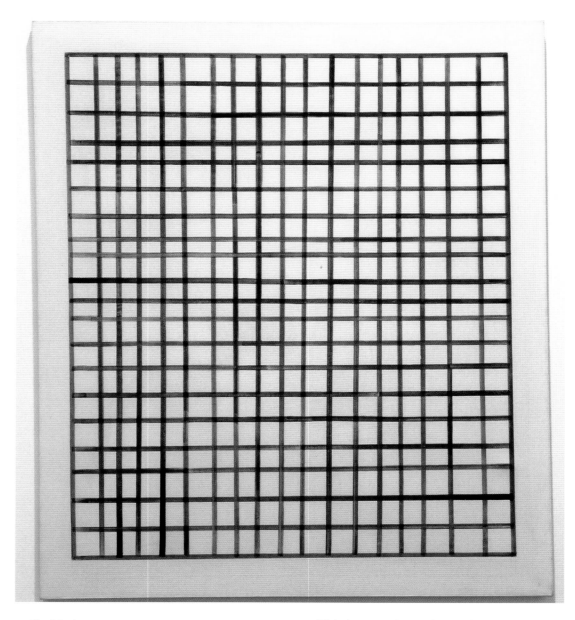

Untitled 1962 felt-tip ink pen on canvas, 42 x 36 (106.7 x 91.4 cm) This is an early work that is part of an ongoing process.

b. New York, NY, USA, 1936. Lives and works in Teaneck, NJ, USA.

Jennifer Bartlett

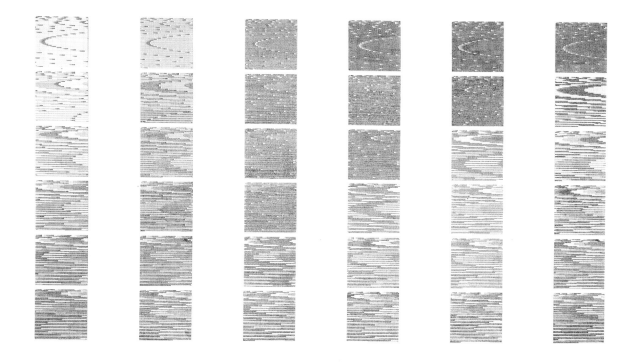

Series VIII (Parabolas) 1971 enamel over silkscreen grid on baked enamel, steel plates; 36 Plates, 12 x 12 inches (30.5 x 30.5 cm) each, 77 x 88 inches (195.6 x 223.5 cm) overall *Series VIII Parabolas* was the first piece that surprised me, that I liked.

b. Long Beach, CA, USA, 1941. Lives and works in New York, NY, USA.

Georg Baselitz

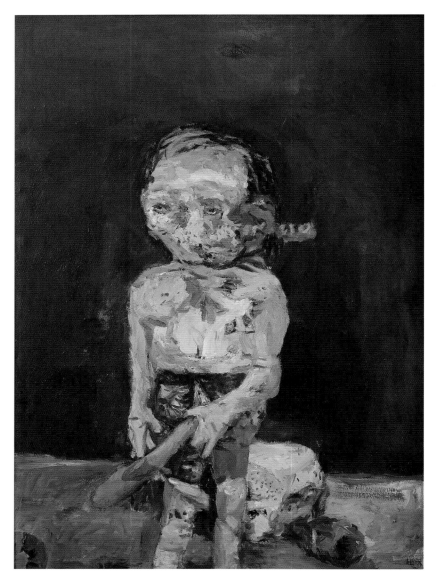

Die grosse Nacht im Eimer (The big night in a bucket) 1962–63 oil on canvas, 97¹/₂ x 70¹/₅ inches (250 x 180 cm)
This painting from 1963 caused a great shock and was aggressively criticized by the public. When I finished the painting, I was aware of its aftereffects. Today I believe that it was good to put my foot down loudly, because you couldn't expect at all that there would be any interest, curiosity or whatever, since there was no talk of painting at that time.

b. Deutschbaselitz, Germany, 1938. Lives and works in Derneburg, Germany and Imperia, Italy.

Tetraeder 1968 10 kg cobalt blue pigment stacked *Tetraeder* is a significant piece from 1968. I consider it one of my first ephemeral sculptures. Left behind by itself, indoors or outdoors, it was exposed to the process of time.

Peter Beard

Reaching Elephant, Kenya June 1960 silver gelatin
photograph, dimensions variable. Photo of Kenyan elephant
reaching for the last branch on a tree in Tsavo Park long before
the 1972–74 die-off of over 30,000 elephants and 5,000 black
rhinos from overpopulation (exceeding carrying capacity) and
laissez-faire mismanagement by National Parks—plus the regret-
table axing of Dr. Richard Laws and Dr. Murray Watson, directors
of the $400,000 Ford Foundation Research Grant studying the
disappearance of the trees in the 8,300-square-mile park, soon
to be nicknamed "Starvo."

The Thinker (Ode to Klee) 1967 pencil on paper, 14 x 18 inches
(35.6 x 45.7 cm) Hospitalized for malaria and hepatitis (in 1967), and
homage to Art School's Josef Albers' Bauhaus friend Paul Klee with
a rapidograph pen and NO RULER!

I consider both these images as my first meaningful
achievement, one in photography and the other in
art. Photography depends on tehnology; drawing
is done with hand and mind. In the case of *The
Thinker*, I did it without a ruler.

b. Tuxedo, NY, USA, 1938. Lives and works in Montauk, NY, USA, and Nairobi, Kenya.

Blast Furnace in Siegen Germany 1961 silver gelatin print, 19⁴/₅ x 23⁴/₅ inches (50.8 x 61 cm) This image was one of the very first we made with the larger 5 x 8-inch field camera. This has also been the negative format we have stayed with ever since.

Bernd Becher—b. Siegen, Germany, 1931. Hilla (Wobeser) Becher—b. Potsdam , Germany, 1934. Live and work in Düsseldorf, Germany.

Robert Bechtle

'56 Plymouth 1963 oil on canvas, 36 x 40 inches (91.4 x 101.6 cm)

The painting that I consider to be my turning point is *'56 Plymouth*, 1963. I was at that time taking tentative steps away from an expressionist painting style toward a kind of realism that I liked to think of as a non-style. *'56 Plymouth* was an ambitious attempt to fuse a modernist, flat-space format, with forms arrayed across the surface (I was thinking of Motherwell's *Elegies*), with an accurately depicted image. I lined up a picture, framed with glass, with an oval mirror and the window looking out from the studio. Both the picture and the mirror contained a partial self-portrait. The lower half of the window was covered by a café curtain which hid the car across the street. As the painting progressed I became more and more dissatisfied by the curtain so I took it down, exposing the car and providing one of those "lightbulb-going-on" moments. I found the experience of painting the car and stucco bungalow provocative and satisfying. Here was subject matter that still was unencumbered with "art" expectations.

I then decided to paint my own car, a '61 Pontiac, which I parked outside my studio window every day between two and four in the afternoon. The changing light prevented working any longer than that. After finishing this painting I wanted to do another. But how, since painting from life seemed clearly impossible? I tried making pencil and pastel sketches, but these proved inadequate for the degree of accuracy I felt I needed. So I resorted to taking photographs to work from. At first, black-and-white prints that I scaled up with a grid, and then color transparencies that I projected. Thus gradually opened up not just a method of working but a whole world of things to paint, my California life and surroundings. I think of it all as following from the removal of the café curtain in *'56 Plymouth*.

b. San Francisco, CA, USA, 1931. Lives and works in Berkeley, CA, USA.

Robert Beck

The Standing Deer 2000 mixed media, 11 x 4 x 5 inches (27.9 x 10.2 x 12.7 cm) I chose this piece to represent my first successful work because it is at once whimsical and unsettling, "arts 'n' craft" and abject.

b. Towson, MD, USA, 1959. Lives and works in New York, NY, USA.

Vanessa Beecroft

VB43 Gagosian Gallery 2, London, 2000, vb43.008.te digital C-print *VB43* could be considered my first work because only after I had done it, did I realize how old in my repertoire that image was. When I was nine years old, I obsessively made pencil drawings that were representations of my four dolls. They could only have orange, red, or yellow hair, and their names were German. When my mother saw pictures of *VB43*, she recognized an aesthetic that had been there for a long time. *VB43* was realized in London, where my father is from and where I lived as a baby. I was always attracted by English-looking features and pale skin tones and felt they were familiar to me and what I was missing after I was taken back to Italy. *VB43* is my most personal project, the one that doesn't really go far from myself, and from which I should step away if I want to grow.

Lynda Benglis

Quartered Meteor (right) 1969 lead, 57¹/₂ x 65¹/₂ x 64¹/₄ inches (146.1 x 166.4 x 163.2 cm) **Goliath** (far right) 1989 stainless steel mesh and aluminum, 95 x 30 x 18 inches (241.3 x 76.2 x 45.7 cm) The work *Quartered Meteor* was processed over a period of five years. The image was the first large water-blown system of polyurethane poured into the corner of a storage facility rented by Gordon Hart, my painter friend and husband and Klaus Kertess, the director of the Bykert Gallery. The work sat, cast directly in the corner, for some time in its original form: iron-oxide, black-pigmented polyurethane foam. I referred to the work as "The King of Flot"—others were doing large- and small-scaled works that experimented with different materials. Of interest were Hesse, Morris, Serra, Saret, and Sonnier with sculpture; and in painting earlier, in the late fifties, Yves Klein. After receiving a Guggenheim in the early '70s, I transposed "The King" into lead and called it "Quartered Meteor." I felt that this particular work had a frontal presence that "looked back at you" as a "being"; this was an aspect that continued with the later poured works as well as the knots. It seems to me that made my work different. Then and at other times, although I was taking a "formal" approach, the result was much more symbolic and romantic, as the forms themselves took on animate qualities.

While also thinking of the issue of painting as well as sculpture, I was making images that seemed to regurgitate from my own body. Likewise, but differently stated, the opposite of "throwing out" from one's own body, physically, was the coiling or knotting, "pulling in." The knotted forms resulted from the natural propensity of the body's reaction to the feelings of contraction and release. *Goliath* is a good example of illusion and allusion, aspects that I desire also. The psychological is symbolic in the work, as is natural phenomena.

b. Lake Charles, LA, USA, 1941. Lives and works in New York, NY; East Hampton, NY; and Santa Fe, NM, USA.

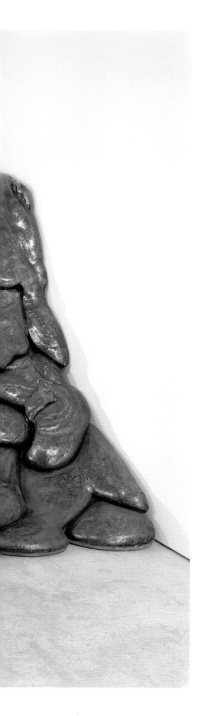

Jake Berthot

Little Flag Painting 1961 oil on canvas, 20 x 20 inches (50.8 x 50.8 cm) Having been raised by my grandparents on an eight-acre truck farm in central Pennsylvania, I loved the seasonal rituals but hated the work.

After being rejected from the navy, and being too inept to make any headway in a commercial art school in Pittsburgh, I studied window display at a school in New York that was one step above the art-school education then offered on the back of matchbook covers.

The bomb existed.

McCarthy and the Korean War were over. As advertised, the Communist threat and J. Edgar Hoover persisted. The arms race was in full swing.

In the big city for the first time, I missed a lot of school, saw a lot of jazz, Miles Davis—classical Miles, Cannonball, Coltrane, and the like, and got into some bad, bad stuff. After a year of good jazz and bad stuff, I knew enough to know that if I hung around long enough, I was going to die. Die real young.

I went south to Florida. Jacksonville. I married my high-school sweetheart, the poet Ginny McKenzie, and dressed windows in a fancy boutique. There was jazz and the Beats. There was Abstract Expressionism. There was *On the Road*, and *Howl*, and Jackson Pollock in *Life* magazine with a fuck-off look like he was James Dean, sitting in Long Island palm grass beside his Model-T. He was way more cool than Picasso.

I was a confused young man.

A part of me still believed in the Eisenhower myth, and I was convinced that if I played it right, I could be a real "growed-up" Ricky Nelson. Yeah, living the life of *Father Knows Best* with a boat, a red convertible, a beautiful wife, and two very well-behaved kids. Of course, an older boy, a younger girl. Later, our son John was born.

There was Martin and the yet to be visible Malcolm. Vietnam lay darkly in the wings.

Then Jacksonville exploded, and the Black uprising began. After some real scary involvement in Jacksonville, my wife and I headed for New York City, the land of integration—not segregation. A happy land, where blacks and whites loved and kissed one another as they strolled down the avenues hand in hand.

I was living in Bed Stuy, Brooklyn, when them happy Negroes damn near burned the place down.

Something wasn't quite straight. In fact, America was real twisted: duplicitous, deceptive, and full of downright lies. So long Ike, goodbye American Pie.

You could say the *Little Flag Painting* art talk gibberish was a total misread of Jasper Johns—which it was—but the guts of it came from being really pissed off. It was the first time feeling and seeing became one.

48   b. Niagara Falls, NY, USA, 1941. Lives and works in Accord, NY, USA.

49

Ashley Bickerton

The Love Story of Pythagoras Redhill 1981 stills from a super-8 film It's funny how ideas can percolate (like love unrequited or unresolved?) for two decades or more. The series of paintings I have worked on in Bali for the past decade came fully hatched from an aborted series (only two completed drawings) I did in a rented loft in NY one summer while still a student at CalArts. Some of the ideas within that series had themselves been percolating for a couple of decades before I found the right way to wring them into form.

What now seems even funnier is the greater time stagger with regard to these rediscovered film clips from some 23 years ago. I realized that my next body of work, still germinating, comes fully and unadulteratedly out of this student project. I had figured out at 21 what I was going to be happy doing at 45. Took a while to get here though.

The film was "very loosely" based on Malcolm Lowry's *Under The Volcano*, well "loosely" as in not at all. The actors were all painted like some Fauvist experiment in genre and the sets were constructed by hand with an intentionally inept realist literalism. The shadow of the slowly turning fan was wobbly in the hands of the drunkest person on the set. It oozed a ham-fisted and clichéd romanticism to the point of the ridiculous, which hopefully would take it to the point of the lucid. There were characters like *The Negative Man*, a fellow painted up like a black-and-white photo negative, and so on. I thought I was making a "New York–New Wave" film although I had never seen one. (It was sadly disappointing when I finally did).

I sometimes do wonder if this film was not my most natural voice, and if all the high-minded and dehydrated conceptualism so in vogue at CalArts during that time and later at the Whitney program didn't somehow derail it, take its piss and vinegar, and replace it with some formally correct procedure. Well, that would be my responsibility anyway, wouldn't it?

Convolutedly, it's now gotten to the point where I am tired of painting representations of people, and I actually want to paint people, paint on them, on their clothes, their backgrounds. This idea came to me, it seemed, independent of anything. Then your e-mail for this book arrived, and I realized it was weirdly serendipitous!

b. Bridgetown, Barbados, 1959. Lives and works in Bali, Indonesia.

Richard Billingham

Untitled 1990 color photograph on aluminum, 41³/₈ x 62¹/₄ (105 x 158 cm) I originally intended to take pictures like this one of my father in bed to paint from later. At the time I quite liked a lot of the paintings Walter Richard Sickert had done in mainly earth colors of very ordinary working-class people in their homes going about their day-to-day activities. I wanted to make some paintings like those and although I did some drawings from life I thought the best source material would be from photographs (Sickert also used photographs as source material). Much later I came to feel that some of these photographs could be seen as works in themselves. The picture here is probably the earliest of those photographs and was taken in 1990. I consider it my first decent work due to its calmness and serenity.

b. Birmingham, England, 1970. Lives and works in Stourbridge, England.

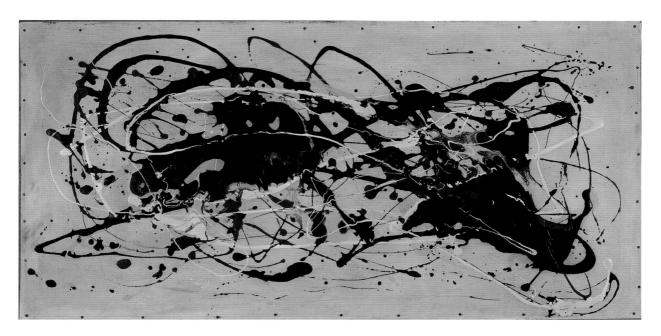

Untitled c. 1963–64 enamel on masonite, 36³/₄ x 72¹/₂ inches (93.3 x 184.2 cm) This painting has been part of my life for almost as long as I can remember. I can still see the basement of the building on West 101st Street where my father was the super, and I remember looking up at him as he drizzled enamel paint in the dim light, and I have some recollection of joining in. I must have been around four at the time. My parents had escaped the disapproval of their parents by leaving New Bedford, Massachusetts, and embracing a bohemian life in New York. The painting was part of that, and while my father eventually drifted away from making art, the flash of connection and power that I felt in painting together with him made my own artistic life possible. Since the time when it was finished, the painting has hung in the living room of every place my parents have lived, and one of my ongoing games was to fashion images from its abstract pours.
—NAYLAND W. BLAKE

b. New York, NY, USA, 1960. Lives and works in Brooklyn, NY, USA.

Peter Blake

Self-Portrait 1949 oil on board, 11¾ x 9 inches (29.9 x 22.8 cm)
This is my first self-portrait, from 1949.

b. Dartford, England, 1932. Lives and works in London, England.

Early Landscape 1968 oil on board, 12 x 16 inches (30.5 x 40.6 cm) When I made this painting I was 19. I don't remember what I was thinking about, but I loved moving the paint around with my brush and with my finger. At the time, I had just entered New York University, and had moved into the city from Long Island. I had just discovered the work of modern American artists like Marsden Hartley, Arthur Dove, Milton Avery, Charles Birschfield, Hans Hoffman, Mark Rothko, and Willem de Kooning—I still love all their work. I think there is a feeling in this early painting that has remained consistent in much of my work, even to this day.

b. New York, NY, USA, 1949. Lives and works in New York, NY, USA. 55

Barbara Bloom

Crittall Metal Window 1972 silkscreen print (1 of 10 images), 25 x 33 inches (63.5 x 83.8 cm) This series of posters was designed and silkscreen-printed in 1972, my last year at California Institute of the Arts. The posters were meant to be well designed, so well-designed as to render them unnoticeable or forgettable. They were meant to be hung individually, not in a group, nor in proximity to each other. They were meant to appear simultaneously in many rooms of a building (like portraits of royalty or dictators). The text: "Crittall Metal Windows — Manor Works Braintree" is legible in a beautiful deco typeface, but the words make no particular sense.

The image of a Modernist house in each version is different, but the difference is unnoticeable.

The effect I was attempting is that noticing a poster would elicit the sense of déjà vu. One wouldn't exactly recall having seen it before, but might vaguely remember the sense of familiarity.

These subjects of memory, of visibility and invisibility, of good and bad design, have remained the ongoing topic of my work for more than thirty years.

I chose *Crittall* as a seminal work to discuss, but I don't want to go without citing a painting I made when I was about seven years old. The work was entered in a local art show and contest. The painting is long gone. My parents have moved many times, and are not the particularly nostalgic sort. I recall that it was a poster-paint-on-newsprint painting of a girl and trees and maybe a jump rope (but maybe I am editing this element in). It was loosely painted and the appealing thing about the painting is that it somehow captured the windiness of the situation. I was unsure as to how I had achieved that effect, but happy that I had.

The painting won second place. I thought at the time that it was probably the windiness that had appealed to the judges, and felt confident that they had singled out this work. I also remember thinking that it was fair that the first-place winner was a hard-pencil drawing by Robby Robe. Robby was a tiny elfish kid, with a pointy nose and ears that were probably less exaggerated than in my memory. He drew all the time, and produced these labored, detailed, obsessive works. I remember thinking that he deserved to get a prize because his work was not "of something." This is the term I used then and only now do I recognize my early appreciation of the abstract and conceptual.

b. Los Angeles, CA, USA, 1951. Lives and works in New York, NY, USA.

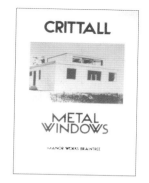

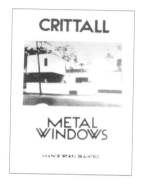

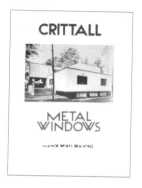

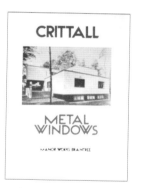

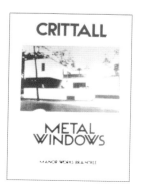

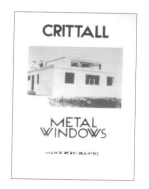

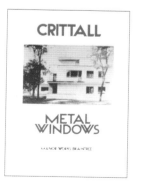

Christian Boltanski

L'attente 1967 installation At the time I was living at my
parents' and in my bedroom I was creating large dolls.
I didn't yet know whether I was doing this to make art
or whether I needed a feminine presence.

b. Paris, France, 1944. Lives and works in Malakoff, France.

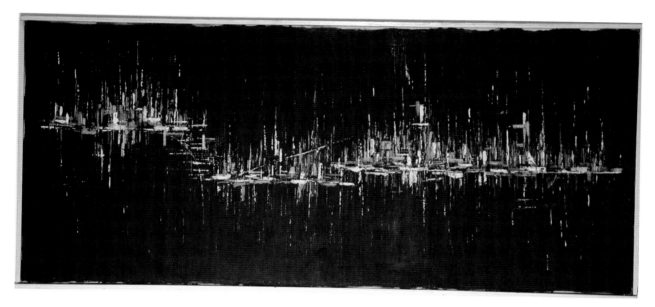

City Lights At Night 1953 oil on canvas, 6 x16 inches (91.4 x 40.6 cm)
Here is a very early oil painting on stretched canvas from 1953. I was eleven years old, and had already studied painting with a professional teacher for three years.

Louise Bourgeois

The Blind Leading the Blind 1947–1949 painted wood, 67⅛ x 64⅜ x 16¼ inches (170.4 x 163.5 x 41.2 cm)

The Blind Leading the Blind refers to the blush I experienced at the side of all of the people around me. My father was promiscuous, so I had to be blind to the mistress who lived with us. I had to be blind to the pain of my mother. I had to be blind to the fact that my sister slept with the man across the street. I felt an absolute revulsion toward everything and everybody, mostly for erotic reasons and sexual reasons. So, when I met an American student who was a puritan, I thought it was wonderful. I married that guy.

UCLA early 1970s, gelatin silver print, 10 x 12 inches (25.4 x 30.5 cm)
This photograph was made when I was a junior
at UCLA in the 1970s. I was uncomfortable
photographing in the world so I began setting up
situations: tableaux using objects, friends, and myself.
I found it when organizing my early negatives.

Cecily Brown

Untitled 1996 oil on canvas, 48 x 60 inches (121.9 x 152.4 cm)
This painting appeared in my first New York show,
in 1997 at Deitch Projects. It was among the first
paintings I made that weren't embarrassed to
be paintings, the first that used color (after years
of black and white), the first that overtly used
the Old Masters.

Step 1982 oil on canvas, 46³/₈ x 35¹/₈ inches (117.8 x 89.2 cm) The action takes place on a border: between dream and reality, life and death, sky and earth.

A monument brought to life or life stiffened in its tracks. A step into the void or a balancing act above it. A leap to the death or to eternal life. A stopped moment. Stopped not because it is so fair, but because there is no other; it is missing, ruled out. A moment stopped in its tracks. The monument to a moment.

b. Moscow, Russia, 1945. Lives and works in New York, NY, USA.

Christopher Bucklow

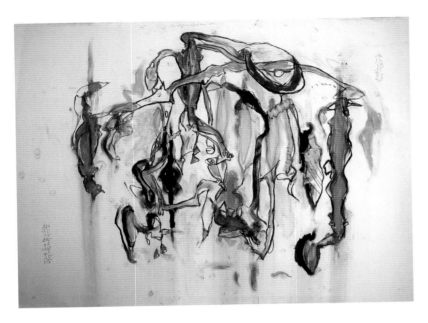

I Will Save Your Life 2002 carbon and pastel on paper, 22½ x 31½ (57 x 80 cm)

The first image is the image I constantly search for.

That first image will stand as the parent of all my work that comes after it.

In the interim I have only the "just sufficient."

There is a phrase in psychology concerning the conditions in which a child will thrive; it is if the mother or father is a "good enough" parent. That parent does not have to be ideal— merely sufficient.

I send you this image as such a parent. In it I see the glimmer of what I have been seeking: a sensual visual vehicle and yet one depicting a detailed conceptual narrative. This glimmer has the title *I Will Save Your Life*—a line from the imagined marriage ceremony of Rrose Sélavy and Bill de Kooning. Rrose's head grafted with Bill's right arm—a mutant marriage—form proliferating and growing wonderfully wrong.

The image has, then, two parents.

It is schooled in this one fact—"all the cells of your neocortex are built by the genes from your mother's DNA—and all those of your rhinencephalon built solely by the strand inherited from your father."

Photo Montage 1958 black-and-white photo, 3 x 4 inches (7.6 x 10.2 cm) When I was about eleven years old, my mother separated from my father and moved to Switzerland, taking my younger brother and sister and myself with her. My mother had entrusted me with the use of her expensive German Rolleiflex camera. Initially, I took typical tourist-like pictures of quaint Swiss chalets and mountain scenes that emulated the postcards I saw in the souvenir shops.

At some point, I was able to conceive the possibilities and the power of illusion that photography offered. In my mind, I imagined a place where small spring flowers would be as big as my brother and sister. I made this photo montage of my brother and sister with "gargantuan" spring crocuses to create this place.

It was at this point that I became aware of my ability to conceive ideas and to effectively realize them.

b. Boston, MA, USA, 1946. Lives and works in Topanga, CA, USA.

Victor Burgin

US77 (detail) 1977 black-and-white photographic panels, each panel 40 x 60 inches (101.6 x 152.4 cm) This panel exemplifies concerns basic to all my subsequent works: the relation of image to text, of real space to imaginary space, of description to narrative, of stillness to movement.

In everyday life (and the mass media that informs it), the relation between words and images is one of dependency: Words are used to explain an image, or images are used to illustrate a text. In *US77*, text and image have independent lives, but enter into mutual relationships. In this example, the keyword "Framed" brings together the frame of the actual photograph on the wall, the frame of the Marlboro poster in the photograph, the frame of the photograph described in the text, and the frame of the mirror in the text. It pins together semantic fields that might otherwise remain separate, shifting the potential meanings of the work to a 'third space' between the real place described in the photograph and the imaginary place of the narrative.

At the time I made this work, I wrote that I thought of the gallery as the "negative" of the movie theatre, and of *US77* as "a sort of static film where the individual scenes have collapsed inwards upon themselves, so that the narrative connections have become lost." Wrapping around the gallery, the twelve-part work *US77* also anticipates the panoramic loops of my later video pieces, and their investigation of spaces of description and narration between the 'still' and the 'moving.'

COURTESY OF THE ARTIST AND CHRISTINE BURGIN GALLERY, NEW YORK.

66   b. Sheffield, England, 1941. Lives and works in London, England and Paris, France.

FRAMED

A dark-haired woman in her late-fifties hands over a photograph showing the haircut she wants duplicating 'exactly'.

The picture shows a very young woman with blond hair cut extremely short.

The hairdresser props it by the mirror in which he can see the face of his client watching her own reflection.

When he has finished he removes the cotton cape from the woman's shoulders. 'That's it', he says.

But the woman continues sitting, continues staring at her reflection in the mirror.

Richmond Burton

Today is a Beautiful Day 1971 ceramic, 12 x 12 x 1½ inches (30.5 x 30.5 x 3.8 cm)

I made this oval platter with my grandmother Manilla Fulton in her ceramics studio. It is signed and dated on the back: Rick, Aug. 28, 1971.

I keep my first work of art in my studio and named it *Today is a Beautiful Day* as an artistic *plat du jour*. Its colors, forms, and elements have reappeared in various ways in my paintings over the years. Two trees, one dissolving into the rays of sunlight and two flowers on a field of green grass silhouetted against a turquoise sky remind me that in making art, the best way to be subversive is to express happiness. I'm still searching for that ideal and sometimes elusive place.

b. Talladega, AL, USA, 1960. Lives and works in East Hampton, NY, USA.

Panorama (never-the-less) 2000 ink on plexiglass with four steel mounts, 61 x 92 ¹/₁₆ x 2³/₈ inches (55 x 234 x 6 cm) *Never-the-less* is part of the "Panorama" series, works on Plexiglas that have opened up a new field of investigation, following my research on photography and space.

Starting from intimate drawings, done in a small format at my studio table, I photograph.

Then after considerable enlargement, these drawings are silk-screened with ink on Plexiglas.

The results are frozen drawings, fossilized in space in front of the wall that supports them.

This extraordinary experience produces these interesting hybrid objects, in which are fused the experience of place, photography, and drawing—these are my new paintings.

b. Toulouse, France, 1952. Lives and works in Paris, France and the Bronx, NY, USA.

Sophie Calle

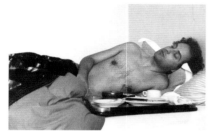  

Les Dormeurs (The Sleepers) 1979 176 gelatin silver prints and 23 text panels, each: 6½ x 8⅛ inches (22.9 x 20.6 cm); plus text panel: 11½ x 9 inches (29.2 x 22.9 cm); overall: 62¾ x 212½ inches (159.4 x 539.8 cm), edition of 5 (French) and 5 (English) I asked people to give me a few hours of their sleep. To come and sleep in my bed. To let themselves be looked at and photographed. To answer questions. To each participant I suggested an eight-hour stay. I contacted 45 people by phone: people I didn't know and whose names were suggested to me by common acquaintances, a few friends, and neighbor-hood residents whose work called on them to sleep during the day (the baker, for instance). I intended my bedroom to become a constantly occupied space for eight days, with sleepers succeeding one another at regular intervals. Twenty-nine people finally accepted. Of these, five never showed up: an agency baby-sitter and I took their places. Sixteen people refused either because they had other commitments or the thing didn't agree with them. The occupation of the bed began on Sunday, April 1, at 5 p.m. and ended on Monday, April 9, at 10

b. Paris, France, 1953. Lives and works in Malakoff, France and New York, NY, USA.

Monday, April 9, at 10 a.m. Twenty-eight sleepers succeeded one another. A few of them overlapped with each other. Breakfast, lunch, or dinner was served to each depending on the time of day. Clean bedsheets were placed at the disposition of each sleeper. I put questions to those who allowed me—nothing to do with knowledge or fact-gathering, but rather to establish a neutral and distant contact. I took photographs every hour. I watched my guest sleep.

Peter Campus

Dynamic Field Series 1970 video My first artwork was thrown away when my family moved to Long Island. It was a painting I made when I was 13. It was on black paper and made with poster paint. I can still remember it: the mast of a ship, with a man in a crow's nest looking out with binoculars at the dark sea.

My first video work, the one that had the same kind of meaning for me as that painting, was one I made in 1970 at the Judson Church. I was alone in the church. I pulled on a rope that raised and lowered a camera that pointed down at me. The rope and video cables hung down, visible in the image.

I had been studying with Chuck Ross. He would talk to me about my work, and I would listen to him. I felt the importance of being open to something other than my own instincts. I saw the work of Bruce Nauman who was making extraordinary video pieces, and I was watching how NASA used surveillance cameras in the space program; the resulting images didn't represent human responses, but were simply a presentation of visual data.

I think of this work, *Dynamic Field Series*, as my first work of art, the first moment I was in my community as an artist, relating to my community with my work.

b. New York, NY, USA, 1937. Lives and works in East Patchogue, NY, USA.

Fan as Eudemonist, Relaxing after an Exhausting Day at the Beach 1975 gelatin silver print, 10 x 8 inches (25.4 x 20.3 cm)

In the summer of 1975 I was about to begin my senior year at the Minneapolis College of Art and Design. I made it my habit, on hot summer days, to ride my bike from my studio apartment next to the Art Institute downtown, to Lake Harriot a few miles away. I would bask in the sun and read by the beach. On that particular day I remember reading *The Anxiety of Influence* by Harold Bloom. After sitting in the sun for a couple of hours, I rode home to my apartent/studio and stayed up much of the night, writing, etc. I made a little sketch, and set up an old fan on a pillow. I used cardboard for the couch and made construction-paper walls, a window, curtains, and an outlet. The Eudaemonists were an obscure group of Greek philosophers who believed that the pursuit of Happiness was the greatest good. My day at the beach seemed to embody this ethic. The Fan as stand-in for Breath, Spirit, or Inspiration was lying on a couch watching TV. I was a member of the first generation of artists to grow up watching TV. In this image I created a place that existed solely for the camera. It was a temporary installation or performance, whose document was more than a document because the primary or only way (rather than secondary way) of experiencing the art, event, or installation was through a photographic reproduction. I had acknowledged that for many, including myself, the experience of Art is achieved primarily through photographs.

b. Lansing, MI, USA, 1953. Lives and works in New York, NY, USA.

Maurizio Cattelan

Untitled 1989 black-and-white photograph and silver frame, 8 X 10 inches (20 x 25 cm)

I lived in a small, isolated town in Corsica until I was twenty. I was somewhat of a loner and I used to play with what was around me—the clouds and the sea. That really was a determining factor in the way I developed and flexed my imagination. I really did spend a lot of time just observing the sea, the repetition of the waves, the simple rhythm through which nature is formed. It was particularly important, because it forced me to find the motivation for work in the "simplest" of things.

b. Padua, Italy, 1960. Lives and works in New York, NY, USA.

Envelope 1964 oil on canvas, 16¼ x 18 inches (41.3 x 45.7 cm) This small painting of a letter was done in 1963–64 when I was backing away from the large, gestural, de Kooning–inspired paintings I had been struggling with as a student. It is one of many paintings I did of objects in my studio that focused more on looking and less on what I knew. It became a new beginning for me.

b. Riga, Latvia, 1938. Lives and works in New York, NY, USA.

Saint Clair Cemin

The Granny Ashtray 1987 bronze, 4¹/₂ x 5 x 6¹/₂ inches (11.4 x 12.7 x 16.5 cm) My career as sculptor began like the universe: with a big bang in which it expanded to considerable size in a very short time. In the first week I produced in the neighborhood of fifty different pieces, in clay and plaster. Among them there were mugs with faces, ashtrays, pornographic bibelots (candleholders), and animals of all sorts (penguins, elephants, etc.). Each piece took from ten minutes to several hours to be made. I made several nudes and transformed one of them into an ashtray (between the legs). I gave her a skull for a head, the body of an old woman, and no arms. It was monumental in its gruesomeness and very dramatic. The art critic Alan Jones, a close friend, had two comments about it: "It is like a spit in the eye of the public," and "It looks like a student of the French Fine Arts Academy from the last century reincarnated as a Hell's Angel." The first comment made me think that I was surely on the right track and the second came to characterize most of my work: Different points of view, different perceptions of the world collide and produce a piece that is a record of their interference pattern. I made the piece in clay; so as not to lose it, I cast it in plaster, following as well as I could the advice of a book on mold-making. One year later, I gave it to a foundry to be cast in bronze in an edition of five.

I still hold on to the artist's proof of that edition, but some copies in plaster found interesting homes, such as that of Robert Mapplethorpe, who told me it was "beautiful."

**Their Freedom of Expression . . .
the Recovery of their Economy** 1984
charcoal and pastel on paper, 80 x 80 inches
(203.2 x 203.2 cm) This was the first
large-format charcoal drawing
I ever did. It was done for a local
exhibition that was part of a
national campaign against inter-
vention in Central America
organized in New York City by
critic Lucy Lippard and a group
of Salvadoran poets in 1983–84.

I thought the drawing would
go into the closet after the show,
since supporters of Reagan and
Kissinger would not like the way
I portrayed them, and people
who didn't like them would not
want to see much of their faces
anywhere. So I didn't want to
make "art"; I just wanted to
do some kind of inexpensive
charcoal-and-paper editorial
cartoon to be seen as a billboard.
To my surprise, I got a new way
of looking at my own work,
and also people reacted very
favorably to the style and content. This evolved into a series
of drawings in the same format
that lasted through the mid '90s.

I had stopped drawing for
almost ten years, and began
to do artist books, prints, and
paintings, but for the last couple
of years I revisited my large
charcoal drawings again thanks

to the current political climate,
and got a second wind with a
new series. Drawing has become
my favorite medium now, and
I can't say enough about how
much I owe to *Their Freedom of
Expression* . . . and how much it
has helped me to develop a lot
of freedom in my own work.

b. Mexico City, Mexico, 1953. Lives and works in San Francisco, CA, USA.   77

John Chamberlain

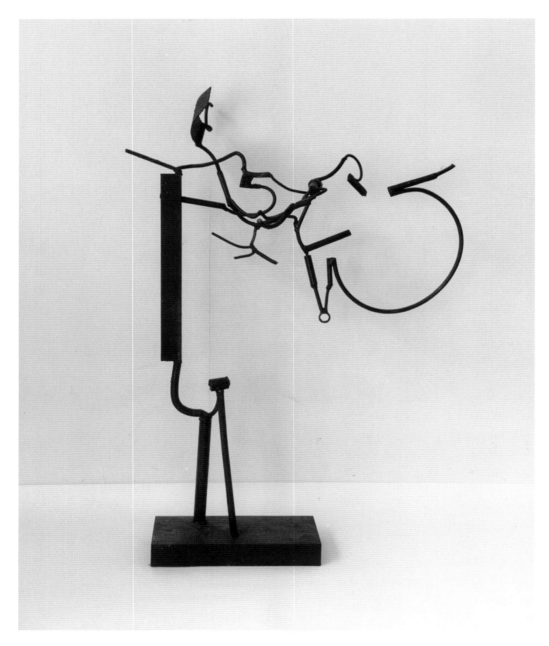

Calliope 1954 steel, 52 x 37 x 24 inches (132.1 x 94 x 61 cm) *Calliope* was the first sculpture I made. Even to this day I still like it.

b. Rochester, IN, USA, 1927. Lives and works in Shelter Island, NY, USA.

(Forever Free) Sam 1992 acrylic latex on paper with penny, 42 x 26¹/₆ inches (106.7 x 26.2 cm) As a young artist seeking to understand the complexities of black representation, I discovered blackface minstrelsy. The compelling subject matter has since had a profound effect upon my professional and creative interests. My initial investigations into the subject of blackface were fueled by my concern for expressing a truth. The research inspired many good works of art, which for me began to scratch the surface of the timeless issue of difference. It was not until I happened upon a photo of the famed actor/comedian Bert Williams in blackface and dressed in a chicken costume that my concern began to blossom into a careful commitment to pursuing the complexities of this challenging subject. While I studied the image, many questions came to mind, which influenced the development of the painting titled *Sam*. Although far removed from the initial impact of the image of Williams staring back at me through a sooted mask, I am reminded of the chilling effect the image had on me. For me this image remains a symbolic summary of yesterday's premonition of the silence and invisibility many often feel in America today.

b. Lafayette, LA, USA, 1967. Lives and works in Austin, TX, USA.

Sarah Charlesworth

The First Human Being 1972 silkscreen print, 16 x 20½ inches (40.6 x 52.1 cm), edition of six In an old photo of a street scene in Paris taken in 1838 by Louis Daguerre, a lone figure of a man, paused in a stationary position while having his shoes shined, appears as the first human being to be photographed. Because of the lengthy exposure times necessitated by these early photographs, people were not initially visible, their mobile forms eluding the camera's protracted gaze. Wide expanses of streets and buildings appear free from human "traffic." This one barely perceptible figure of a gentleman, a small detail within a larger cityscape, became the basis of a silkscreen print which I made in 1972.

While it was still five years before my first show and the initiation of the *Modern History* series, the demarcation point that marks the beginning of my recognized work, I fix on this print as my "first mature work" because it stands for me as a threshold, a foreshadowing of the concerns upon which my mature work is grounded.

While I have been an artist my whole life, having drawn, painted, postered, and photographed throughout my childhood and through college, the threshold that this particular piece represents was one in which my attention, my vision, shifted from the primarily visual to the conceptual and philosophical significance of sight.

At the time of this work, I was in a Master's photo workshop with Lisette Model and was searching for the meaning of photographs while taking variously dynamic or ironic pictures of whatever. I had been stimulated by the early conceptual work of my friend and teacher Doug Huebler and by Joseph Kosuth. My first photo of the first human being to be photographed interrupted my frustration with picture-taking and crystallized an orientation to which I still abide, the thrill of the conceptual and the ideational significance that attends and extends from the life of images within culture. This work predates the idea of "appropriation" as a keyword and recognizes the act of meaning as part of the continious fabric of shared visual culture.

b. East Orange, NJ, USA, 1947. Lives and works in New York, NY, USA.

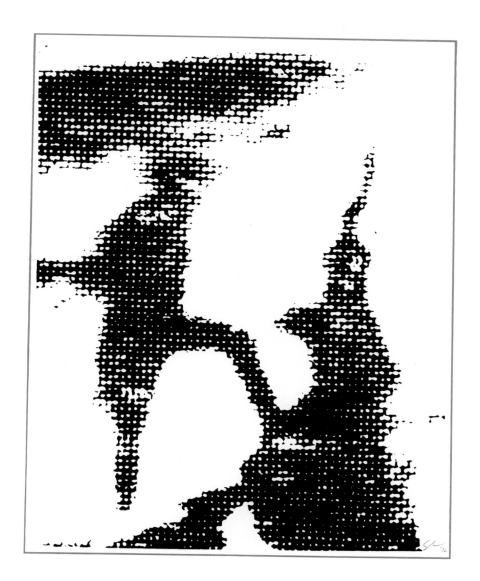

Sandro Chia

The Idleness of Sisyphus 1981 oil on canvas in two parts, 10 feet 2 inches x 12 feet 8¼ inches (309.9 x 386.7 cm) There are two reasons for this choice:
1) It is probably the single work of art I most identify with, as it represents a metaphor for my life as an artist. Just like Sisyphus is condemned to the never-ending toil of carrying a rock to the top of a mountain just to see it roll straight back to the bottom of where he started, so am I to the task of painting a blank canvas where just as I'm finished filling the empty space I've got to start all over with the next one in a seemingly never-ending mission.
2) The acquisition of this painting by The Museum of Modern Art represents one of the major turning points in my career.

Untitled, Childhood Drawing 1943

finger paint on paper, 15 x 19 inches (38.1 x 48.3 cm) Although I did everything early, for some reason I did not talk until I was two and a half years old. Within six months of uttering my first word, I began to draw, and when I was four, I did a finger-painting that prompted my nursery-school teacher to tell my mother that I was gifted in art. By five, I was attending classes at the Art Institute of Chicago, taking the bus every week to go downtown where I became lost in a visual world that became more real to me than my everyday life. My course was set from my first visit to those Saturday classes; I would become an artist and—despite the fact that few women were included in the museum's collection—I was utterly convinced that I would make a contribution that would assure my becoming part of art history, a goal that has guided my life.

Dale Chihuly

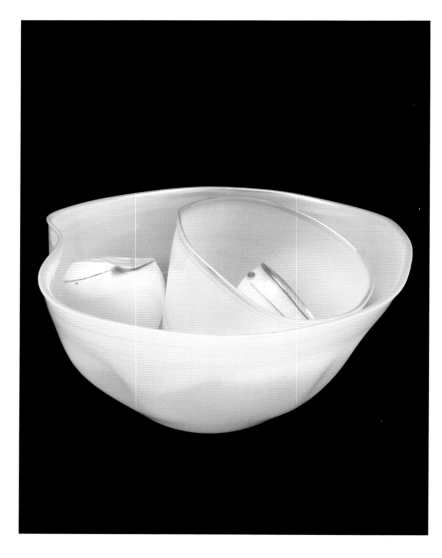

Pink Basket Set with Blue Lip Wraps 1978 handblown glass, 9 x 10 x 7 inches (22.9 x 25.4 x 17.8 cm) I saw these Indian baskets at the Washington State Historical Society, and when I went back to Pilchuck and started making the basket series, it was the first time I really used the fire, heat and gravity to make a form. I let it wrinkle from the heat, and made the glass very thin. This was a breakthrough for me, and for my work from that point on. The Baskets really started what was to be the most typical Chihuly work, I guess, because the Baskets led, really, into the Seaforms.

William Christenberry

Tenant House I 1960 oil paint on linen, 79½ x 85 inches (202 x 216 cm) I was always taken, even as a youngster, with the vernacular architecture of my region, and I was hoping to find a way to come to grips with the landscape that was so familiar to me. My training is as a painter, so I wanted to use painting as a primary means.

This painting is the very first one, and actually preceded my making color pictures of such structures in the landscape. The painting has quite a few expressionistic overtones—the emphasis on gesture, surface quality—that were beginning to be prevalent in American painting, mainly in New York, a world which I only had access to via magazines or books.

It was right after this that I began to use the camera as a tool, not in order to paint in a photo-realistic way, but as a color reference for the paintings. So there was a cross-fertilization of painting to photography, photography to painting. By 1961 I was making more and more photographs of similar things in the landscape. The first person to encourage me to take the little photographs seriously was Walker Evans himself, when I went from Alabama to New York.

Christo and Jeanne-Claude

Dockside Packages Cologne Harbor 1961 (installation view) Rolls of paper, tarpaulin, and rope, 16 x 6 x 32 feet (480 x 180 x 960 cm) At the same time as our first personal exhibition, at the Haro Lauhus Gallery in Cologne in 1961, we created our first temporary outdoor environmental work of art. The gallery was near the waterfront of the Rhine River.

For the *Dockside Packages* we used several stacks of oil barrels and large rolls of industrial paper, covering them with tarpaulins secured with ropes. With the permission of the Port Authority, all the materials were borrowed from the dockworkers. *Dockside Packages* was composed of separate parts of various sizes. The temporary work of art remained for two weeks.

Wood Rock 1988 wood-laminated rock, 22 x 15 x 15 inches (55.9 x 38.1 x 38.1 cm) I had this rock that I really liked. But I decided it wasn't rock-like enough—so I covered it with wood to make it more so.

b. New York, NY, USA, 1959. Lives and works in New York, NY, USA.

Chuck Close

Big Self-Portrait 1967–68 acrylic on canvas, 108 x 84 inches (274.3 x 213.4 cm) I was trying to get away from what I had been doing in the past—Abstract Expressionist–inspired work like that of Willem de Kooning and Arshile Gorky. I was trying to work differently. I always depended on virtuoso art marks. Knowing what art looked like, I could make interesting art marks but they ended up looking like de Kooning's art marks. I had so many habits that were associated with the tools that I used—the paint, the brushes. I got rid of all that stuff. I got rid of the tools I had facility with and I got tools that I didn't know how to use. I'd use an airbrush because it was associated with commercial stuff and not with fine art.

At first I made this 22-foot long nude but the scale still wasn't big enough. I had been photographing the finished nude painting and I had film left in the camera. I decided I wanted to make it even bigger yet, so obviously the one part of the figure to make bigger was the head. I was the only one in the room and I turned the camera on myself and I took these photographs. I sort of backed my way into it.

I didn't even think I was making portraits. I called them "heads." *Big Self-Portrait* was the first. It was a proving ground. Using black paint on white canvas forced me to make decisions early. I wanted to give my hand something specific to do. I worked within a grid from left to right and top to bottom instead of working all over at once. A lot of it had to do with my learning disabilities. I'd break a big insurmountable problem into bite-size pieces.

I wanted to make the head so big it was a *Gulliver's Travels* experience. I wanted to get it so big that it was hard for the viewer to experience it as a whole. I wanted to force the viewer to scan it, to experience it almost like it was a landscape he or she was traversing.

I didn't realize at the time that, in the process of constructing these self-imposed limitations that would guarantee I could no longer make what I was making, I kicked open the door for a whole other body of work. I'm totally surprised that nearly 40 years later I'm still making work based on the human head.

b. Monroe, WA, USA, 1940. Lives and works in New York, NY, USA.

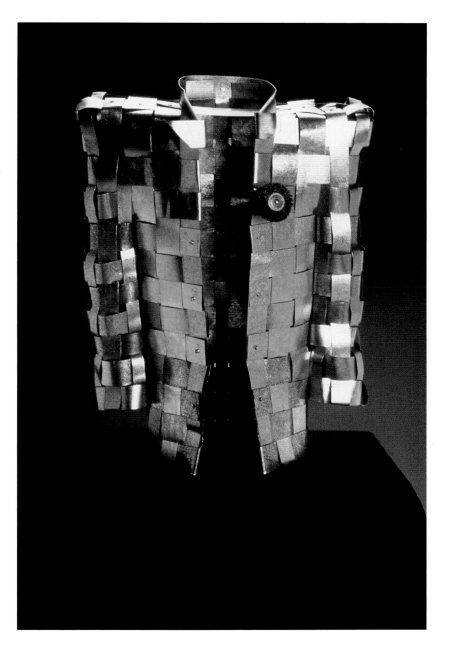

Illinois Jacket 1988 woven steel, life- size

Once, when I was invited to a dress-up party, I was compelled to step out of my bohemian uniform and buy a fancy suit. Unfortunately, though, I didn't have fancy money. But I hit every thrift- and near-thrift store I could find until I found something. When I did it was tailor-made, Italian silk. Two pieces. Early '60s style. Shiny like silver. In the inside breast pocket there was an invitation to some corporate event. It had a Chicago address. Instantly I begin to refer to the suit as "Illinois Suit." Being such a big fan of jazz and all, and now the proud owner of such a jazzy suit, I couldn't resist calling the jacket my "Illinois Jacquet" after the famed Louisiana sax player from the Lionel Hampton big band. Eventually, in my household, the word "Illinois" became synonymous with the word "jacket." Oh, and that work of art called *Illinois Jacket* looks just like the real thing.

b. Somerville, NJ, USA, 1955. Lives and works in Mine Hill, NJ, USA.

Hannah Collins

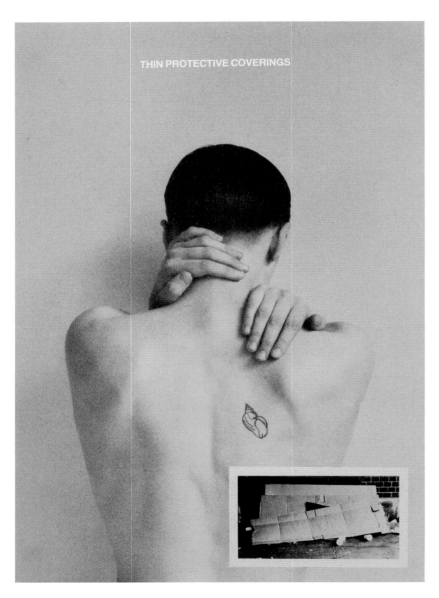

THIN PROTECTIVE COVERINGS

THIN PROTECTIVE COVERINGS
1986 printed card based on photocollage,
8¹/₂ x 6 inches (21 x 15 cm) This card for
Matt's Gallery in London was
the first work that combined my
own body image, wrappings, and
materials in an imaginary place
for the body, drawing (as a tattoo
on my back), and limited color in
a minimalist sense, together with
words. It brought together my
own body, drawing, writing, collected materials in their context,
and color into one image and as
such was effective: A lot of my
friends kept this card on their
walls for years so its small format
was useful.

I went to a local tattoo parlor,
which at the time was a bit more
risque than today and gave them
the drawing to tattoo onto my
back. Then my friend Maureen
Paley from Interim Art in London (who was just starting her
gallery and before that was a
photographer) took the photo,
and Robin Klassnik of Matt's
Gallery produced the work as a
card for my first really complete
show of cardboard works. I still
of course have the tattoo but
never have to look at it.

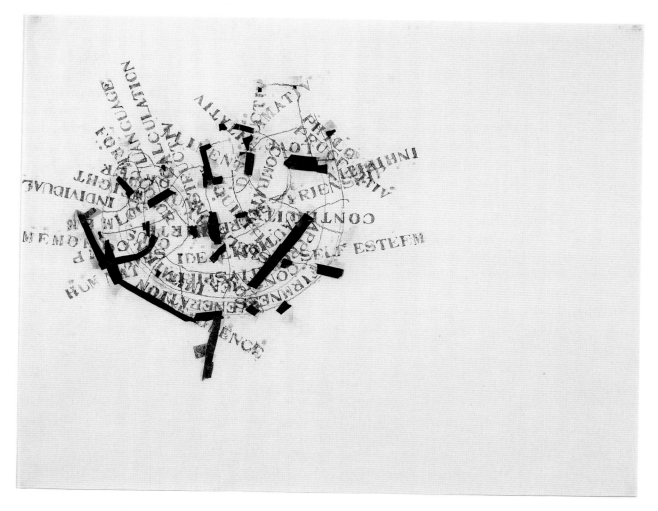

Phrenology 1985 ink, charcoal, and collage on paper, 19 x 24 inches (48.3 x 61 cm) *Phrenology* was the earliest work included in my first solo exhibition. I drew a phrenological skull diagram upside down and askew. This symbol of human order and intention is isolated and set adrift on the page. The rubber-stamped labels indicating personality traits (self-esteem, combativeness, etc.) are enlarged and overemphasized and run outside of their boundaries, thus creating their own chaotic form. Fragments of black paper are taped to the drawing in an attempt to define the contours of the skull.

I feel these notions of frustrated meaning and conflicting gestures are expressed in just about all of the art I make.

b. Seattle, WA, USA, 1956. Lives and works in Los Angeles, CA, USA.

George Condo

The Cloud Maker 1984 oil on canvas, 26 x 32 inches (66 x 81.3 cm) *The Cloud Maker* was painted at Tenerife in the Canary Islands in 1984. I went there after spending some time in Madrid and Cologne. It was created on the 23rd floor of a 1960s high-rise looking out over the ocean. This was a time when back home in New York people were experiencing a proliferation of grafitti: Artists such as Crash, Toxic, A-1, and Lee were exhibiting at the Sydney Janis Gallery. They were famous for their "tags," a way of writing their names that identified them as artists. This appears to have been my inspiration along with the will to create a synthetic found object—recontextualized in the language of art rather than everyday life without being an appropriation.

b.Concord, NH, USA, 1957. Lives and works in New York, NY, USA.

Project 1998 oil on canvas, 30 x 40 inches (76.2 x 101.6 cm) I had always wanted to make a picture of something that no one had ever seen before. I built a housing project out of cake and candy and started making paintings of it. When I looked at *this* piece, I felt like I was seeing a totally new world.

b. Melrose, MA, USA, 1965. Lives and works in New York, NY, USA.

Petah Coyne

Untitled #245 (Tree Stump) 1985–86
mixed media, 63 x 65 x 68 inches (160 x 165 x 172.7 cm) In 1985, a more seasoned and quite revered sculptor kindly informed me that I was not considered a serious sculptor. A serious sculptor makes things that stand on their own, not hang from the ceiling as was my proclivity. And the sculpture should be made of materials that are strong and everlasting, not the dead fish and swamp muck I most often used.

My response: to make my first real sculpture? . . . . One filled with all the conundrums possible. Seemingly a root, but would a root really stand? And made of what? Not natural materials. And buried inside, something not suspected. Real Sculpture?

b. Oklahoma City, OK, USA, 1953. Lives and works in New York, NY, USA.

Knotted Strong 1969 In 1969 I studied in the Cheltenham College of Art. The foundation year included courses in drawing, painting, ceramics, and printmaking. Toward the latter part of the year we were told, "now we will make a sculpture." We were shown a store-room full of various materials, and after selecting some odds and ends, we started work. I was not particularly enthusiastic about this exercise, but by the end of the first day I was hooked. Making something without any purpose—nobody could tell me what to do and nobody seemed to have a clue about what was good or bad. So much freedom and so many constraints and so much responsibility.

I had already applied for a painting course at the Wimbledon School of Art, and after a summer working in a foundry in Yate, near Bristol, I arrived to start the course. Thirty students in one room and Roger Ackling and Jim Rogers running the show. Lots of interesting discussions and information but little indication of what to do. Thank you both! In case I never got around to it before.

After several weeks and me already beginning to wonder whether or not art school was the right place for me, I bought several large balls of string and started cutting them up and tying knots in them. Why? A mixture of desperation and resolve to at least do something. It was indeed a great relief to be doing something. Working, looking, thinking, feeling, learning.

Michael Craig-Martin

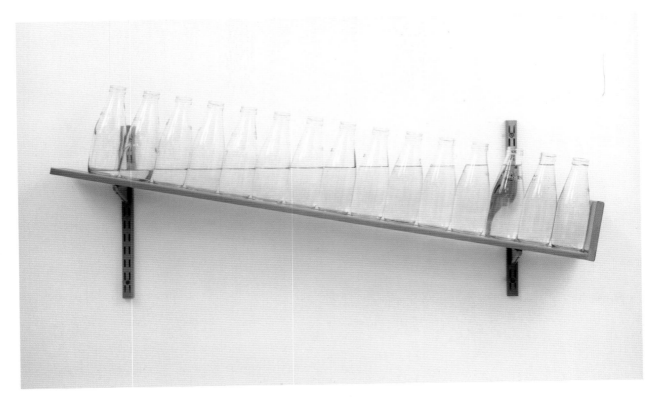

On the shelf 1970 objects and water, 20 x 42½ x 6 inches (51 x 109 x cm), edition of three I did some other works earlier than this that I consider 'successful', that 'worked,' that I was happy with, that other people liked, that got critical attention, that were bought by good collectors or institutions, etc.

But this is the first piece that I think of as genuinely and still-to-this-day representing me properly. It is the first work where I consider that both the concerns and the voice are unmistakably mine.

This was the first work I did using only readymade objects: standard shelving units, milk bottles, tap water. I had become aware at the time that although the physical appearance of ordinary objects is almost entirely determined by considerations of functionality, artworks using them in readymades invariably set aside or denied their functions. Duchamp did not put wine bottles on the bottle dryer, nor did he want the urinal to be peed in. I set out to try to make artworks based on the ordinary usage of the ordinary objects they employed: shelves hold bottles, bottles hold water, water finds its level.

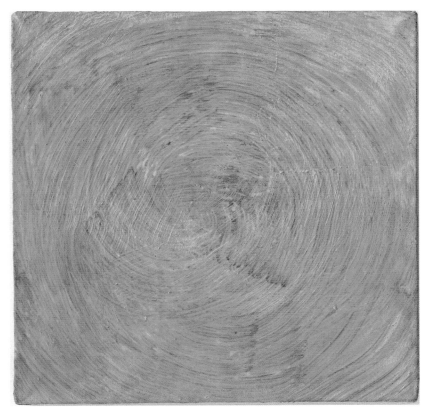

Work No. 3: Yellow Painting Acrylic paint on canvas, 12³/₄ x 12³/₄ inches (32.5 x 32.5 cm)

I started numbering my works because I wasn't happy with titles made of words. They meant too much and added too much extra, and I wanted a way of treating everything the same, big or small, whatever it was made of, whatever it was. Using numbers—just like catalogue numbers—seemed a good way of doing this. All numbers are equal.

When I started numbering my works I went back and gave numbers to old ones. I got quite self-conscious about it—about which numbers I gave to which works—and found that I didn't want to have a "Work No. 1." It was too much. I couldn't live with it. WORK NO. 1, MY FIRST WORK! NO WAY! The point of the numbering was to try to give all works the same value—to treat everything the same—but the number one just was not the same. Not all numbers are equal.

And so I tried to make a kind of fade-in. I started with three, put five next, and went on up from there.

b. Wakefield, England, 1968. Lives and works in London, England.   97

Gregory Crewdson

Untitled (baseball field through window) 1987 C-print, edition of three, 20 X 24 inches (50.8 x 60.7 cm) I made this photograph as a graduate student at the Yale School of Art in the late 1980s. It was part of a larger series of photographs that explored the inter-section of everyday life and theatricality. The photographs were made in and around various small towns in northern Massachusetts. The photographs used this setting as a back-drop to explore the psychological underside of the American vernacular. At the time, I was interested in establishing a photographic style and sensibility that hovered between photographic realism and cinematic unreality.

During the summer of 1987 I spent many nights making photographs around the perimeter of a minor league base-ball park in Pittsfield, Massachusetts. Although I am a great baseball fan, I had little interest in picturing the game itself. Instead, I focused my attention on how the surrounding neighborhood was illuminated by the stadium lights at night. I was entranced by how the artificial lighting transformed this ordinary suburban tract of land into a place of mystery and wonder. For me, this was the most beautiful place in the world.

This photograph was taken through a picture window in a house overlooking the baseball park. The window is used as a framing device that separates the interior and exterior spaces. For me, the strange, celestial light that illuminates the nocturnal landscape suggests a narrative event that is just out of reach of the viewer. As a young photographer, this picture was of particular importance to me in that it clearly mapped out the scope of my artistic ambitions. It is remarkable to me now how deeply connected this early work is to my current practice. Almost every aspect of my photographic production—the use of cinematic lighting; the nocturnal, luminous palette; and the implied voyeuristic viewpoint—is clearly evident in this image. When I view this photograph now, it confirms my belief that that each artist has a single story to tell and that the struggle is to reinvent that story over and over again in pictorial form.

b. Brooklyn, NY, USA, 1962. Lives and works in New Haven, CT, USA.

Russell Crotty

Surf Drawing (blue) 1990 pencil and ballpoint pen on paper, 120 x 240 inches (304.8 x 609.6 cm). Installation view, "Frontier Tales," Los Angeles Contemporary Exhibitions. This drawing was the result of a long series of books I had been doing while at the same time attempting to be an abstract painter. I came to the realization, with a little help from some friends, that the real work was the books filled with drawings of collected and imaginary fragments of California coastal escapism with a bit of degradation thrown in for good measure. From my books, I borrowed the gestural sequences of stick figures riding waves to make very large-scale drawings, some with up to forty-thousand images, as a sort of printout of my remembered and, to a large degree, desired experience. *Surf Drawing (blue)* was the first of these.

Lumella 1977 oil on canvas, 13³/₄ x 9³/₄ inches (35 x 25 cm) It is an image in the dark on the Adriatic Sea, a small sea. Therefore the title.

b. Morro d'Alba (Ancona), Italy, 1949. Lives and works in Rome and Ancona, Italy.

John Currin

Untitled 1985 oil on canvas, 66 x 48 inches (167.6 x 121.9 cm) For the first time it wasn't about style. I had just been dumped, so I was completely hysterical and pathetic, but also egomaniacal. Those emotions are like the holy trinity of painting.

Raggedy Ann in a Walnut Shell: Age 4 1978 paper, pencil, magic marker, tape, and walnut shell, 1½ x 1 x 1½ inches (3.8 x 2.5 x 3.8 cm) I remember making this piece at my kitchen table and being really frustrated as I accidentally cut off Raggedy Ann's left arm and repaired it with tape. Looking at the way she is dressed, I don't see much of a change in how I dress the people in my paintings today. Raggedy Ann, Holly Hobby, Laura Ingalls Wilder from *Little House on the Prairie*; the pinafore, patterned dress, and utilitarian shoes seemed to have stayed with me.

The walnut-shell cradle idea came from the story of Thumbelina. I was and still am obsessed with miniatures. The smaller and the more detailed, the better. It was always about creating another reality that existed in a separate space. Raggedy Ann lived out her adventures when people weren't around, and tiny Thumbelina lived with the flower fairies. When I make my work today, I like to think that the image in the paintings is just a small moment in the life of the characters.

b. Poughkeepsie, NY, USA, 1974. Lives and works in Brooklyn, NY, USA.

Bruce Davidson

b. Oak Park, IL, USA, 1933. Lives and works in New York, NY, USA.

Widow of Montmartre, Paris, France 1956 silver print, 11 x 14 inches (27.9 x 35.6 cm) In 1956, I was given an appointment at the Magnum Paris office to show Henri Cartier-Bresson my *Widow of Montmartre* series of photographs that I had completed several weeks before our meeting. At that time, I was a 23-year-old American soldier stationed at the international headquarters of the Supreme Allied Powers in Europe just outside of Paris. There, I had become friends with a French soldier, Claude, whose mother had invited us to lunch at their apartment in Montmartre. After a leisurely meal, I stood on their balcony that overlooked Montmartre with its view of the Moulin de la Galette and other historic buildings. It was at that moment that I noticed an elderly woman slowly making her way up the steep and winding Rue Lepic. She wore a dark coat and a wide brimmed hat, and reminded me of a puppet on a string. I lifted my camera to my eye and made my first picture of Madame Fauchet. My friend told me that the woman was the widow of a French Impressionist painter who had passed away years before. She lived alone in a garret above them that was laden with her husband's paintings and other memorabilia scattered throughout the dwelling. We knocked on her door, and she greeted Claude with a kiss of affection and invited us into her chambers for a glass of wine. I visited the widow from the army camp a number of times riding up Rue Lepic on my motor scooter that she called my "horse." This encounter grew into a warm and lasting friendship. It manifested in a group of photographs that reflect the respect and feeling I had for this woman who was a bridge to a past era. This series of photographs led me to Henri Cartier-Bresson and in turn, to Magnum Photos. I became a member in 1958.

Nancy Davidson

Untitled 1975 crayon on paper, 96 x 200 inches (243.8 x 508 cm) I remember watching a videotape of Philip Guston talking about his paintings. He stopped in front of a painting and remarked, "I remember when that came off."As soon as I started thinking about my "first" piece I knew exactly the piece I wanted to select. I remember my excitement during the process of making it. I had set up "a priori" conditions before beginning. Because of this process I did not know how it would appear until I completed the piece. This was my first piece that connected a large scale, bilateral symmetry, and curved forms. These combined elements became my focus for years. When I began to make sculpture with latex inflatables in 1992, these elements reappeared in my work in a strange combination vastly different in visual appearance yet maintaining a relationship to the human body.

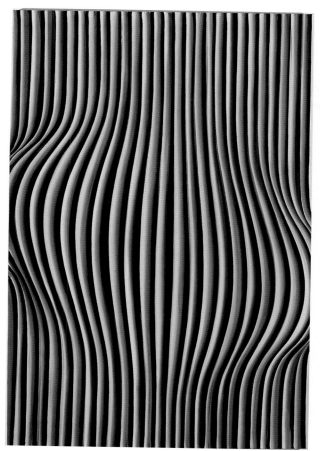

Umm...#1 & #2 (Sidewalk Series) 1993 oil on canvas, 90 x 60 inches (228.6 x 152.4 cm) each *Umm...#1 & #2* is one of the first diptychs in which I used the Modernist "stripe" to create an image that functioned like a covering. I wanted this representation to simultaneously reveal and conceal an underlying form and be suggestive of a draped body. It was an attempt to make a mimetic image where the repeated gesture creates a skin and the act of painting becomes like the caressing of the form. While the format of the diptych documents a physical memory it also reminds one of the slapstick humor of the double take. This image was informed in part by a childhood memory of a gigantic swinging advertisement for pantyhose comprised of plastic forms reminiscent of women's backsides. In a funny way I think it was my attempt to put the "sex" back into abstract painting.

b. Toronto, Canada, 1965. Lives and works in New York, NY, USA.

Richard Deacon

Performer, Assistant, Observer New Arts Lab, London, January 1970 six documentation stills of a performance by Richard Deacon, Ian Kirkwood, and Clive Walters The photographs are part of a sequence documenting a week of performance at the New Arts Lab in London in 1970. At my instigation the three of us absented ourselves from college during a week of assessments and worked on a continuous public performance in the space at the New Arts Lab. The materials that we used were defined by us each "bringing on the first day something that the other might need as a performer." The photographs are mostly concerned with the fragmentation of a small wooden crate. The reasons for considering this action appropriate as #1 are:

(a) It was carried out in the public domain.
(b) It was an act of independent from the institution.
(c) The collaborative aspect has always been of importance to me.
(d) There was no plan.
(e) It was interesting.

The Story of Beard 1992 16mm black-and-white and color film with optical sound, eight minutes, dimensions variable The reason I have chosen *The Story of Beard*, is not that I particularly like the work (actually I'm quite embarrassed by it), but that it was the first time I really understood how to use narrative. It was also my first edited film as well as my first film with sound. Some of the things I worked out when making this film prefigure in my decisions today, and this is why it is such an important early work. I forget now why, or what started it, but I had embarked on a research project on the topic of hair, which led me for a while to accrue vast amounts of information on the subject in The British Library in London. This found knowledge soon became an impediment, as too much research often can, and I remember absolutely clearly that moment when I realized that the only way through it all was to use fiction. In fact, in just one evening, I developed a story that became the voice-over to the film. This method of collating material—from hitherto unremembered bits of information to previously collected sounds and images that suddenly find their context—is very much the unconscious process I rely on today, although its manifestation may appear very differently. This is why *The Story of Beard* is so important, as it was my first formulation and understanding of a working process with film.

Wim Delvoye

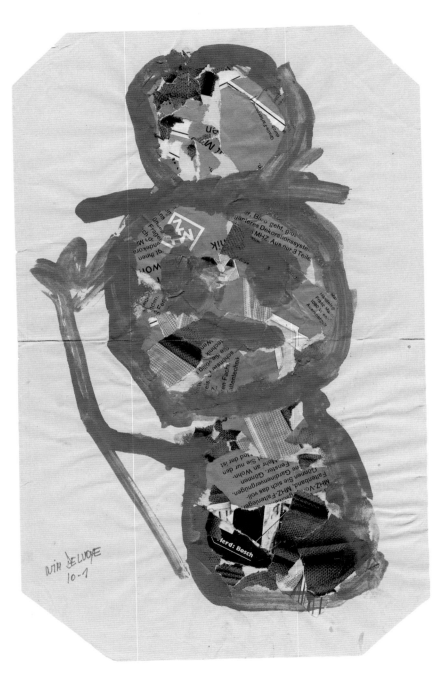

Untitled (snowman I) January 10, 1968 collage with paper and watercolor pasted on folded paper, signed by teacher (Ria Valcke), 16 7/8 x 10 1/2 inches (42.7 x 26.7 cm) I am very much interested in the question "When did my work start to become art and how?" and—generally speaking—in the division between art and life. I am very interested in the crossing of art and life and in uncovering the class-related rules and social mechanisms that come with this division.

b. Belgium, 1965. Lives and works in Ghent, Belgium and Berlin, Germany.

Drei Oefen 1992 C-print on Diasec, 67¹/₁₀ x 85⁴/₅ inches (172 x 220 cm) This was the first image that somehow successfully (to my liking) translated a sculpture of mine into a pictorial context that is also valid in its own right. It shows a vitrine of three gas ovens which I saw in Belgium years ago, but of course at the same time the objects mimic an Esperanto of minimal art. Besides, the work provides a nice double take in the way it's representing itself and its topic, as it shows its main actors straightforwardly on display—as the image itself happens to do too.

Mark di Suvero

Che Farò senza Eurydice 1959 weathered timber, rope, and nails, 84 x 104 x 91 inches (213 x 264 x 231 cm) I chose *Che Farò Senza Eurydice* as a first pivotal sculpture as it is the first all-wooden sculpture I made in my studio in the South Street Seaport. I consider it my first open cubist sculpture that dealt with space in a way that wasn't being dealt with in France. With its exhibition at the Green gallery in 1960, along with other similar wooden works, this sculpture launched my career. It changed my life.

b. Shanghai, China, 1933. Lives and works in New York, NY, USA.

Jan Dibbets

Perspective Correction 1967
black-and-white photograph, 42¼ x 42¼ (115 x 115 cm) In February 1967 I stopped making paintings and started to research the peculiar manifestations of photography. The photograph represented here was not the first perspective correction I made. There had been several tryouts in my sister's garden as well as on the Dutch beach.

This one was made later in the year 1967 in the garden of my parents' home. It was the first time, imperfect as it is, that something workable came out.

Through this photograph I realized there might be a lot more photography than just making more nice photographs. Photographs could question photographs.

b. Weert, Amsterdam, The Netherlands, 1941. Lives and works in Amsterdam, The Netherlands and San Casciano dei Bagni, Italy.

Philip-Lorca diCorcia

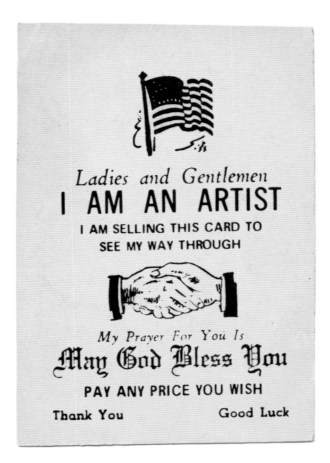

Untitled (I Am An Artist) 1973 off-set lithography on card stock, 2 x 3½ inches (5.1 x 8.9 cm) The mid-'70s marked the first flourishing of conceptual art, which proposed a radical immateriality and break from the tradition of craft in art. At the base of this was the assumption that anyone could be an artist simply by calling himself or herself one. This assumption produced a lot of bloated, self-absorbed work with little sensual reward, and a self-reflexiveness bordering on narcissism. By producing and distributing these cards, which are copied from the ones given out by blind and dumb panhandlers, I was both participating in and deriding the conventions that conceptual art had established. I consider it my first mature work because it is still relevant today thirty or more years after making it as a student.

b. Hartford, CT, USA, 1951. Lives and works in New York, NY, USA.

115

Rineke Dijkstra

Selfportrait, Marnixbad, Amsterdam June 19, 1991

C-print, edition of six, 45³/₅ x 36⁷/₁₀ inches (117 x 94 cm) After I finished art school I worked on commission for a couple of years. I made portraits of business-men, actors, writers, and artists for magazines and newspapers. At a certain moment I felt I wanted to do something else, something more substantial, something more personal. Working on commission means that you constantly have to deal with the self-image of people and with the expectations of a magazine. I took two months off to think about it, but no idea came up. It was summer and I had just had a good holiday. On the last day of these two months I had a bicycle accident and broke my hip. I stayed in bed for two months and once I could walk again I had to swim every day to recuperate. One day I looked into the mirror after swimming and saw the mark of the goggles around my eyes. It looked like a scar. How beautiful, I thought, just the image of the past five months. I photographed myself then, full-length after swimming thirty laps, too tired to strike a pose. At first I thought the photo was awful, but later I found it revealing. The absence of a self-conscious pose seemed to show a different layer, a hidden part. Even the bathing suit became important as it shows the figure very clearly, giving the impression of nakedness, of vulnerability, of greater truth.

b. Sittard, The Netherlands, 1959. Lives and works in Amsterdam, The Netherlands.

Mark Dion and Jason Simon

Artful History: A Restoration Comedy 1988 Film Still

Artful History: A Restoration Comedy 1988 Film Poster

Artful History: A Restoration Comedy (1985–88)
My first serious or mature work, *Artful History* had three distinct incarnations. First, it materialized as an installation at the Hoboken-based gallery Four Walls in 1985. Then, it was transformed into a publication piece titled "Tales from the Dark Side," for Thomas Lawson and Suzanne Morgan's *REAL Life Magazine* in 1986. Finally, a half-hour, broadcast-quality documentary film was produced in collaboration with Jason Simon. This work, titled *Artful History: A Restoration Comedy*, was the most complex and successful articulation of the project.

The thematic of the broad project revolves around a series of bizarre and pathetic case studies of the events that befall a number of paintings that enter a commercial art-restoration studio. The paintings are 'improved' by the studio based on contemporary taste, commercial viability, or simple hucksterism, mirroring the wholesale rewriting of history we experienced during the Reagan years.

I've always had a passion for the documentary tradition, particularly at the height of its most rigorous self-analysis and reinvention during the period after 1968 to the mid-1970s. Jason was also fascinated by this period and he expanded my technical and intellectual landscape with his expertise in both filmmaking and film history. It is hard for me to look at this film today; it seems like a greenhorn endeavor. However, I must acknowledge that a significant amount of my methodology is already expressed in the *Artful History* project. —MARK DION

Hitchhiker 1989–90 oil on sackcloth, 59⁴/₅ x 89 inches (152 x 226 cm) In *Hitchhiker* I was attempting to bring the viewer much more into the painting than I had considered in earlier works. I was hoping that the open-endedness of the road and the lack of a fixed narrative would make a painting that was as much about the viewer's imagination as my own. Also I used the material in a more open way than I may have before: The paint wasn't overtly trying to describe space but was trying to suggest it. The truck, which I painted last was necessarily plain painting.

b. Edinburgh, Scotland, 1959. Lives and works in Trinidad and Tobago, West Indies and London, England.

Leonardo Drew

Number 8 1988 cardboard, fabric, metal, rope, and wood, 120 x 108 inches (304.8 x 274.3 cm) *Number 8* is "other." "Otherness" being that thing that "becomes," that "is," and before *Number 8* the concept of "other" did not exist.

b. Tallahassee, FL, USA, 1961. Lives and works in Brooklyn, NY, USA.

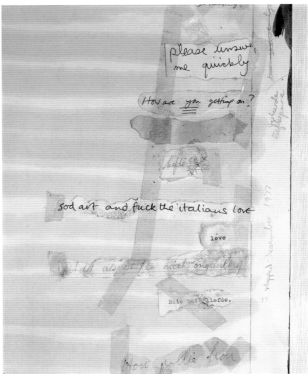

Don't Talk to Strangers (detail), 1977

mixed media, 49¹/₅ x 61²/₅ inches (125 x 156 cm)

Don't Talk to Strangers had the tone I like. It was funny and sad at the same time. It was about art and life at the same time. I realized that for me art was like making love letters for strangers, whatever form it takes.

Jeanne Dunning

Untitled 1982 partially glazed stoneware, installation in the women's bathroom in the art building, Oberlin College, OH I chose this piece for two reasons. First, because even though it is in a totally different medium, it is so related to the work I am known for. And second, because it ended up having an unexpectedly long life and impact. It is a sort of guerilla installation that I built in the women's bathroom in the art building during my last month as an undergraduate student at Oberlin College in 1982. The walls of the bathroom stall were completely covered with writhing biomorphic forms made of fired and partially glazed stoneware. I call it guerilla because I just put it there, wired it to the stall walls with picture-hanging wire and plywood, without anyone's permission. And then a few weeks later I graduated and left, assuming it would be taken down by the powers that be. I discovered much later that the piece stayed. For years afterwards, more recent Oberlin College students that I happened to meet would somehow realize that I was the person responsible for the weird installation in the women's bathroom stall and would tell me that it was still there. I had the impression that it became mildly notorious, or maybe a sort of secret shared experience among the students who prowled the art building. I heard that people used the cavities in the undulating forms as ashtrays, which oddly pleased me because I liked the idea that it had become such a fixture in the bathroom that people were using it.

 b. Granby, CT, USA, 1960. Lives and works in Chicago, IL, USA.

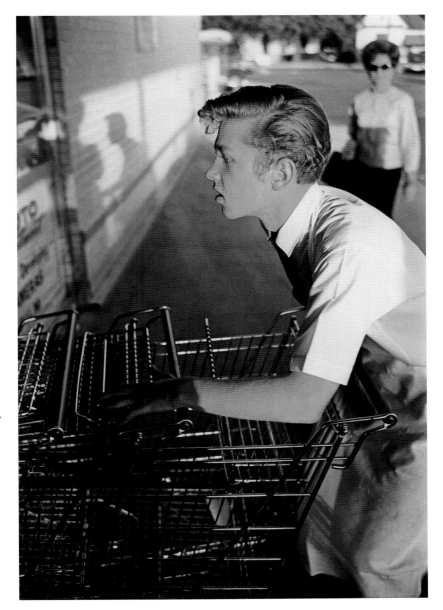

Untitled 1965 C-print, 8 x 10 inches (20.3 x 25.4 cm) This was my first successful color image. It was the first frame of that first roll of color negative film.

I had tried some color negative film several years before, but I didn't expose it correctly. I had been overexposing my black-and-white work. But when I tried this with the color negative film, it was worthless, colorless. I threw it away.

I was going to do some shopping in the supermarket. This boy happened to be outside, pushing shopping carts.

The photograph was taken with a Canon VT rangefinder camera outside of Montessi's supermarket on Madison Avenue in Memphis, Tennessee, around 1965.

Nicole Eisenman

Skeleton Monster 1996 ink on paper, 20 x 15 inches (50.8 x 38.1 cm) I wanted to make a scary Halloween drawing for a friend. I drew this in a loose and scribbly way with ink and brush on paper, which was a new choice of materials, and was really excited to have made something I couldn't have predicted. It's a dancing skeleton-insect-thing with a large dick. I've stuck with this Don't Think Too Much Just Do approach to drawing but this was the first of its kind.

b. Verdun, France, 1965. Lives and works in New York, NY, USA.

Expectations 1992 outside light projection, pink filter, lens, dimensions of length variable, beam at eye level. Installation view, suburb of Copenhagen, Denmark This work is a very early piece comprised of a beam of light projected out of doors, across the urban landscape of Copenhagen's streets, buildings, and people. It represents an urban horizon line of expectations projected upon the dream of suburban utopia, the dream of a good life the right way—a horizon that is constantly imploding.

b. Copenhagen, Denmark, 1967. Lives and works in Berlin, Germany.

Mitch Epstein

Topanga Canyon, California 1974 dye transfer, 16 x 20 inches [40.6 x 50.8 cm] In the autumn of 1974, I embarked on a zigzag road trip from New York City to Los Angeles. Once in LA, I set myself up for a three-month stay to make pictures in a city that I knew next to nothing about. I relentlessly drove and walked the streets and canyons with a Kodachrome-loaded Leica in hand. I attended public events listed in the local newspaper to see what I might find to photograph. Often a day's work would yield nothing more than long drives and small clues to future drives. However, on occasion, I would come across a situation of extraordinary photographic possibility. *Topanga Canyon, California 1974* was one of those. At a harvest fair in the hills north of Los Angeles, I came across four archetypal California girls fondling a snake, while an abandoned pink-clad baby slept on the hay a few yards from them. The photograph frames the relationship between these girls, their snake, and the baby in the hay. I saw in this picture—and others I made at that time—a new prospect for turning the ordinary into theatrical tableaux.

b. Holyoke, MA, USA, 1952. Lives and works in New York, NY, USA.

Inka Essenhigh

Wallpaper for Boys 1986 oil on enamel, 56 x 54 inches (142.2 x 137.2 cm) This is the first painting where I made a conscious decision to get rid of all the messy paint. One day I went into the studio and decided I was just going to do a line drawing. I put down one background color and started to draw; I didn't change anything. This was also the first time I allowed myself to make a decorative pattern—two-dimensional, like wallpaper, and cutesy, which was new for me. It was the first clear painting I made without all the problems of making a painting attached to it; with this painting I knew I had removed all those problems within my own head. I was more excited than ever about painting.

Pink Auto Reflection ca. 1968 oil on masonite, 3 x 4 feet (91.4 x 121.9 cm) This picture could or could not be number one, but if it isn't "it," it's close.

It dates from the late '60s when I finally decided painterly did not necessarily mean loose with lots of drips, that it was OK to use photographs, and that you could have no better subject than the streets of New York.

b. Keewane, IL, USA, 1932. Lives and works in New York, NY, and Maine, USA.

Tony Feher

Center of the World Hangers 1995 clear glass bottles with plastic caps, water, cotton sash cord, variable dimensions A list of firsts in no particular order. First time. First day of school. First love. First kiss. First fuck. First job. First drink. First joint. First arrest. First trial. First conviction. First appeal. First lawyer. First surgery. First car. First flat. First apartment. First time away from home. First time abroad. First time in Paris. First in line. First day of spring. First up. First out. First at bat. First base. First across the finish line. First hole-in-one. First gun. First kill. First time out. First day back. First down. First goal. First cigarette of the day. First show. First review. First run. First edition. First flop. First pair of shows. First win. First loss. First marriage. First hit. First divorce. First date. First stop. First start. First lie. First in the pool. First in the Hearts of Men. First to die. First dollar. First dime. First cook. First week. First month's rent. First year. First step. First flight. First in flight. First orbit. First call. First book. First snow. First child. First born. First tooth. First word. First world war. First day of peace. First day after. First jump. First album. First single. First day of the rest of your life. First birthday. First degree. First blowjob. First mate. First cold of the season. First bell. First shit. First shower. First shave. First in the bathroom. First wave. First light. First language. First punch. First landing. First grade. First rate. First "A." First "F." First string. First stitch. First take. First act. First starring role. First to the top. First deputy. First officer. First President. First course. First crossing. First out of the chute. First time I ever saw your face. First cut. First time I realized life was a series of firsts, then you die, which is a first.

Wicker Queen 1998 mixed media, height approximately 44 inches (112 cm) I have always been moved by melancholy, nostalgia for childhood, and the decay of time. *Wicker Queen* was the first time I conjured up these feelings of weakness and sadness by using the formal image of a collapsing sculpture. Before that piece I had attempted to do the same through the idea. I would try to create a realistic image of a woman and her tears, for example. I emulated Kiki Smith so the work looked like that. Now I felt an excitement and freedom through being able to say what I want to say but through the form only. *Wicker Queen* said it all but was still quite mysterious since it was not "realistic." There was such an amazing liberation in the actual making of the form too, since it involved throwing stuff together in any which way it landed. The whole thing couldn't be planned and that "of the moment" quality is what made the piece have more meaning than anything else I had made before.

b. Fort Defiance, AZ, USA, 1971. Lives and works in New York, NY, USA.

Hans-Peter Feldmann

Fritz 2003 various materials, height approximately 57 inches (145 cm) I would like to offer you my first work, but I'm unable to do so because I have no idea what my first work was. But I can offer you a picture of a work, which I did a few years ago, and which I consider my "first work."

It's me, in front of a wall, with my head a bit down, trying to find out something, and I even did not know what this "something" was about.

So I took a doll of a boy around 10 years old. The doll was built in the beginning of the 1950s, when I was 10 years old.

I put the doll in this position, which I think comes close to what I want to express.

Moses Soyer's Studio 1956 black-and-white silver print, 16 x 20 inches (40.6 x 50.8 cm) I had no idea, no certainty, no complex dialectic—only a prodigious gift and magnificent influences. The image speaks of a melancholic romanticism and direct empathy. It arrested its time and went unnoticed by me and anyone for years until its rediscovery by me in a backward perusal of my worth. A wonderful gift.

b. Brooklyn, NY, USA, 1941. Lives and works in Martins Creek, PA, USA. 133

Eric Fischl

Untitled 1969 oil on canvas, 60 x 84 inches (152.4 x 213.4 cm), missing or destroyed It is hard to single out one painting as a breakthrough painting, but this particular work does have some significance for me in this regard. I was a student midway through my second year of art school when it was painted and it was the first painting to take me into and then out of the depths of creative darkness. It was the first painting in which everything I thought I knew about art had to be abandoned. This canvas resisted every preconception I had about what art is supposed to be. What my ideas were or what my painting style should be meant nothing to this holy mess I was creating in my studio. It was the first time I had come face to face with *not* knowing. Every decision I made was sent back like so many empty envelopes. Nothing could satisfy or complete it. In a moment of utter frustration, I exploded. I threw my palette and my brushes at canvas and watched as the turpentine dissolved the shapes I had placed there. In a fit of defiant indifference, as an act of giving up or giving in, I painted what I thought was an absurd image of this white floating bed and then I left the room.

When I returned, I was calm. I was emptied out and I was calm and in this calmness I saw the painting and I finished it. I made no demands on it nor tried to return it to something within my own familiarity. I simply painted what needed to be painted. I had no idea of its "meaning," nor did I care. What I trusted was that there was an internal logic. That was all.

To this day I have no idea of what this painting means. It pleases me to remember the quality of the struggle. I am certain that had I not prevailed I would not be the artist I so desperately wanted to become. I also have come to realize that while so many of my paintings have centered their dramas on or around the bed, it was never the bed that was in doubt. It has always been the chaos that the bed causes.

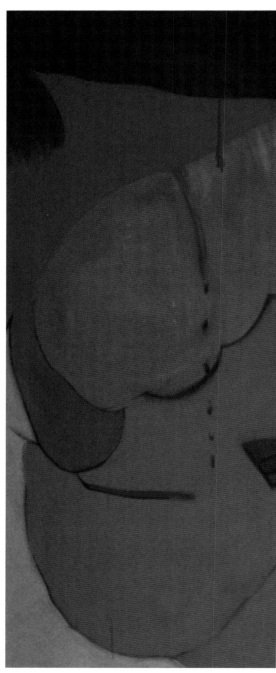

COURTESY OF THE ARTIST.

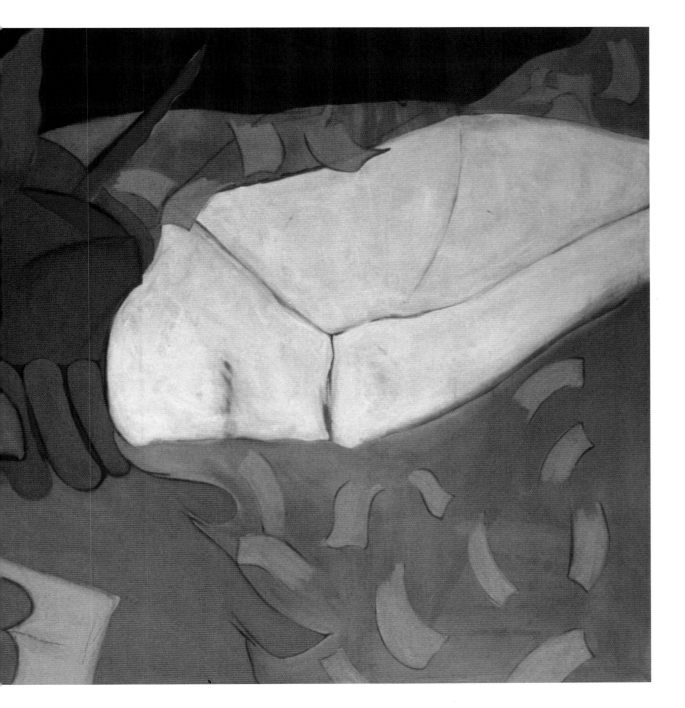

Peter Fischli & David Weiss

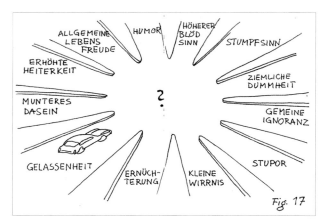

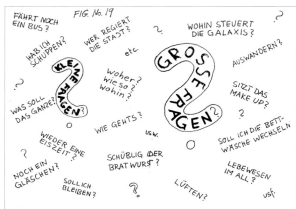

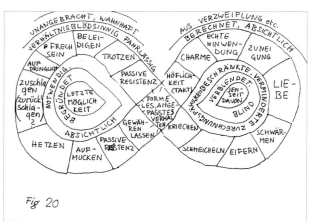

Ordnung und Reinlichkeit (Order and Cleanliness) 1980–
2003 photocopies on paper, each 13 x 18 inches (33.6 x 46 cm), edition of 12

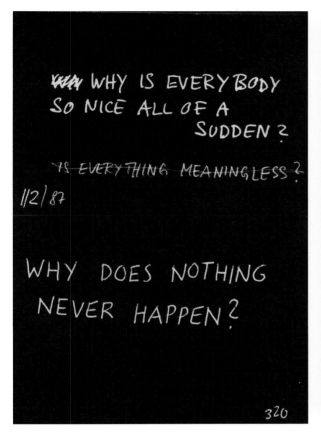
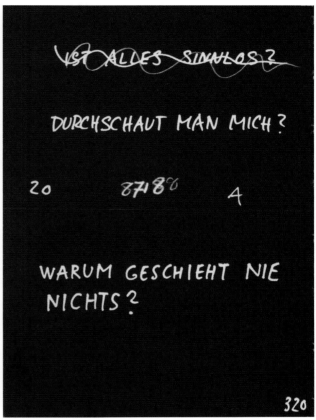

Pages from the English and German editions of the artists' questions book *Will Happiness Find Me?* 2003

Sylvie Fleury

Burn Outs No Car This is not the original first "burn out" I did but I bet it looked a bit like this . . .

    b. Geneva, Switzerland, 1961. Lives and works in Geneva, Switzerland.

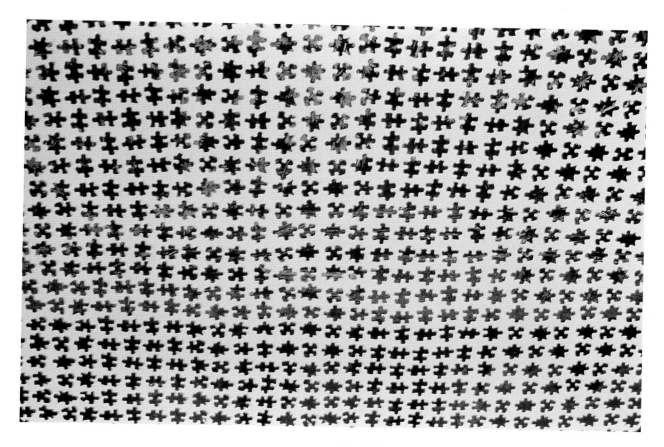

Untitled 1990 jigsaw puzzle, 42 x 60 inches (106.7 x 152.4 cm) This piece gave me a clear point of departure conceptually—putting something together (solving), and at the same time, taking it apart; circular logic.

b. St. Louis, MO, USA, 1965. Lives and works in Conway, MA, USA.

Katharina Fritsch

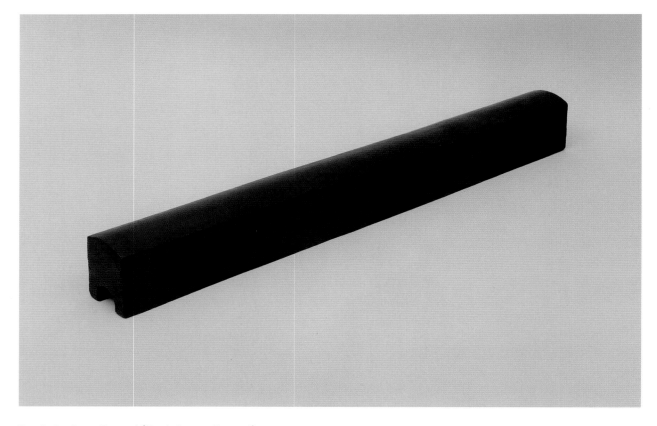

Dunkelgrüner Tunnel (Dark Green Tunnel) 1979 colored wax, 3¹/₈ x 3¹/₈ x 31¹/₂ inches
(7.9 x 7.9 x 80 cm), edition of two The work *Dunkelgrüner Tunnel* was one of four
1:100 models for outside pieces.

I did the piece when I started to work at the Kunstakademie
Düsseldorf in the class of Fritz Schwegler.

It was a kind of minimal summary of the melancholic memories
I had of my childhood in the Ruhrgebiet and the Bergische Land
with its old industrial buildings and dark landscapes.

Rose-Covered Cottages, Summer 1996 1997 oil on canvas, 12 x 12 inches (30.5 x 30.5 cm) When asked to choose a painting, this is the first one that came to mind. I don't know, it's just about the feeling I had after I made it.

b. Stamford, CT, USA. Lives and works in New York, NY, USA.

Ellen Gallagher

Untitled 1992 oil, pencil, and paper on canvas, 22 x 22 inches (55.9 x 55.9 cm) This painting was made while I was living in Boston. During those years I was involved with the Dark Room Collective, a group of young writers and artists based in Cambridge, Massachusetts.

I started using penmanship paper in my work in 1992. And, I think I knew by then the collective was drifting apart. The use of paper as a support seemed like an ideal way to communicate freedom, however idiosyncratic and inscrutable. Likewise, that freedom is only made possible through the amnesia of the penmanship paper. In this state, my characters are forced to repeat their lines. And with each repetition, experience themselves anew. Which, then, isn't a repetition. It's an ever-shifting loop where these densities and gaps are created.

After Liberty 1989 postcard, situation, 6 x 4 inches (15 x 10 cm) I made the work *After Liberty* in 1989 when I was living in Harlem, New York, when I was totally broke and the only studio space I had available to me was my lap. During the day I was working in Tribeca as Richard Prince's assistant and at night I was making art on my lap by reworking postcards, magazines, and newspapers. *After Liberty* was thus the first serious piece I made after leaving art school.

b. Johannesburg, South Africa, 1968. Lives and works in Brussels, Belgium. 143

Ralph Gibson

Untitled (Man with Rose) San Francisco,1960 silver gelatin print, 9 x 12½ inches (22.9 x 31.8 cm) This image dates from 1960. I was in my first semester at the San Francisco Art Institute and was struggling through a maze of confused emotions that seem to be an art student's reality. I was living at the Stella Hotel on Washington Street in North Beach paying $4 a week for a small room with a clean sheet provided every Thursday.

I would pin photographs on the wall across from the bed and study them for weeks on end. There seemed to be very little motion or growth in my work and my impatience was unbearable. The night before, I had come back from printing at school and pinned up this image.

Upon awakening the next morning my eyes went directly to this photograph and as I lay there I knew that this was the very first photograph that showed any indication that I might eventually find personal expression as a photographer. It was a very important moment for me. I also learned at that moment that the Muse would throw just enough crumbs to survive, and that real satisfaction as an artist was not going to come for a long time.

b. Los Angeles, CA, USA, 1939. Lives and works in New York, NY, USA.

George the Cunt and Gilbert the Shit 1969 magazine
sculpture. Made for and first published in 1970 in *Studio International* but
with the "offending" words censored; also shown in a glass case to invited
viewers at 3 p.m. on May 10, 1969 at the Robert Fraser Gallery, London.

Starting out as artists we wanted to be the first to
insult us.

Bruce Gilden

Untitled 1969 black-and-white silver print, 16 x 20 inches (40.6 x 50.8 cm) Coney Island is a classic subject for New York street photography. I knew it from the work of Leon Levinstein, Lisette Model, and Weegee, amongst others. It featured characters not in the mainstream, had the clean background of the ocean, and was easily accessible. This photograph was the first image from my own work that really excited me in that I felt it was on a par with the images I admired from Coney Island.

b. Brooklyn, NY, USA, 1946. Lives and works in New York, NY, USA.

84 Diagrams 1989 printed Ingres paper, archive boxes; each box 8.5 x 12 x 1 inches (21.6 x 30.5 x 2.5 cm) An image from my first exhibition at Karsten Schubert Gallery, London in December 1989. The work comprised four boxes of building designs that were exhibited in a display case and also passed around by visitors to the exhibition during the opening as individual sheets of paper. The work was a parallel activity, one of a number that I developed at the time which involved operating in territories just alongside art. On any given day I might produce 10, 50, or 100 building designs. A selection were printed on colored Ingres paper for this exhibition and available in a set of 84 individual designs. The exhibition remains important to me as a functional model that involves the sharing of documentary evidence of activity. An engagement with the built world remains at the core of my work, yet never again in such a straightforward and direct way. In a sense the exhibition functioned as a series of collected works in advance of rather than at the end of a long period of thought.

b. Aylesbury, England, 1964. Lives and works in London, England and New York, NY, USA.   147

Jim Goldberg

My Uncle Ran A Ski Resort 1971-2003 Polaroid and text, dimensions variable

My UNCLE RAN A ski/SUMMER resort iN CONNECTicuT, though it wASN'T much of A resort. He WAS A CoMMUNIST who fought for the right for AMEriCANS to be Able to visit CubA; he lost AT the SuPreme CourT level. LATer he RAN for SeNATor. He lost that ALSo, but he wAS ALWAyS SOMEONE I AdMired. THE ONLY MEMENTOS I hAVE from him ARE A book ABOUT STALIN ANd AN old PolAroid CAMERA.

THE SUMMER before COLLEGE I worked AT his "resort". (It wAS the SUMMER I hAd my toNSils out ANd heMorrhAGEd blood iNTo A SiNk.) It wAS my first SUMMER AWAY from home before beGiNNiNG STudies iN theology. A buNch of old, miscreANT reGulArS ANd I were hired to do odd jobs. ONE NiGhT I WAS out with my COUSIN WALKiNG the GrouNds ANd WE SAW A WOMAN GiViNG A MAN A blow job through the CUrTAiNS of AN openWINdow. THE MAN WAS lyiNG ON A bEd, WATchiNG TV, ANd lookiNG bored; I hAd NEVER SEEN ANyThiNG like this ANd COUldN'T believe iT. A few dAyS lATer I lost My VirGiNiTy to A GirL iN the TowN.

I beGAN my STudies but reALiZED soon thereAfter that I didN'T hAVE the discipliNE for theology. I becAME A photoGrApher. This picture is the first self-portrAit that I took.

b. New Haven, CT, USA, 1953. Lives and works in San Francisco, CA, USA.

Nan Goldin

David at Grove Street, Boston 1972

gelatin silver print, 20 x 16 inches (50.8 x 40.6 cm)

My earliest photographs, taken at age 15, were primarily of David, and then of other friends and lovers with Polaroid cameras given to us at my Summerhill-type Free School. At 18, I started to photograph David and drag queens we lived with in Boston using a 35-mm camera. This portrait of David as a teenage queen, taken in 1972, is a marker for me of the transition from snapshots to my "art," which many others still call snapshots.

b. Washington, DC, USA, 1953. Lives and works in New York, NY, USA and Paris, France.

Leon Golub

The Bug (Shaman) 1952 lacquer and
oil on canvas, 50 x 38 inches (127 x 96.5 cm)

Primitive and insane art gave me
a handle by which to take ahold
of the world . . . not the world
of New York painting related to
European tradition, but a world
which had inexplicable qualities
to it.

b. Chicago, IL, USA, 1922; d. New York, NY, USA, 2004.   151

Guillermo Gómez-Peña

The Loneliness of the Immigrant 1979 performance I left Mexico City in 1978 to study art in California—"the land of the future," as my lost generation saw it. Six months after my arrival in Los Angeles, I decided to spend 24 hours in a public elevator wrapped in an Indian fabric and rope as a way of expressing the profound feelings of cultural isolation I was experiencing as a newly arrived immigrant. I was unable to move or talk back. My total anonymity and vulnerability seemed to grant people the freedom to confess to me intimate things about their lives—things I didn't want to hear; to abuse me verbally; even to kick me. I overheard two adolescents discussing the possibility of setting me on fire. A dog peed on me, and at night, the security guards threw me into an industrial trashcan, where I spent the last two hours.

To me this piece was a metaphor of painful birth in a new country; a new identity—the Chicano; and a new language—intercultural performance. I quote from my performance diaries: "Moving to another country hurts much more than moving to another house, another face, or another lover. Immigrants constantly experience in their own flesh the bizarre Otherness of absolutely incomprehensible situations, symbols, and languages. As a new immigrant, I hope this piece will help a little bit to transform our insensitive views on immigration. In one way or another we all are, or will be, immigrants. Surely one day we will be able to crack this shell, this incommensurable loneliness, and develop a transcontinental identity. I hope I will still be alive to experience it."

The strong emotional responses from my involuntary audiences made me realize what an idoneous medium performance was to insert my existential and political dilemmas into the social sphere. Eventually, the "loneliness of the immigrant" became a kind of urban legend in the Chicano community. I was 24 years old.

COURTESY LA POCHA NOSTRA, SAN FRANCISCO.

b. Mexico City, Mexico, 1955. Lives and works in San Francisco, CA, USA.

153

Antony Gormley

Land, Sea and Air II 1982 lead, fiberglass, Land (crouching); 17³/₄ x 40¹/₂ x 20⁷/₈ inches (45 x 103 x 53 cm), Sea (standing); 75¹/₈ x 19⁵/₈ x 12¹/₂ inches (191 x 50 x 32 cm), Air (kneeling); 46¹/₂ x 27¹/₈ x 20¹/₂ inches (118 x 69 x 52 cm) How to make bodies into vessels that both contain and occupy space? The series of three-part lead works are the first works in which I used my own body. I was trying to map out the phenomenology of the body and to find a new way of evoking it as being less a thing, more a place; a site of transformation; and an axis of physical and spatial experience.

Land, Sea, and Air II is the second of these works: three body cases that attempted to associate a perception with a posture, and a posture with an element. For the first time, the lead carapace is divided by a vertical and horizontal grid, a system I used from this point onwards. Land has its earholes open and listens to the ground, Air kneels and listens to the sky with its nose holes open, and Sea faces out to the horizon with its eye holes open.

Two Rocks 1980 oil on canvas, 58¼ x 101¼ inches (148 x 257.2 cm)

Two Rocks is a painting I made after being in the American Southwest for the first time, in 1980. People had told me for years that I'd be astonished when I saw the desert, but its net effect was greater than that. Since I'd started painting landscapes about three years before, I had stuck by the idea that only something imaginary should be considered worthwhile subject matter. After seeing the desert, and the utter strangeness of it, I abandoned that notion.

The photo I took there at Lake Powell is quite different from the painting. Eventually I realized that my imagination, and the transformation that occurs during the making of a painting, would always creatively and positively interfere with the photographic source. The painting is also seminal in that the cipher it represents, the two rocks themselves, read to me in so many different ways at once: a portal, a warning, hands, two bodies, twins. They are at once matter-of-fact and a riddle. They feel both remote and inviting. I've revisited this dialectic many times since in my work.

b. Cleveland, OH, USA, 1953. Lives and works in New York, NY, USA. 155

Dan Graham

Schema (March 1966) magazine pages My first, most uncompromising and absolute work is the magazine piece *Schema (March 1966)*. Instead of relating self-referentially to the white cube of the gallery, it relates to the information system and to mass production in terms of disposable magazine pages.

Each published example of this piece appeared as an isolated page in different magazines. The work cannot be exhibited except through its placement in a magazine. If it were placed within an art magazine, a page would be situated in relation to reviews of gallery shows, articles and reproductions of artworks, and it could analyze the function of the magazine in relation to the gallery system.

Conventionally, art magazines reproduce secondhand art which exists first, as phenomenological presence, in galleries. Turning this upside down, *Schema (March 1966)* only exists by its presence in the functional structure of the magazine and can only be exhibited in a gallery secondhand.

I wanted to make a 'Pop' art which was more literally the logic of a consumer society. I wanted to make an art-form which could not be reproduced or exhibited in a gallery/museum, and I wanted to make a further reduction of the 'Minimal' object to a not necessarily aesthetic two-dimensional form (which was not painting or drawing): printed matter that is mass-produced and mass-disposable information. Putting it in a magazine page meant that it also could be 'read' in juxtaposition to the usual reproduction art, art criticism, reviews, reproductions in the rest of the magazine and form a critique of the magazine (in relation to the gallery structure).

Variations of *Schema (March 1966)* generated themselves through the work's self-defining decomposition in terms of its printed appearance as a two-dimensional page printed with physical 'informational' characteristics such as the quality of paper stock, the amount of black type proportionate to unprinted paper, the point size of the type, etc. Physical place is reduced to the present appearance of information in terms: The work is composed as it decomposes into the constituent material elements of its context. Its place pertained to both the work's internal grammatical structure and to the external physical position it occupied.

Each publishing of this work is inherently unlike the others and in different magazine issues the specific meanings (content) inevitably change with the context of its placement. A magazine page thereby generates its meanings from the overall context in which it is published, particularly the pages immediately surrounding it. The meaning of the work is contingent upon the specific meaning of each of its appearances; collectively it has no one meaning.

This work functions as both art and art criticism. Magazines determine a place or frame of reference both outside and inside what is defined as 'Art.'

b. Urbana, IL, USA, 1942. Lives and works in New York, NY, USA.

Schema for a set of pages whose component variants are specifically published as individual pages in various magazines and collections. In each printed instance, it is set in its final form (so it defines itself) by the editor of the publication where it is to appear, the exact data used to correspond in each specific instance to the specific fact(s) of its published appearance. The following schema is entirely arbitrary; any might have been used, and deletions, additions or modifications for space or appearance on the part of the editor are possible.

SCHEMA:

(Number of)	adjectives
(Number of)	adverbs
(Percentage of)	area not occupied by type
(Percentage of)	area occupied by type
(Number of)	columns
(Number of)	conjunctions
(Depth of)	depression of type into surface of page
(Number of)	gerunds
(Number of)	infinitives
(Number of)	letters of alphabets
(Number of)	lines
(Number of)	mathematical symbols
(Number of)	nouns
(Number of)	numbers
(Number of)	participles
(Perimeter of)	page
(Weight of)	paper sheet
(Type)	paper stock
(Thinness of)	paper
(Number of)	prepositions
(Number of)	pronouns
(Number of point)	size type
(Name of)	typeface
(Number of)	words
(Number of)	words capitalized
(Number of)	words italicized
(Number of)	words not capitalized
(Number of)	words not italicized

Rodney Graham

75 Polaroids 1976 75 flash Polaroids mounted on 15 panels, wood, dispersion, lamp, 145⅝ x 145⅝ x 145⅝ inches (370 x 370 x 370 cm) *75 Polaroids* comprised 75 flash photos of nature taken at night and mounted in an-eye level frieze around three interior walls of a purpose-built room. It was first shown at the Pender Street Gallery in Vancouver in 1976 in an exhibition with Robert Kleyn. This work is important to me because it opened up the possibility of other works dealing with nature and light in an installation context: Out of it came *Camera Obscura*, 1979, and *Illuminated Ravine*, 1979, for example.

b. Abbottsford, Canada, 1949. Lives and works in Vancouver, Canada.

Joanne Greenbaum

Untitled 1992 oil on canvas, 36 x 20 inches (91.4 x 50.8 cm) My first oil painting that I actually still have is of a squirrel in a tree with snakes slithering up the sides. The sky is orange. I did that when I was ten years old. The one I chose to show here is one I did ten years ago. What strikes me now is how similar they actually are: something on the sides, something in the middle. I remember at the time rereading Lucy Lippard's pivotal book, *From the Center*. (I had read this in college and worked really hard to reject her premise.) It was the first painting I did when I realized that I didn't have to use a lot of paint. I kept it because it's from a time when I was working completely in privacy and trying out new things with staining veils of color (hello Morris Louis) and graphic elements. It felt liberating to make a painting with two colors that took perhaps one day. I made lots of these but this one is the first that made me realize I could do anything. I still use a no-color background for most of my work, and that too was freeing. It was a blank page in which to act with the paint. This felt like a performance in my studio. The red shapes are almost like a stage set with the green in the middle as the internal action. This painting was the first instance when I stopped being claustrophobic about the paint surface. This marks the period when I started to use color as a found object. The paintings have since become more complicated and imbalanced, but I try to hang on to the feeling of honesty and directness that this one has.

b. USA, 1953. Lives and works in New York, NY, USA.

Timothy Greenfield-Sanders

Portrait of Orson Welles 1979
silver gelatin print, 11 x 14 inches (27.9 x
35.6 cm) *Portrait of Orson Welles*
was a pivotal image for me as
a young photographer. I was 27
when I shot this photograph for
Life magazine on September 1,
1979 in Toronto, Canada on
an enormous, cold film set.
I was so thrilled to meet one
of my heroes. Here was Orson
Welles, director, producer, writer,
and star of *Citizen Kane*, in the
flesh. I had dozens of questions
for him.

"What was your favorite of all
your films?" I asked Mr. Welles.

"Oh, I don't play games like
that," he replied.

And there in an instant I
realized my mistake and more
importantly understood my role
as a portrait photographer. I was
there to make him feel comfortable, not to act like a tourist or
fan. I should have asked him
what he needed: a drink of water,
a cup of coffee, a more comfortable chair. I should have been
trying to put myself into his shoes
because even for the most famous
and photographed people in the
world, a photo session is always
complicated both psychologically
and emotionally. Ever since, I've
tried to be aware of that.

b. Miami Beach, FL, USA, 1952. Lives and works in New York, NY, USA.

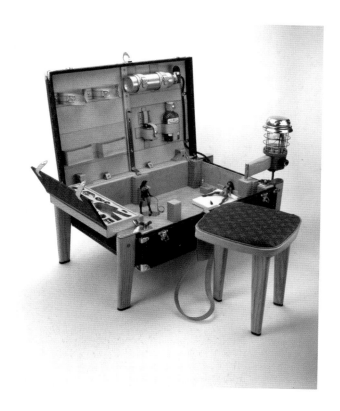

Getaway–Louis Vuitton 1999 genuine Louis Vuitton "Alzer" suitcase, leather, pressed suede, brass and brass with 18 kt. gold-plated surfaces, American red oak, Dewar's White Label scotch whiskey, drinking flask, cigarettes with box of matches, collapsible three-legged stool with Louis Vuitton monogrammed canvas seat, customized gas-powered lamp, two handcrafted anatomically correct female roommates with a collection of miniature accessories in a retractable side case. Opened: 27$^1/_2$ x 38$^3/_8$ x 41$^3/_8$ inches (69.9 x 97.5 x 105.1 cm). Closed: 7 x 26 x 17$^3/_8$ inches (17.8 x 66.04 x 44.1 cm) I made so much over-the-top sculpture—so much craziness. But no matter how successful my work was, it never really made people happy. I always felt like it was missing the thing that made you lust after it.

One day I was shopping with my wife on Fifth Avenue and we stopped by the old Louis Vuitton store. I had been in the store before, but on that day I just loved the way the store made me feel. We had been talking about traveling all morning and it just hit me—Bang—I thought, "I want it *all*, I want the whole kit. . . the trunks, the store, my beautiful wife, the sales ladies, the carpeting, the switch plates. . ." I stared intensely at one large trunk with a bunch of drawers in it and I turned to my wife and said, "it's like a fucking sculpture," and she said, "you should buy one." So I did.

Ouch! It was expensive; but it was one of the first pieces I worked on in the studio that was sold before I finished it. Today I manufacture my own brand of custom-made trunks covered in my own trademarked "TG" logo. It's funny looking back on it now and realizing it all started on a sunny afternoon in midtown. Fifth Avenue rules!

b. Brooklyn, NY, USA, 1969. Lives and works in New York, NY, USA.

Cai Guo-Qiang

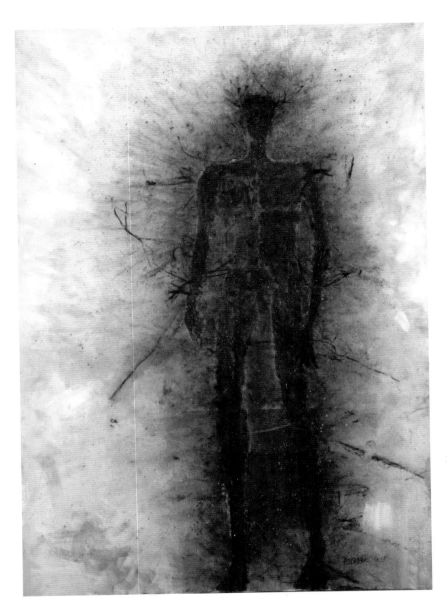

Self Portrait 1989 exploding gunpowder on oil on canvas, 65³/₄ x 46¹/₂ inches (167 x 118 cm)

I consider this my "first" work not because it is literally the first artwork I ever made, but because it was a catalyst for a focus and development of my ideas. It was the first time I ever created a self-portrait using exploding gunpowder on top of an existing image. I first painted the image in 1985 with oils, and in 1989 the painting was reworked with gunpowder.

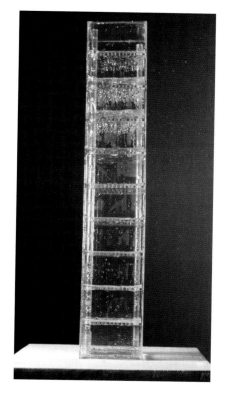

Cleaning Women at Documenta 1959 (above) black-and-white photograph **Rain Tower** 1962 (right) acrylic, plastic and water, 32³/₄ x 4 x 4 inches (83.2 x 10.2 x 10.2 cm) Assigning the lofty status of "first work" to any of my productions only reflects how I think about this at any given moment. In the past I considered different works, and today's choice will not last. For the purpose of this publication I select two complementary items: a photograph and an object.

The photograph is one of many photographs I took backstage at Documenta in 1959. At the time I captured two cleaning women amid paintings stacked against the walls, I didn't think of making art. Over the years, I have learned not to have a definition for what constitutes a work of art.

If *Rain Tower* of 1962, the object of my choice of today, is turned upside down like an hourglass, the enclosed water drips through the holes of its nine floors down to the lowest compartment. The viewer has to get involved physically.

b. Cologne, Germany, 1936. Lives and works in New York, NY, USA.

Peter Halley

The Big Jail 1981 acrylic and stucco on canvas, 72 x 72 inches (182.9 x 182.9 cm) I painted *The Big Jail* in 1981. It was the first large painting I made in which I transformed a rational square into a prison. However, in this painting there is also a symmetrical pink triangle behind the prison bars. This motif was leftover from my previous work in which human figures were represented by upright triangles. Later I learned that the Nazis forced people who were gay to wear a pink triangle on their clothing. Then, in the late 80s, the pink triangle became a symbol of the AIDS activist movement.

b. New York, NY, USA, 1953. Lives and works in New York, NY, USA.

Ann Hamilton

Untitled (suitably/positioned) 1984 man's wool coat and pants, wooden toothpicks, 60 x 33 x 10 inches (152.4 x 83.8 x 25.4 cm) It may seem unlikely that standing still for several hours, self-consciously displayed as an objectified presence wearing a suit covered with a dense surface of protruding toothpicks would be the moment when I felt that first real "a-ha" recognition of my own work . . . but that was the moment. While standing there I caught a glimmer of the difference between picturing relationships and demonstrating them; my first glint of understanding that a work is made of a series of acts and that those acts collectively embody meaning. I started with a dark blue or black man's suit purchased from the Salvation Army. Then I attached to the fabric thousands of black-painted toothpicks by twisting their sharp, glue-covered tips into the weave of the fabric.

This took a long time. It kept my hands busy and made me feel like I was doing something while I waited to understand what it might be. I thought it might need to be an object and went about trying to make or find an armature to hang it on when Melinda Hunt, a fellow student, said to me, "Your body is an armature. Why don't you just wear it?"—which, at the time, seemed easier than learning to weld.

When I put on the toothpick suit I looked like a porcupine with its defenses up, but with a completely wrong camouflage for the spare white space of my studio. I had been thinking about the relative contextual protection of camouflage. But standing still on public display for almost three hours wasn't about being camouflaged. Though physically covered I was nonetheless exposed. I became interested in the ambiguity of that position. I made no eye contact, but stood feeling the presence of the room, of people entering and exiting, people standing near or far, behind or in front of me . . . absorbing the presence of my breathing and the circulation of my blood . . . feeling myself animate the exterior skin while I became the inanimate armature within it . . . feeling part of everything happening in the room but also separate . . . feeling that every moment of standing there was the same and that every moment was different . . . feeling so self-conscious that I might lose my self-consciousness was all a part of that experience.

Afterwards I still wasn't sure if the suit was an object, or if I should name it as a performance, or a sculpture. But that no longer seemed to matter. What mattered was my recognizing a way of coming into presence that I wanted to experience again.

Richard Hamilton

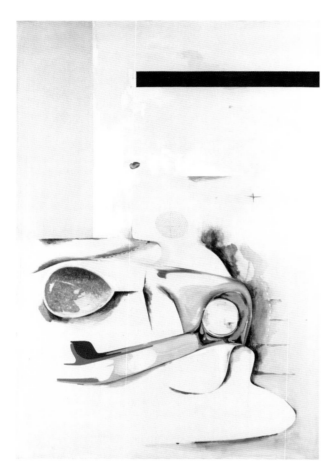

Hommage à Chrysler Corporation 1957 oil, metal foil, and collage on panel, 47³/₅ x 31³/₅ (122 x 81 cm) A seminal exhibition with the title "This is Tomorrow" was organized at the Whitechapel Art Gallery in 1956. The show displayed 12 integrated structures each produced, ideally, by a group of three individuals: a painter, a sculptor and an architect. The presentation conceived and constructed by John McHale, John Voelckler, and myself was seen as one of the major successes of the exhibition. We sought to articulate certain ideas that had formed an important part of the discussions taking place within the Independent Group at the Institute of Contemporary Arts for several years previously. These were: first, the popular arts as expressed in the mass media, and secondly, our concern with the perceptual tools used by human beings to interpret visual information.

A few months later I became frustrated by the separation between our extramural interests and the artworks we produced. I was alone in my determination to break down the barriers between "Pop art"—the name we gave to the wonderfully inventive art seen in film, TV, automobile design, etc.—and Fine Art, which at that time was moving from Abstraction to Minimalism so rapidly that it seemed to me to be disappearing up its own arse. Unable to convince my friends that concerted action might make sense, there was no alternative than to go it alone. *Hommage à Chrysler Corporation* was the first painting I made that emerged from an aesthetic constructed in my own head—with a little help from my friends and some intense looking and thinking about Marcel Duchamp, in 1957 a mind-blowing experience.

b. London, England, 1922. Lives and works in the blissful countryside of Oxfordshire, England.

Chris Hammerlein

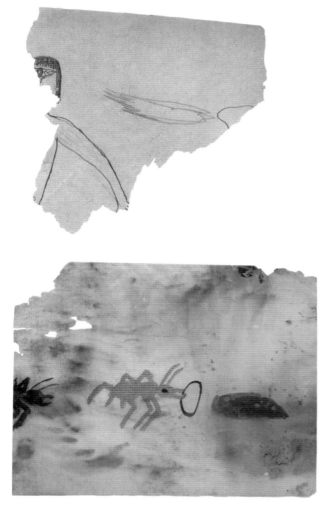

Untitled (Childhood Drawings) 1965 These fragments represent nascent descriptions of life as I imagined it as a boy artist. My identity personally has always, it seems, been wedded to my identity as an image-maker and I've always considered the silent image the spokesman for my worldview.

b. Cincinnati, OH, USA, 1962. Lives and works in Brooklyn, NY, USA.

Jane Hammond

Untitled (179, 124, 74, 118, 26, 247, 64, 136, 260, 275, 200, 183, 56, 244, 105, 62, 237) 1992 oil on canvas with metal leaf, 70 x 86 inches (177.8 x 218.4 cm) I grew up near the shore. We had a pond on our property. I was rescued in a flood. My mother sold frog's legs. I was the victim in a lifesaving class. My family was always clamming.

I've made a number of water paintings: magicians doing the old glass-of-water trick; a snowman with a fire under him; an open book of lifesaving techniques; a bear serving drinks; a ballerina before a curtain painted with octopus gatherers; a male/female couple, each with my head, having sex on a raft. Someone else pointed this out to me. I couldn't see it.

I collect facts. I make fictions of these facts. I start with an idea. I usually end up with something else.

I was thinking here about a portrait of the conductor and his players, the artist and her instruments. (That's my head on Esther Williams's body.) I'd be on the ladder, half-in, half-out, surrounded by images in my lexicon.

As I worked, the images called out the numbers I'd assigned to them ten years before. It was becoming a self-reflexive portrait of my system, my way of working, or so I thought.

Later twenty students in Cincinnati each wrote an essay on it. One said, "This is the artist, and these are all her lovers. Their ankles are chained to the bottom of the pool and they're calling out how many years they have been there."

Every essay was different but many involved conflict, ambivalence, and sexuality.

I've chosen this painting because it braids together my original concept and intention, a slippage into something juicier and less knowable, and a spark to the associative contributions of its spectators.

b. Bridgeport, CT, USA, 1950. Lives and works in New York, NY, USA.

Mona Hatoum

The Light at the End 1989 angle iron frame, six electric heating elements, 65³/₈ x 64 x 2 inches (166 x 162.5 x 5 cm). Installation view, the Showroom, London The *Light at the End* is the first work in which I was able to combine a minima approach with a strong content that is implied rather than directly stated. It is also the first work in which I was able to explore the phenomenology of materials, in this case heating elements, offering the viewer a situation that is experienced intensely on the physical level and then meanings and associations that come out of that initial physical experience.

San Guinefort 1991 mixed media, 57½ x 104⅜ x 33½ inches (46 x 265 x 85 cm) The medieval legend of San Guinefort tells of a father who left his son alone at home, and upon returning found his dog with bloodstained jaws. He guessed that the dog had attacked his son, and decided to behead it. Entering his son's room, however, the father found the cadaver of a snake and realized his mistake. He decided to build a sacred sepulcher for the dog who had protected his son. The place of the sepulcher became a pilgrimage site for the parents of children in danger. Devotion to him was forbidden by the Catholic Church, and San Guinefort later took human form and is now known as the protective saint of children.

I actually wanted to make a video; I wasn't at all interested in sculpture, and San Guinefort was my first work with the medium. Chance made me come up with the idea. I unexpectedly received a medical supplies magazine at the same time I got a book of short stories about the saint dog. I immediately knew what I had to do. And I ended up developing a series of other works around this one, which gave me a lot of confidence in the medium. I was thrilled. Making this work became a sort of rite, lasting in time. Whenever I pat the dog's back it brings me luck. I do it carefully, so as not to disturb his sleep.

Todd Hido

#1536 1995 chromogenic print, 20 x 24 inches (50.8 x 61 cm) I never planned on taking pictures at night and I didn't have much experience with photographing houses either, but something made me stop when I saw this home. I knew I needed to photograph the place.

I felt very nervous when I was making the series of long exposures. I felt like I was intruding somehow, but my desire to make something interesting overcame my fear and hesitation.

I didn't change or manipulate the light in any way. There was already something a little unnatural and strange about the scene—it looked to me a like a little model.

I was struck by the brightness of the light inside the house and how the bushes seemed to hide and shelter the structure from the outside world. I couldn't help but wonder what the occupants' lives were like—I couldn't know, so I made stuff up. The house reminded me of ones from my childhood.

I've gone on to photograph homes for years now—I never would have guessed that this pursuit would have been what keeps me up at night. I guess that's how the good ones are—they get to you when you're not expecting it.

Production element for Impressions d'Afrique 2003 (backwards transcription excerpt) Such an easy question, "What was my first work?" And yet each time I begin the thought—a kind of trace—and land on some island of "a work," a bewildering erasure occurs that acts like a kind of survival mechanism. For if I were to establish said point of departure, as it were, my peripheral vision of my own trajectory would become strangely moribund. Nevertheless, with the thought there, I can't help but explore how it resonates and throws me around a hall of mirrors, so to speak. Intricate psychedelic felt-tip pen drawings that I covered my bedroom walls and ceiling with as a young psychonaut come to mind. Or was it thousands of tape loops of recordings of anything and everywhere, pseudo multi-tracked on a reel-to-reel tape recorder with three heads? There was the case of the *Hole in the Wall* that established a physical/conceptual möbius insert and yet the duality had to be broken—by speech, the body, and machine languages?

No, probably none of the above. As soon as my focus racks to the past, the present becomes vague and quickly susceptible to the doubt truck that is always collecting. Suffice to say, I must occlude myself from meandering through the past and bring forth what is now vibrating in the present—that which keeps me alive on the head of a still point.

(3)

b. Santa Monica, CA, USA, 1951. Lives and works in Seattle, WA, USA. 173

Susan Hiller

Dedicated to the Unknown Artists (details) 1972–76

305 postcards, charts, maps, one book, one dossier, mounted on 14 panels, each 26½ x 41½ inches (66 x 104 cm) I found the first 'rough sea' postcard in a Brighton sweetshop in 1972 and shortly afterwards, another one in Weston-super-Mare. Soon I had a collection of more than 300. I was intrigued by the sublime drama of the pictures and equally fascinated by the subtle permutations, variations, and versions created in multiple printings, reprintings, and retouchings by anonymous hands, the unknown artists of my title.

I played with the postcards on and off while making paintings and live events for groups of people. More and more intensely I felt the two ways of working were pulling me in contradictory directions just like my dual trainings in art and in anthropology. Finally, at some point in 1973, I realized that using cultural artifacts as basic materials could be a starting point, a way to integrate many things, including myself. But it wasn't until 1974,

when I was artist in residence at the University of Sussex, that I had the means to begin serious, concrete work on Dedicated to the Unknown Artists.

In those days I never considered a work finished until it was exhibited or otherwise used by an audience. Dedicated to the Unknown Artists was virtually completed in 1974, but my artist-in-residence exhibition was suddenly postponed and I simply left the piece behind to go traveling for a year in India, Afghanistan and Indonesia. When I got back, I rented a wide-keyboard electric typewriter and painstakingly typed up large charts laying out what I had discovered about the postcards; the charts were ultimately mounted alongside them. All my findings were included in "Notes" analyzing the material and the process of making the work, and, more significantly in retrospect, proposing that my role as an artist in Dedicated to the Unknown Artists was to function as a curator collaborating with the works exhibited by discovering, validating, and presenting them.

b. Tallahassee, FL, USA, 1942. Lives and works in London, England.

The piece was installed in 1975 missing one element, a small book
of images called *Rough Sea* which I had designed in 1974 to function as the exhibition catalogue. In 1976, after further delays, the
publication was finally printed and *Dedicated to the Unknown Artists* was
exhibited in its complete form.

Thomas Hirschhorn

Jeudi 17.1.1991–Jeudi 28.2.1991 1992 wood, cardboard, paper, prints, adhesive tape. Exhibition view, Hôpital Ephémère, Paris,1992 **233 Travaux** 1992 wood, cardboard, paper, prints, plastic foil, adhesive tape. Exhibition view, Hôpital Ephémère, Paris, 1992 The exhibition at the Hôpital Ephémère was one of my first exhibitions. I chose this exhibition as my "first work" because it was the first time I wrote a text about one of my exhibitions and about my work. With the following text and with writings in general, I wanted to clarify and understand what worked out and what did not function with my work. The text helped me distance myself from the work I had made. The writing helped me be aware of mistakes and what was lacking. But as well, the texts I wrote about my exhibitions served as self-encouragement to continue working.

About my exhibition at the Hôpital Ephémère. 3.1 - 4.19 1992
(Text written in April 1992, translated by Andreas Riehle)

I am not satisfied with my exhibition. This dissatisfaction does not come from the concrete result of the exhibition or from an obvious failure. On the contrary, I rather have the feeling that something concrete actually happened, the visits of Max Wechsler, Adrian, Ian, Francesca, Aude Bodet, Madeleine Van Doeren and Jean Brolly's purchase, and also my next exhibition project for the Shedhalle in Zürich and the perspective of future exhibitions in Luzern, Bern and Ivry. And then the discussions with the artists here, at the Hôpital Ephémère, their invitation to talk about my work, and so on. But in spite of all these concrete and positive events and reactions, an "unsatisfied feeling" prevails.

I finally assimilated these events and reactions as positive and they can be considered as positive, although these positive aspects are based on a misunderstanding. Is this misunderstanding created by a commitment or by something speculative?

My dissatisfaction comes from the part of the exhibition where the works are on the ground ("233 travaux"). I wanted my paper sheets, cartons, wood pieces to conquer their presence in the exhibition autonomously, beyond justifications. I wanted to be radical. I wanted to expose them to the danger of whatever would become of them. I entirely assumed the possibility that the work could be hurt by the context. I thought of the beggar that we bump into on the street corner and how we feel more embarrassed about having touched him than about his being a beggar. I thought of the dead bodies during the urban war in Yugoslavia. Of the meaninglessness of the civil victims killed by "accident." What a shame that the beautiful white walls of the exhibition space are not being used? No, shame comes from the dead without reason. Is it a shame that my work does not show its power on the white walls? No, to witness Iranian women stoned by their own families, that is a shame. I wanted all my works to be displayed in the same way. Whether large or small, made of wood, paper or carton I wanted each work to be considered for itself. I wanted no arrangement with large, small, wood, paper, carton work. Nor did I want any other fixing system. I wanted the visitors to walk around my work, find their way in a space where everything is put on the same level. The works can be considered from a non-authoritarian stand point. I didn't want to make a demonstration by hanging all the works on the wall. Instead of hanging my work, I prefered putting it on the floor, like a display. It is the first time that I don't hang my work but put it on the floor instead. What is important is my decision to show the works. It was not a set decision, but resulted from the display process. As a consequence, the result comes from a process and not from a concept.

I want to add that the decision to put the work on the floor instead of on the wall wasn't thought out thoroughly. Because all energy was taken up for this specific decision and every other question as, how much space to leave around each work, or how to seperate the works, all of these other issues became minor issues, and I regret it. There was not enough energy left to resolve these questions.

I am not satisfied, because this part of the exhibition wasn't good and it could be misunderstood. I want to be simple and clear. However I don't feel that this exhibition isn't right or just, but it lacks the force, the strength, the power which is present in a single work. I didn't want it to be so. Because I assume that when my work is showed, it can be showed everywhere and in any condition. I believe my work is powerful even when it is packed, or stored in the dark. My work doesn't need an attractive presentation. My work just simply exists. I think my work is not subordinated to a specific space. My work can be shown on the wall, put on something, on the ground or in a room. My work can also be carried in jacket pocket. To be exact, this should be checked out. This exhibition shows that everything is possible, this is also a meaning for this exhibition, I said to myself: I can do what I want with my work. I have no doubt that it is possible, but is it really necessary? I want my work to be necessary without any possible misunderstanding (I don't care if it is understood, what is important is the will). I must look for the mistake or the mistakes. One mistake is that I didn't take the time to try out all the different possibilities once I had chosen to put the works on the floor. I didn't go far enough to actually do it. Would it have been better to distribute the works on the floor without coordinating them, would it have been better to show the works with larger intervals? Would it have been better to cover the exhibition space with the two other works ("Jeudi 17.1.1991–Jeudi 28.2.1991" and the video "Périphérique") exhibited? About this, I have no clue, because I didn't try it out. Another mistake was that I am the one that chose the location, I fought for it myself, and elaborated it with a set idea, instead of letting things come from the works. I can say it now, because I had originally planed to hang the works, and finally put them on the floor. As reaction, instead of action. And also, I created a pressure which was not necessary before starting the set up, by asserting to do it in a certain way. (Because, finally I did not even stick to what I had planed and asserted, and it wasn't good)

My conclusions show: too remote from the works. Must have less time. Fewer wills. Do it simpler.

Nicky Hoberman

Glacé Cherry 1996 oil on canvas, 90⅛ x 52 inches (229 x 132 cm)

This painting still feels like a landmark: It is my first big canvas. I did it in the space of a single frenzied twelve-hour stretch. I now work much more slowly, in even, concentrated, bite-size spurts. This piece, however, was a huge challenge at the time; I can still feel the excitement and giddy newness in making it. I don't work from prepared sketches; instead, I dive straight in, drawing with paint on the canvas so that every painting has a fresh start that may result in an unexpected, exciting outcome, or else end in total failure. *Glacé Cherry* depicts Dinos Chapman's daughter, but that isn't important; above all, it's the very start of my portraying unsentimental, powerful, yet distorted young girls. The figure, dressed in contemporary clothes, is floating against a flat turquoise ground, her hair flying, her left arm outstretched beyond the picture frame as her feet disappear below while she smiles enigmatically.

b. South Africa, 1967. Lives and works in London, England.

ONE 1988 charcoal tempera on paper, 36 x 48 inches (91.4 x 121.9 cm)

Drawing has always been and continues to be a vital practice for me. In 1988, a year and a half after finishing grad school at the Pratt Institute, I made a drawing I called: *One*. At that time I recognized the beginning of something new in my work. What I recall about the process of making and experiencing that work is as follows:

In my notes from that time, I mention the potential of affecting movement in space, actually "dictating the viewer's movement" by establishing an experience that required one to walk in a circle. It was my hope to establish an improvisational collaborative experience using the viewer to "complete the work" by his or her movement around it. In one sense the work was primarily a traditional drawing, charcoal on paper, made with sixteen pieces of paper stapled together. I exploited the flexibility of the material I was working with and created a freestanding, cylindrical drawing. "The drawing was impossible to view all at once and had to be walked around to be seen."

Upon reflection, I am reminded of the influences of other artists who inspired me at the time. Certinly the drawings of Richard Tuttle were very compelling. The innovation I saw in his drawings opened me up to new potential and freedom in my own practice. I responded to space, the interaction with individual viewers and the "object" as equal integral components that became the work itself. I sensed the importance of a connection with each viewer; believing, as I still do, that "art" exists internally in each individual and is awakened and brought forth by the invitation to "experience" presented by an "object."

When deciding to title this work *One*, I was using the title to highlight a moment when something sig-

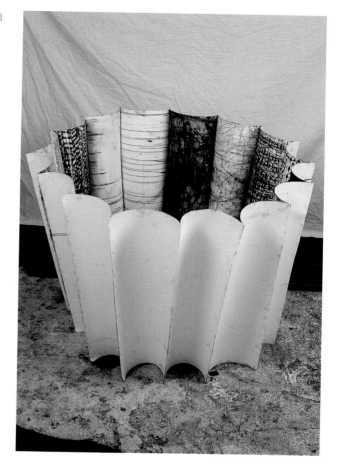

nificant had occurred in my thinking and the realization of these thoughts in the physical manifestation of the work. The awareness of the potential "material in everything," including the language I attached to the work in the title, still resonates from *One* for me.

b. Spokane, WA, USA, 1957. Lives and works in Brooklyn, NY, USA.   179

Howard Hodgkin

Interior with Figures 1977–84 oil on wood, 49¼ x 56¼ inches (125.1 x 142.9 cm)

Interior with Figures is a picture which, perhaps more than many others, suggested a way forward at the time I painted it. Not because of the (for me) unusually explicit subject matter, but because I managed somehow to contain this in a pictorial space without having to conceal it completely. Otherwise there is nothing more to say, except that, like so many other artists, I hope that every new picture is a new first time.

b. London, England, 1932. Lives and works in London and Wiltshire, England.

Kurmittelhaus Wenningstedt | 1979 C-print on Kodak paper, 15 x 22 inches (38 x 57 cm) Wenningstedt is a small place on Germany's northernmost island in the North Sea: Sylt. I used to spend many summers on this island. Out of curiosity and out of interest in public spaces I was looking around for suitable places to photograph. This photograph is among the first I took and is still one of my favorites. A "Kurmittelhaus" is a place where people take their cures.

b. Eberswalde, Germany, 1944. Lives and works in Cologne, Germany.

Jenny Holzer

Messages to the Public (above) March 15–30, 1982
Spectacolor sign. Installation view. Times Square, New York
Truisms (left; detail of window installation) Dec. 12–30,
1978 photostat Franklin Furnace, New York.

ABUSE OF POWER COMES AS NO SURPRISE
ACTION CAUSES MORE TROUBLE THAN THOUGHT
BOREDOM MAKES YOU DO CRAZY THINGS
EXPIRING FOR LOVE IS BEAUTIFUL BUT STUPID
LACK OF CHARISMA CAN BE FATAL
MONEY CREATES TASTE
RAISE BOYS AND GIRLS THE SAME WAY
YOU ARE GUILELESS IN YOUR DREAMS

182   b. Gallipolis, OH, USA, 1950. Lives and works in Hoosick, NY, USA.

Einhorn/Unicorn (top) 1968-69 pencil on paper, 11³/₅ x 8¹/₅
inches (29.7 x 21 cm)
Einhorn/Unicorn (bottom) 1970 fabric, wood, dimensions variable

in the dazzling heat
from the undulating field
a small white rod
approaches you . . .
I first saw her in the street, she walked past me,
whilst I was still lost in my own "unicorn" day-
dreams—the strange rhythm of her gait, of putting
one step in front of the next. . .

All was like a reverberating shock of my own
imagination. Her movements, a certain flexibility,
knowing precisely how to use only her legs, with
the rest of her body, from head to hips, frozen still.

Drinking coffee, talking politics, and me franti-
cally wondering how to convincingly explain my
idea. She is 21 years old and ready to marry.

She is spending her money on new bedroom
furnishings.

I try to tell her that I want to build a particular
instrument for her, a kind of rod to go on her head,
and that this rod is made of wood and is supposed
to emphasize her manner of walking.

We spend the next weeks trying to determine
the right proportions for her body, establishing the
weight and height of the object, and doing distance
and balance exercises.

The performance took place in the early morning, outside in the open countryside. Mist lies in the
fields, the sun captures this apparition, the return
of the unicorn.

Her consciousness is heightened with almost
electric vibrance; nothing can stop her trance-like
journey, measuring herself against every tree and
cloud in sight. And the wheat caresses her hips, but
not her bare shoulders.

b. Michaelstadt, Germany, 1944. Lives and works in Zell-Bad and Berlin, Germany and Paris, France. 183

Roni Horn

Ant Farm 1974-75 performance, ant farm dimensions: 48 x 72 x 4 inches (121.9 x 182.9 x 10.2 cm) This is perhaps the work that cued me to what I was about. It helped me understand my relationship to the audience. It showed me how the experience itself becomes the key, and then it did so in a way that incorporated many idioms—sculpture, performance, and even an element of drawing.

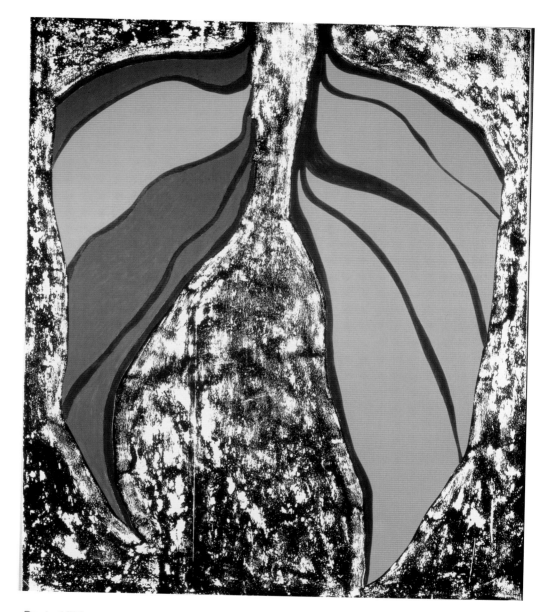

Roots 1993 enamel paint on Formica, 72 x 86 inches (183 x 218.5 cm) After having made conceptual works that completed themselves without a need for me, I needed to take part again in the creative process. This painting describes how I had to reach down to gather the nourishment to breathe again, and the fear that weeds, not flowers, may emerge.

b. Kent, England, 1962. Lives and works in London, England, and New York, NY, USA. 185

Callum Innes

From Memory 1989 oil on board, 39 x 29³/₁₀ inches (100 x 75 cm) This work came at a stage when I had emptied every single image out of my work. It became a starting point. I had been keeping a book of linear sketches of various plant forms. In this case I used a linear drawing of a wild cucumber plant. I decided to sink the silhouette into the corrugated cardboard so that the image became part of the fabric and therefore part of the history of the material.

Motel Modern 1982 enamel paint, wood, fiberglass, aluminum, and textiles, dimensions variable. Installation view, the Inn of Tomorrow, room 343, Anaheim, CA, October 23–24, 1982. Installation continued at the Richard Kuhlenschmidt Gallery, Los Angeles, CA, October 26–November 20, 1982. *Motel Modern* was the culmination of five years of submersion in Southern California thrift stores and swap meets, including two years at CalArts, surveying the progression of utopian design through planned obsolescence to Goodwill oblivion and eventual rediscovery. *Motel Modern* emerged as my first body of work conceived as an ensemble for a specific site.

Today the Inn of Tomorrow is remodeled beyond recognition, complete with mansard roofs. Modernism has come in and gone out of style several times, knocking down the fence that *Motel Modern* sat on between high and low art, between kitsch and camp, and between irony and sincerity.

b. Kenosha, WI, USA, 1955. Lives and works in Palm Springs and Santa Monica, CA, USA. 187

Bill Jensen

Smoked Oysters 1971 hand-ground oil on canvas, 8 X 6 feet (2.4 x 1.8 m) This was my first painting done after I moved to New York. I would consider it my first mature painting, the start of my own voice.

b. Minneapolis, MN, USA, 1945. Lives and works in New York, NY, USA.

Problems 1992 acrylic on board, 28 x 32 inches (71.1 x 81.3 cm) How weird that this painting is from a long time ago. I guess it is over thirteen years old maybe. It is a painting from my first years in San Francisco. I had lived there for about four years. It changed me a lot to see life in close quarters in that city. Lots of different types of people. I started painting the things I saw around town and the people I began to know. I was, I think, pretty anxious in my mind back then, and that is why I painted everything so harsh and fast back then. I was really anxious. I never made art like that until I moved to that town. It really informed my mind and I am a different person now because of the magic of San Francisco.

b. USA 1968. Lives and works in Portland, OR and San Francisco, CA, USA.

Jones Beach Piece 1970 performance, performers: John Erdman, Susan Rothenberg, George Trakas, Joan Jonas *Jones Beach Piece* was my first outdoor performance. (*Wind*, 1968, choreographed for film, was based on *Oad Lau*, an indoor piece.) *Jones Beach Piece* consisted of a series of actions or signals performed a quarter of a mile away from the audience, who were standing on a small hill overlooking a mud flat that was surrounded by grassy dunes, serving as wings where performers could hide and emerge at unexpected times and places. Deep landscape space alters the viewer's perception of sound and image. In my earlier *Mirror Works*, 1968–71, the mirror was the transforming device. Later video performances involved many devices from mirror and outdoor works. The closed-circuit video system—camera, monitor, projected image—multiplied, delayed, and transformed the subject or image in simultaneous live and captured sequences. This image of the hoop represents one of the defining moments for my work. The structure consisted of movements one after another like beads on a string.

As the performance was seen in the distance, which flattened images and delayed sound, most photographs of the work were taken in rehearsal. To move closer the photographer entered the action. This particular image includes Susan Rothenberg in the hoop with George Trakas and John Erdman rolling it. I am is standing in the distance. There was something magical in performing outdoors. Moments never to be repeated. Landscape has continued to play a significant part in my work.

Brad Kahlhamer

Bear Butte 1998 oil on canvas, 16 x 14 inches (40.6 x 35.6 cm) *Bear Butte 1998* was the first painting in which I could confidently associate color—in this case, yellow—with a spiritual experience.

b. Tucson, AZ, USA, 1956. Lives and works in New York, NY, USA.

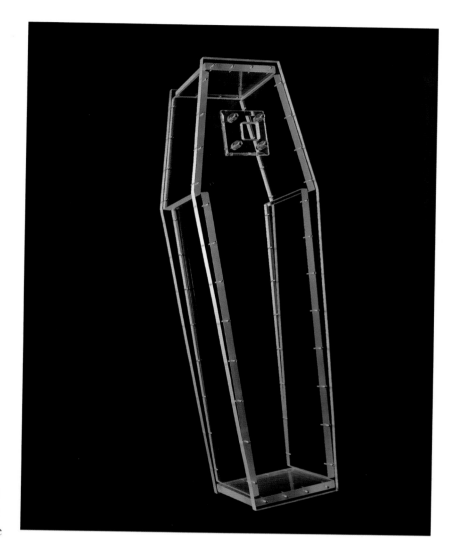

Station (Bullet-Proof Casket) 1990
bullet-proof Plexiglas, one-way screws, 23 x 75
x 17 inches (58.4 x 190.5 x 43.2 cm) I choose
this work because I feel that it,
among all my early sculptural
work, best embodies the idea of
enclosure, the play with perme-
able barriers that create interior
spaces, and the sense of the
beyond. All of these became key
aspects of my subsequent work.

Nadav Kander

Diver, Salt Lake, Utah 1997 color print, 30 x 40 inches (76.2 x 101.6 cm)

Most of my recent work focuses on the footprint of humanity upon the landscape. This image is no exception—it deals with something serene and at the same time unsettling. When I take photographs, I am not portraying the answers but rather asking the questions so that the viewer is left with more intrigue. Some of the projects I am working on at the moment involve an element of digital manipulation; however, this one, surprisingly has not been retouched in any form.

b. Tel-Aviv, Israel, 1961. Lives and works in London, England.

**As if to Celebrate I Discovered a Mountain Blooming
with Red Flowers** (above) 1981 mixed media and pigment, 42¹/₈
x 120 x 120 inches (107 x 305 x 305 cm). Installation view, Tate Gallery, London
The Earth (right) 1991 fiberglass, pigment,dimensions variable.
Installation view, Palacio Velazquez, Parque del Retiro, Centro de Arte
Reina Sofia, Madrid

*As if to Celebrate I Discovered a Mountain Blooming with
Red Flowers* is a work that makes clear my attitude
to sculpture. If one can say the history of sculpture
is the history of material, *As if to Celebrate . . .* , in
its celebratory material, is a non-material presence
for sculpture.

The Earth, ten years after *As if to Celebrate. . .* ,
does away with the object completely. It is the first
non-object.

These are two works I refer to constantly. They
are a measure of what I feel I need to do.

b. Bombay, India, 1954. Lives and works in London, England.   195

Alex Katz

Winter Scene 1951-52 oil on composition board, 24 x 23⁷/₈ inches
(61 x 60.6 cm) This was the most successful example
of allover landscape painting that I had done at
that time.

b. Brooklyn, NY, USA, 1927. Lives and works in New York, NY, USA.

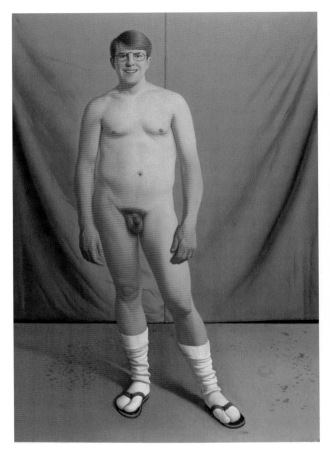 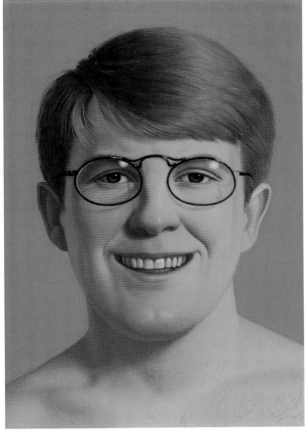

Self-portrait 1995 oil on birch, 27 x 17.5 inches (68.6 x 44.5 cm)

This is the last painting I finished while in graduate school at UCLA. I came into the school making paintings that were influenced by twentieth-century psychological figuration. Otto Dix, Rene Magritte, Hans Bellmer, Francis Bacon, and a lesser-known American named Gregory Gillespie were important artists to me at the time. But soon after entering the program, I realized that psychological figuration had little relevance for me and had no relationship to my lived experience. I wanted to continue to use the figure but eliminate the psy-chological as it had been interpreted in Europe for the past hundred years: an interpretation that came out of Romanticism, Expressionism, and Surrealism, and was almost always expressed through images of pathology. This was the first painting in which I felt that I had purged those elements from my work. Instead of making a painting that tried to show the psychological interior of the subject, I began to investigate the complex relationship between the figure in the painting and the viewer, a concern that remains relevant for me today.

b. Indianapolis, IN, USA, 1966. Lives and works in Brooklyn, NY, USA.

Mike Kelley

Chicken Brooder 1978/1990 galvanized sheet metal, wood, felt, electric lights, 37 x 32 x 36 inches (94 x 81.3 x 91.4 cm) I would consider *Chicken Brooder* to be my first mature work of art. I made it in 1978, during the last year of my graduate studies at CalArts. *Chicken Brooder* is just that, a simple wooden structure fitted with electric lights used to hatch eggs. I built it from instructions found in a craft magazine that I purchased at a local flea market. It looks exactly like the one pictured in the magazine. When I entered CalArts my work was still very much influenced by my undergraduate training in painting at the University of Michigan in Ann Arbor. My paintings and drawings were part Rauschenberg sloppy formalism, part Jim Nutt sub-pop. I was also toying with performance and installation in response to images I had seen of works by Joseph Beuys and Rudolf Schwarzkogler. At CalArts, which was dominated at the time by Conceptualists of the image/text variety, I had an artistic crisis. Not knowing what to do, I decided I would simply copy something to see what would happen. The image of the chicken brooder found in the how-to magazine attracted me, and even came with instructions on how to build it. Making this piece required me to work with materials I had not been accustomed to using and opened my eyes to the possibility of working with craft materials—materials not associated with fine art practice. Following upon this, I made a series of birdhouses, then similar structures with no apparent use. Later, I began to work with found craft items such as homemade blankets and stuffed toys. Materials such as these attracted me because of the specter of class affiliation that clung to them. This was not something that was of much interest to the art world of the late '70s and early '80s and I found it invigorating.

COURTESY OF THE ARTIST AND METRO PICTURES, NEW YORK.

b. Detroit, MI, USA, 1954. Lives and works in Los Angeles, CA, USA.

Mary Kelly

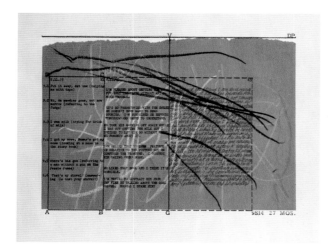

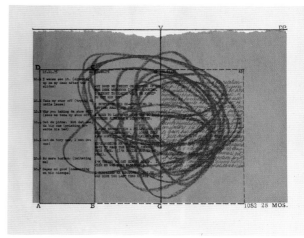

Post-Partum Document 1973–79

Documentation III, analyzed markings and diary-perspective schema, ink, pencil, crayon, sugar paper; 1 of 10, 11 x 14 inches (27.9 x 35.6 cm) each

First child,
First extended project, third part:
His first drawings,
My first narrative.
First major exhibition,
First woman to show there,
First press, big scandal, much
debate:
Is it art?
Women's work?
Why Lacan?
Second thoughts:
Yes, because I say so.
No, not exactly.
To interrogate the interrogation
rather than the object
First, and then . . .

William Kentridge

Tropical Love Storm 1985 charcoal and pastel on paper, 39³/₈ x 27 inches (100 x 70 cm) This drawing was based on a photo of Brassaï, and I would regard it as a seminal or first work because it came after a break of not drawing for two years. I decided to work without interrogating the work before it was done—which had paralyzed me for these two years. So I drew the photograph without thinking about the questions that arise around making a copy, or the nature of the couple drawn. Making the drawing answered a need to be back in the studio and showed that work could start from an unclear thematic impulse and find its raison d'etre somewhere along the journey of its making. The drawing functioned as a huge release from the brakes on working which I had placed on myself and opened the way for other drawings less derivative than this one.

b. Johannesburg, South Africa, 1955. Lives and works in Johannesburg, South Africa. 201

Anselm Kiefer

Am Meer 1970 oil on canvas, 60⅝ x 46⅞ inches (154 x 119 cm) This painting is part of a series of other paintings and is one that I have not burnt or destroyed. It comes from pictures of me in the different European countries.

b. Donaueschingen, Germany, 1945. Lives and works in Ribaute, France.

Miss Ivy Cavendish (Oxford) 1958

pencil on paper, 21 x 16³/₈ inches (53.3 x 41.6 cm) I had just left the army and started on the GI Bill at Oxford University, drawing from life every day in the Ashmolean Museum. It was 1958 and this was not my first drawing there, but, after a year or two of brushing-up my drawing each gloomy day, I believe this one was a breakthrough in confidence and the skill to draw on my early canvases. I'm 73 now, and I think I can draw as well as any Jew who ever lived, or better, because I've passed a lot of water since Oxford—to paraphrase the immortal Sam Goldwyn.

b. Cleveland, OH, USA, 1932. Lives and works in Los Angeles, CA, USA.

Imi Knoebel

Raum 19 (Room 19) 1968 fiberboard and wood, 77 parts of varying sizes. Created and built when I was at Kunstakademie Düsseldorf. With the exploration of the ins and outs of many possibilities, I laid the foundations for my creative development.

b. Dessau, Germany, 1940. Lives and works in Düsseldorf, Germany.

Buffalo Dance 1973 acrylic on canvas, 70 x 67 inches (177.8 x 170.2 cm) I had been trained as a hard-edged, geometrical abstractionist in the '60s, the era of formalist dominance. Upon leaving graduate school, I began to ease into a more intricate, personal, obsessive approach to those works. I found that the geometrical structure could contain a variety of touches.

Early during the winter of 1972, I was invited to the Tamarind Lithography Workshop in New Mexico to create lithographs. While there, I visited Native American pueblos, as well as national parks and monuments, absorbing the rich hues of earth and rock, the nuanced iconography of patterning in woven carpets. To differentiate for myself the many colors in my prints, I developed a variety of surfaces (cross-hatchings, dots, dashes, strokes, overlays), which produced a rhythmic repetition.

Returning to New York, I began to add those textures to my large canvases. *Buffalo Dance* was the first which successfully absorbed the strata of land, the light of dusk on the mountains. I inserted more and more detailed passages, which evoked the markings of native pottery

without directly appropriating them. This was perhaps a proto-Pattern Painting. Later, I studied the decorative motifs of many cultures, deliberately integrating them into my art, but *Buffalo Dance* was a gift, inspired by fragments of memory.

Guillermo Kuitca

Nadie Olvida Nada 1982 acrylic on hardboard, 9¹/₂ x 11¹³/₁₆ inches (24 x 30 cm) Nineteen eighty-two was an intense year in Argentina. In April, the Falklands War began and there were daily signs that the military dictatorship was coming to an end. There was a feeling of euphoria in Buenos Aires but, just twenty, I was burned out; the years of the dictatorship and my own adolescence had left me confused. I had secretly determined to give up painting. I had begun to write and rehearse my first play with a friend.

I spent afternoons in my studio, but I did not work. Gradually I began to paint, but without enthusiasm, just making faint lines with the brush. I sometimes imagined that if I held the brush, still the easel would be the thing to move, not my hand.

My work from this period has small, faintly-painted figures seen from the back. Soon thereafter, the image of a bed appeared in a painting and in this piece (*Nadie Olvida Nada, 1982*) I placed it in the foreground.

The bed was a place but also a possibility. At the moment I painted it I must have felt a great attraction to the material. My approach was, for me, outside any tradition; I didn't think of any other artists using beds. I felt that I had discovered it, that I was the first man on earth to see a bed, that my experience with it went beyond my experience as an artist. Something like "Hey look, here is a bed, and it is a wonderful thing" as if it were a natural, and not a cultural fact.

The bed is a place for sleep, love, birth, and death but for me this everyday object was a space whose pure presence anticipates events that have not yet occurred; in other words, the painted bed was also a plan. The plan we inhabit.

Over the years, the bed became apartment, city, map, theater, diagram—in short, the vehicle and center for operations for all my future work.

b. Buenos Aires, Argentina, 1961. Lives and works in Buenos Aires, Argentina.

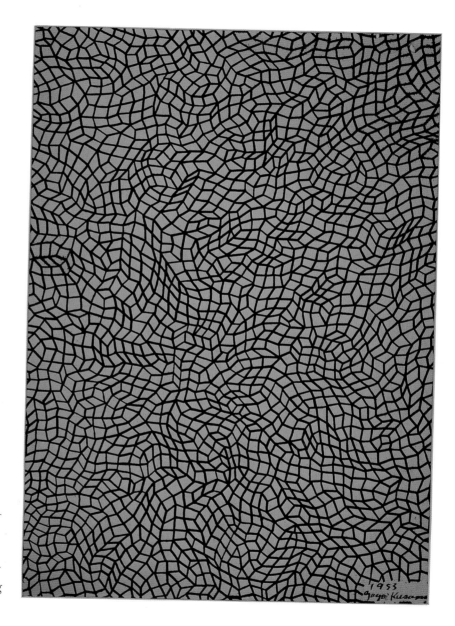

Growing Net 1953 Chinese ink on paper
17 x 11¾ inches (43 x 30 cm) This is one
of my early works and is the
one that formed the basis for my
works through my career. Taking
off from this, I have been creating art pieces continuously to
this day. The polka-dot paintings
I made then have developed into
my works today.

Robert Kushner

Pomegranates and Lilies 1974-75 acrylic and ink on taffeta, 91 x 173 inches (231.1 x 439.2 cm) This piece was the beginning of a long chain of experiments and working methods that continues to influence me today.

In 1974, I had been working intensively with the performance format, utilizing costumes of my own construction. Solo and group performances began in 1970 and were presented in galleries and alternative spaces.

There was a separate, independent body of work involving the use and reinterpretation of motifs derived from decorative textiles. Working with decorative material was a knowing and political position that I and my colleagues openly embraced. At the time, I was painting large-scale motifs on taffeta, cutting up the lengths of fabric and recombining them into unstretched paintings. Most of the forms were derived from Chinese cut paper designs. In the case of this painting, I combined the motif of an open pomegranate, a lily with its dagger shaped leaves, and an abstracted image of water. I felt that by drawing and redrawing these images, re-combining them in different ways, I could come to "own" them, much as a nomadic weaver would eventually own motifs that were repeated over and over on her loom. In the spring of 1974, I had the great good fortune to travel extensively in Turkey, Iran, and Afghanistan, looking at historical Islamic monuments and absorbing a foreign (very foreign) culture firsthand. Everything was different: the landscape, the food, the clothing, the cultural conventions and customs. As a costumer, one of the garments that interested me most was the chador, or veil that Muslim women wore in Iran. When I returned home that summer, I began to experiment with very loosely interpreted variations on the chador as part of costume/performance experiments. By cutting the corners off of an orthogonal painting, I could use the painted expanse as a chador. When viewed on the wall, it was a shaped painting where the shape was anything but arbitrary, rather it was defined by its function as a garment.

This painting, *Pomegranates and Lilies*, was one of the first large-scale costume/paintings that I created at that time. The painting was hung on the walls of the gallery as seen in this photograph. However, during the performance, the two-dimensional painting became a three-dimensional, kinetic form surrounding two nude models who then walked and posed in this two-person chador (an unheard of, and probably considerably irreverent concept in Iran). I loved the idea that to fully understand the painting, the viewer had to see it as a costume in movement. And to fully appreciate the juxtapositions of the motifs of the costume, it had to be seen hung flat as a painting. Painted surface became sculpture with the support of the figure, and sculpture then once again became painting when the garment was removed from the body.

Over the years, these ideas changed and morphed. There was an entire series of *Persian Line* costumes and performances. And then a series of *Persian Line: Part II* costumes and performances. By this time, the lessons that I learned about edges, cut and full, how patterns meet on the selvages, how objects can move aerodynamically in performance, took root. In many ways these early experiments with form and variation have continued to influence me far beyond their importance as individual works.

Jim Lambie

18 Carrots 1996 carrots, household gloss paint, dimensions variable *18 Carrots* was first produced for a 1996 group show in Copenhagen called "Sick Building". There were many fruit and vegetable shops on the walk to the gallery.

I liked the carrots, and thought about making a painting with them. The carrots were held by the green stems, dipped in a bucket of orange gloss paint, then thrown up onto a shelf.

b. Glasgow, Scotland, 1964. Lives and works in Glasgow, Scotland.

Tropicana Pool Water, Guitar Strings, and Mercury

1987 Cibachrome print, 19¹/₄ x 12³/₄ inches (48.9 x 32.4 cm)

Somehow my first successful work of art was never photographed. At the time I wasn't too aware of the necessity of documenting pieces or that images of artwork are seen more than the works themselves are experienced. This may have been why for some time I turned to photography. After a few years of making images, I began to want to make objects again. It was at this time that this photograph was made.

Tropicana Pool Water, Guitar Strings, and Mercury is a combine sculpture, but back then I started calling the pieces in this vein "Cultures." I began calling them this, because I was mostly using scientific containers to combine the various elements that make up the physical aspect of each piece. I was also facinated by the way words like "culture" and "media" function across social and scientific contexts. Tropicana pool water, guitar strings and mercury are inside a specimen jar and this is one of my first "Culture" pieces.

It was the spring of 1987 and Cindy Bernard, Martha Godfrey, and I decided to have a one-night show at the Tropicana Motel in West Hollywood. I made this piece speficically for the exhibition and photographed it poolside the morning after the show. I like the piece as an object and as a photograph even though the two modes operate differently. To some degree this adaptability is the success of this/these works. The photograph functions as documentation of the sculpture, and as a work of art in itself. The sculpture is well-represented by the photograph because it is pictured in the environment from which it was made and refers to the culture it was made to reflect—a Hollywood rock/punk motel

where Paul Morrissey filmed Warhol's *Heat* (or maybe it was *Trash*).

Anyway, the poetics of material, in this case the liquid translucence of chlorinated water, the linear complexity of coils of guitar strings, the shimmer and poison and uncanny weight of the mutable element mercury, combined with the poetics embedded in the words for these materials, call up a rather detailed sense of a place in a certain era. This seems similar to the way a particular smell can conjure up a memory of being somewhere and thereby trigger a feeling for the space. Perceptually these works function quite differently from smell in that they hopefully share its "transportive qualities" but aren't bound to a specific memory. The photograph also invokes the Southern California rock mystique of the Tropicana but it does so as an image. Using various modes to bring something up for contemplation and to be experienced was a beginning of sorts for me.

b. Sacramento, CA, USA, 1960. Lives and works in Los Angeles, CA, USA. 211

Jonathan Lasker

Illinois 1977 oil on canvas, 60 x 47 inches (152 x 119 cm) This work first determined the characteristics of my art. It is literally number one in the master slide book of my work. I always think of it as the beginning of my oeuvre. Every image preceding it is catalogued with a letter (a, b, c, d, etc.). This painting came to me at the end of my student days at CalArts. I remember being very determined to create a breakthrough. As happens with many discoveries, it occurred while I was searching for something else.

Before *Illinois*, I was creating works influenced by a short-lived art movement known as Pattern Painting. The idea behind this movement was to make pictures which reiterated the flat surface of the canvas through repetitive patterns, either representational or abstract. In a way, it was a perverse literalization of the populist reception of abstract painting, in which one is to regard an abstract piece as décor, if one is to regard it at all.

My own work, at the time, looked like what would have happened had Claude Monet taken a small section of dabs of color in one of his landscapes and enlarged it all over a canvas surface. The resulting image was an abstract pattern which represented the color sensations of nature.

However, doing a variation of a passing mode of art would not meet my goal to become a significant artist. I was very aware of this and was determined to make a painting unlike others had seen. Therefore, I began investigating various alternative formal devices.

Eventually, I began thinking very intensely about the color white, especially ways it could function in a painting: as an allover ground, as background, as light, as a neutral color, as the absence (or presence) of all color, etc. At the same time, I was doing charcoal drawings on white paper. These were mostly tentative outlines of biomorphic shapes. One day I decided to paint these white, biomorphic forms on top of a subtle blue-green pattern painting, which I thought I had finished. The idea was to put white in the foreground instead of using it to imply negative space in the background. This device immediately created a battle for hierarchy between figure and ground which fascinated me.

Still, the boundaries between the forms and the background were too abrupt, so I reiterated the edge of the forms by painting the outlines of the shapes, off-register in black, into the wet white forms. Days later I added a black shape in the upper right-hand corner to create an optical tension of background versus foreground between the shapes. I remember spending days afterwards transfixed by this painting. I felt that something had happened in this picture, that the painting itself was an occurrence, and that each time I looked at it I was witnessing that occurrence. I had never gotten this feeling from anything I'd created before.

I continued experimenting with this painting. At one point, I looked at *Illinois* on its side, using the right edge as the bottom. In that position the painting remained abstract, but its forms and background color could also be constructed as a seascape. I called that view of the painting *Sideways Bay*, while in the upright position it remained *Illinois*. Later, when I decided to solely pursue abstraction, I abandoned the alternate view of this work. The painting has had only one title, *Illinois*, since that time. I selected abstraction because I did not wish to form narratives. One intent of my work is to make the viewer see how he or she views a picture, and that is best done using abstract forms which are relatively neutral.

In *Illinois*, the background pattern is very passive

b. Jersey City, NJ, USA, 1948. Lives and works in New York, NY, USA.

in relation to works I made just weeks later. Elements, which would later roar are only whispering in *Illinois*. The contrast is relatively muted. The pattern, consisting of a gray-green-blue softly scumbled over a bright blue, compares to later grounds the way a speckled tweed fabric, which appears solid gray from a distance, compares to a bold, bright plaid.

The dialogue between figure, ground, and line which has remained constant in my work was initiated in *Illinois*. It was also the first time I used layered forms. In *Illinois*, the layering is effected by painting brushy, impastoed white forms with scrawly black lines upon a decorative ground. The white shapes were developed elsewhere, namely in a drawing, and felt very autonomous from the ground, both in physical texture and in sensibility. Layering, of course, had been used by many painters before me. However, I feel that I came to an idiosyncratic conception of layering in *Illinois*.

Among other concerns, Modernist painters have been obsessed with creating a literal reflection of what a painting is—the reiteration of pigmented marks forming a flat surface on a canvas—because this is actually what you are looking at when you look at any painting, even if you subjectively think it is a picture, for example, of a tree. The tree is always an illusion. Thus, one goal of Modernism has been to bring objectivity to painting. Although I regard my work, for many reasons, as something other than Modernist, I see this formal objectivity to be a critical tool in creating a rigorous painting.

With *Illinois*, my idea was to stress the literality of form in painting by using layering to go forward into three dimensions instead of painting my picture laterally into a two-dimensional flat surface. Through this use of layering, I felt that my white forms became things which were on top of another

thing, a painted surface. Therefore, I felt that my paintings were pictures which could be disassembled into component "things of paint." If each element in a picture could be seen in this way as having an autonomous, physical presence, it would make possible paintings which created illusionistic space yet always grounded the viewer with respect to what he or she was literally viewing.

For many, the direct connection between *Illinois* and my later work may be difficult to recognize. What is important is that I was able to see the qualities in *Illinois*, which led to my current work when I painted it. Half the battle of creating an important work of art is to create it and the other half is to see its possibilities.

For about two years after *Illinois*, each painting I did was a means of understanding what was so compelling to me in this picture. It still remains ineffable to me. Sometimes I feel that I am still painting it with each new work I make.

Annette Lemieux

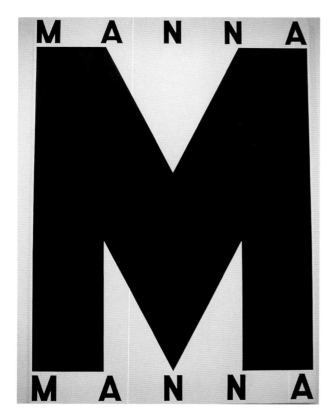

MANNA 1983 oil on canvas, 79 x 55 inches (200.7 x 134.6 cm)

While creating works on paper (charcoal on black paper) that were different versions of the cross, I noticed that they were Xs or Ts, and not crosses at all. Some sort of alphabet was taking over.

I remember creating a large charcoal drawing with an upside-down triangle at the top center, and two right-side-up triangles at the bottom. Looking at it I realized it was an M.

So, I then created an M drawing. After seeing it, the word MANNA came to mind. Perhaps it was food for thought.

I created the big M, and on the top and bottom of the canvas was the word MANNA.

It was during the time of neo-expressionism and "MANNA" didn't look like "Art" with a capital A at all. Some thought it was a sign for the photo shop down the street called "Manna."

I remember feeling very excited and sick to my stomach at the same time. What have I done? And can I do it again?

Zofia Borkowska, 1904–1983 1983 gelatin silver print, 12 x 18 inches (30 x 45 cm) There are a number of portraits and other photographs from this period, but I remember feeling that this was the first really "real" picture that I took—that the picture was something in and of itself, apart from me, yet somehow loaded with my own experience.

This is a photograph of my grandmother in her casket. I remember wanting to take a picture at the viewing and somehow worrying that it was the wrong thing to do—like rubbernecking (staring) at an accident, something voyeuristic. So, I just stood there. And, then, my mother leaned over to me and asked me if I would take a picture. She wanted a record, I suppose. And I was the one with the camera. Already, I knew I was a photographer.

Anyway, although I had already taken lots of pictures, and considered myself a photographer, I remember this moment very clearly. Also this was the first picture I truly struggled with in the darkroom. I worked over and over to get the print just right. The pillowy white satin, the deep grays and blacks of her hands, her face, the photo she's holding. I printed the image over and over—first choosing between frames, then printing the picture darker and lighter—changing the contrast and tone of the print.

Peter Hujar, a wonderful photographer who I was lucky enough to know slightly, saw this picture in my first show. He criticized the print—asked me questions about why I printed it the way I did, and asked about a spot I hadn't retouched out. He was so adamant with me—don't ever be sloppy in the darkroom, he said. If you leave a spot in, you have to know why. That conversation was such a gift to me, and from that conversation I began thinking, really, about how I wanted to print my pictures, and why.

I began to understand, then, with this picture, that there isn't really such a thing as a good print, but rather only an appropriate print—one in which the tonal values, color, and density are all working with the image to create the photograph.

When you sent your request, this was the first picture I thought of. I hadn't thought about all these reasons before, but, well, here they are.

Alfred Leslie

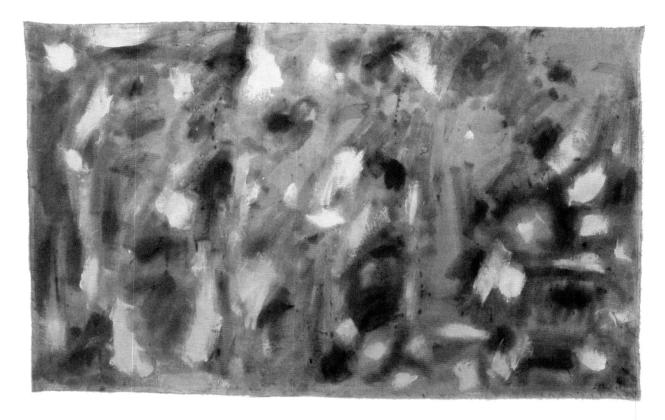

Mid-Winter Painting 1949 automobile enamel on housepainter's
dropcloth, 6 x 9 feet (1.8 x 2.7 m) When I began my first spot
paintings in 1946, I couldn't make them work.
They were raw enough for me—mooned the pieties
of the European touch—but were never able to
be realized in a single gulp, and looked worked-
over. Getting a brush to move across a large coarse
raw cotton duck surface nonstop in real time was,
simply put, a fucking bitch. With *Mid-Winter Painting
1949* it all came together and I came to regard the
painting as singular, a key moment.

b. New York, NY, USA, 1927. Lives and works in New York, NY, USA.

Untitled 1987 oil on linen, 27 x 21 inches (68.6 x 53.3 cm) The webbed structure of this painting was one of the first that I made using a dry brush working on a canvas that was already covered with wet oil paint. This allowed the brush to function like a pen or pencil, because one no longer needed to pause and reload it with paint. Instead, the brush could continue its impression indefinitely, permitting me a new degree of freedom and spontaneity.

I then found that after more layering of paint the resulting monochromatic surface could be rubbed with paint of a different color so that the original structure emerged from within the surface of the painting—similar to the way a chemical agent retrieves an image from film or photosensitive paper.

This fusion of an image with the skin of the last layer of paint suggested a number of emotionally contradictory states: flatness and depth, front and back, texture and smoothness, the ephemeral and the tactile, positive and negative. And since that time I have found that the combination of these two processes, which began with this painting, first established for me a basis for working with oil paint that allowed me to separate and reintegrate different stages and processes of making a painting. I have continued to find these possibilities interesting and productive not only in painting, but also in drawing and printmaking.

b. Colombo, Sri Lanka, 1947. Lives and works in New York, NY, USA.

David Levinthal

Untitled, From "Hitler Moves East"
1975 gelatin silver (Kodalith) print, 8 x 10
inches (20.3 x 25.4 cm) During 1974
and 1975, while I was living and
working in New Haven, I took
this photograph as part of a
series entitled "Hitler Moves
East." Interestingly, when the
book *Hitler Moves East*, was first
published in 1977, my "constructed" photographs were often
mistakenly described as being
documentary photographs
(something that occasionally
still occurs even now). Having
photographed toy soldiers and
other toy-based dioramas since
1972, I had been striving to
achieve a blurring of the line
between fantasy and reality,
envisioning and projecting the
fantasy images of our minds and
their physical manifestations as
represented by toys and objects.
This photograph will always
represent for me one of the first
times that all of the elements
that have become my "style"
over the past thirty years were
joined perfectly together.

b. San Francisco, CA, USA, 1949. Lives and works in New York, NY, USA.

Glenn Ligon

Untitled (I Am a Man) 1988 oil and enamel on canvas, 40 x 25 inches (101.6 x 63.5 cm) In 1985, after a disastrous semester in the Whitney Independent Study Program, I started inscribing text from pornographic magazines onto monochromatic, expressionistically painted surfaces. They were terrible paintings, but they were an attempt to figure out how to make a break from the abstract work I was doing at the time. I had also become interested in late Philip Guston paintings. Guston had shifted his practice from abstraction to figuration to better address the political realities of Vietnam-era America. I was also looking at Jasper Johns, Cy Twombly, and Robert Rauschenberg as models for the use of text in art; and was being introduced to the work of Lawrence Weiner, Joseph Kosuth, and other conceptual artists, and watching the films of Yvonne Rainer and Isaac Julien. All of this was about creating (irreconcilable) possibilities for myself, but the various trajectories that my work was to take were based on my love of and belief in painting.

I struggled with these text paintings for a couple of years until I saw a photo of Percy Sutton in the *Daily News* in 1988. Manhattan Borough President in the '60s and '70s, Malcolm X's lawyer, and producer of *Showtime at the Apollo*, Percy was one of those old-time Harlem power brokers. In the photo he was sitting in his office, holding a framed poster up for the camera. The poster had a white background and big, blocky, black letters that said, "I Am a Man." Striking black sanitation workers in Memphis had carried it, and it was the strikers that Martin Luther King, Jr. had come to Memphis to support when he was assassinated in 1968. When I saw the poster I knew that it would make an interesting painting, even before I was aware of the history of the image. I had an old canvas in the studio that seemed around the right size, so I painted it over with white enamel and oil paint and painted letters in black enamel on top of that. The painting turned out to contain many elements that would characterize my work over the next ten years: the use of a found text that referred to a particular social or political history; a simple, graphic composition; and an anthropomorphic presence.

Because I had painted the painting so haphazardly, with alternating layers of enamel and oil paint, the surface immediately began to crack and yellow, and I was afraid that it would all fall off the canvas. A couple of years ago I asked my friend Michael Duffy, a painting conservator at The Museum of Modern Art, to do a "condition report" on the painting, detailing all the conservation issues he would address if he were trying to restore it. Michael took a photograph of the painting and covered the photograph with notes, pointing out cracks, discoloration, and paint loss. The condition report seemed to me not only a record of the painting's aging, but also of the distance between one historical moment and another, the instability of signs and their meanings, and shifting views of (black) masculinity and the civil rights project. Almost fifteen years after it was made, that painting still seems to me as if it had come from the future and it still tells me things about my practice and the work to come.

220   b. Bronx, NY, USA, 1960. Lives and works in New York, NY, USA.

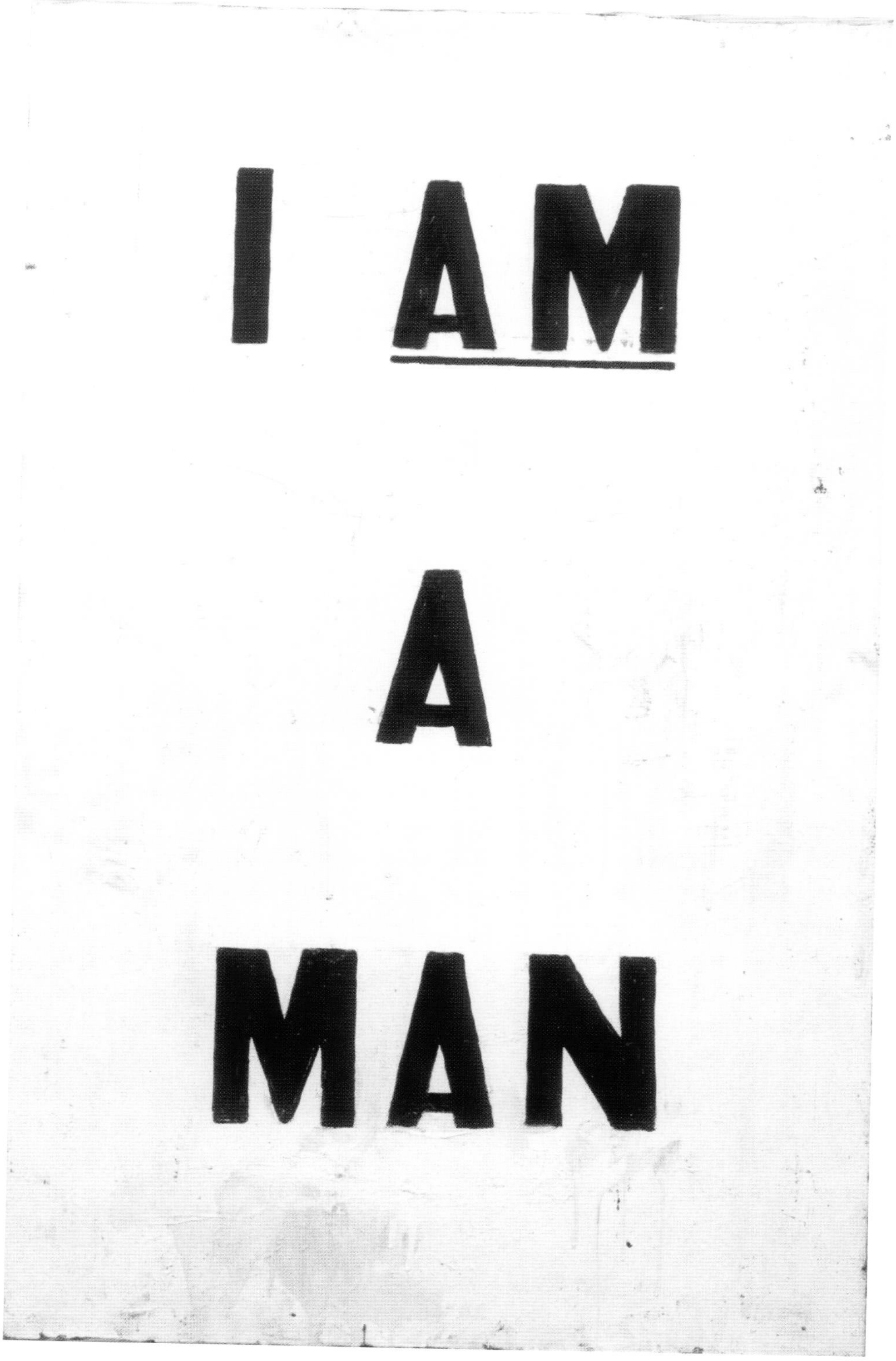
I AM
A
MAN

Donald Lipski

Gathering Dust (detail) 1978–79 mixed media, dimensions variable In 1972 I was a ceramics major at Cranbrook Academy of Art in Bloomfield Hills, Michigan. I started saving little sculptures that I had been making all my life—out of twigs and leaves, matches and paper clips—stuff I picked up off the street or off my plate in a restaurant. I had an insight that these humble things were a simple manifestation of the basic human instinct to make things, that they had a sort of purity and honesty. I thought that saving them might lead me somewhere. It has.

b. Chicago, IL, USA, 1947. Lives and works in New York, NY, USA.

Audition Four: Kathleen and Max (top) 1994 framed chromogenic print, 49 x 61 inches (124.5 x 152 cm) edition of four **Audition Five: Sirushi and Victor** (bottom) 1994 framed chromogenic print, 49 x 61 inches (124.5 x 155 cm), edition of four *Auditions* was the first work I did after graduate school and was a continuation of the work I did for my thesis exhibition. During this time I was thinking a lot about the difference between a motion picture and a still photograph. In my first film, I had been inspired by Cassavettes's and Truffaut's use of non-actors and thought the children they worked with brought an interesting ambivalence to the screen. Even in a narrativized situation there was a way in which it was still a document of a child having an experience. With *Auditions*, I was referencing a scene in Truffaut's film, *L'Argent de Poche* (Small Change), where the two main characters kiss in the stairwell. I had the idea to photograph the re-creation of this scene as a set of auditions, and worked with a class at a local public school to develop the project. The individual photographs separated the moment from its contextual narrative, while the full group of five implied a structure that undercut the more romanticized associations of the scene, emphasizing the documentary side of the project. The structure also gave the set of pictures a durational aspect. As the day progressed, the light moved across the bottom of the stairwell. When viewing them as a group, you get a sense of the real time it took to make the photographs.

b. Norwood, MA, USA, 1964. Lives and works in Los Angeles, CA, USA. 223

Richard Long

A Snowball Track, 1964 Looking back, *A Snowball Track, 1964*, was my first landscape work made from the materials of a place. (The location was a stone's throw from where I was born.) It was made quickly, intuitively, and opportunistically. The image is just a direct result of its making—pushing and rolling a snowball until it was too big to push. The image is a track, an ephemeral mark of movement, and the first of a metaphorical trail of many similar traces I have made along walks in different landscapes around the world.

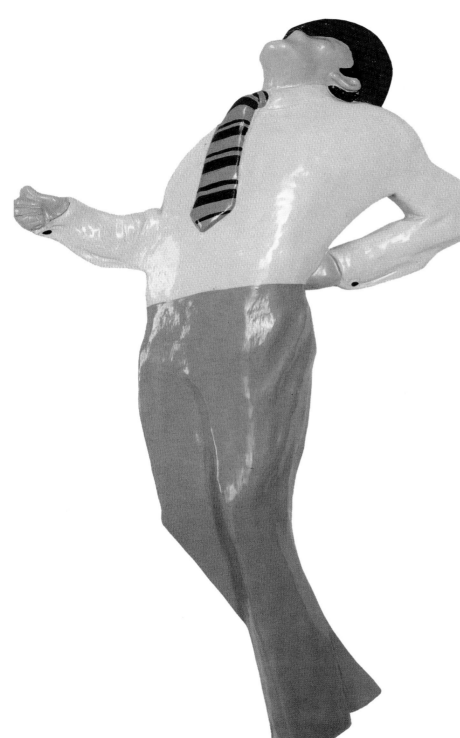

The American Soldier 1977 enamel on cast aluminum, 28 x 16 x 5 inches (71 x 41 x 13 cm) *The American Soldier* is a seminal piece in my body of work because it not only represents the beginning of my later series "Men in the Cities" (1979–83), but also coincides with my discovery of R.W. Fassbinder's films. (Both the relief and title are based on Fassbinder.) For me this piece presents an isolated figure in a pose of dualities: dying or dancing.

b. Brooklyn, NY, USA, 1953. Lives and works in New York, NY, USA.

Andrew Lord

Vase, dish, and cup. Cézanne set 1978 ceramic, height of vase: 9²/₅ inches (24 cm) In 1976 I had a studio in the Netherlands and travelled often to Paris to look at paintings made there at the end of the nineteenth and beginning of the twentieth centuries; by Cézanne, Picasso, and the Impressionists. I tried to understand how Picasso, Cézanne, and Monet had looked at objects and how they had observed light and shade. In my studio in Rotterdam I painted the objects that I was making as if through other artists' eyes. When a particular kind of light fell across a plate or vase, I recorded it with brushstrokes I'd seen in paintings. I discovered that styles of different painters could be reached at different times of day: late Monet at dusk; Impressionism through the bright; fractured light of Dutch mornings; and Cézanne through the broad blocks of Dutch afternoon light.

Sculpture for Livingroom/Public Lounge 1978 furniture, 11 x 11 feet (3.4 x 3.4 m) I was a scientist before becoming an artist, doing drawings and painting signboards on the side as a way of compensating for an art world I did not even know existed. When I first became interested in art in 1978, I was immediately drawn to works that defied my received notions of what constituted art. I did a number of performances in my first art class before realizing *Sculpture for Livingroom/Public Lounge*, but these works were limited to the parameters of the classroom. *Sculpture for Livingroom/Public Lounge* is the first work of mine that is fully realized in a larger contextual sense. I think it is also imbued with many ideas that carry forward into my later works—ideas such as the division between public and private space and how identity negotiates this divide. I was very much drawn to American avant-garde art of the 1960s and 1970s, particularly Minimal art. I think I found it shocking for its 'purity' and repressive qualities (which, conversely, were strongly expressed). One day, I was at home and came across a furniture store flyer that was inserted in the local newspaper. There was an image of a three-unit modular sofa piece, configured to look like the letter U. I immediately thought about the affinity of this image to images of minimal works I had only been recently introduced to. I imagined inserting another piece of identical modular furniture into this configuration, effectively closing it off to form a square. I thought how logical such an action would be, and how ironic in that the conversational space would become idealized and yet denied.

MacDermott & MacGough

A Friend of Dorothy 1947 1986 oil on canvas, 8 x 6 feet (2.4 x 1.8 m)
Our first artworks were small, morbid genre paintings.
Lovers throwing themselves off a cliff, a woman tied to
a log headed for a buzzsaw operated by a man wearing
a stove-pipe hat and cape, or a decorative Edwardian
teapot on a floral tablecloth.

We made the type of paintings that we would like to
see hanging in our home. The kind that would not offend
elderly ladies, since our first studio was in an abandoned
church parlor.

Influenced by a mural painted by Stuart Davis at
a New Jersey soda fountain, we were drawn to the
abstract words that jutted over the walls spelling out ICE
CREAM, SODA, CANDY, or DONUTS.

While visiting Julian Schnabel in the Hamptons one
summer, he presented us with one of his large canvases to
paint on. We were used to small, parlor-sized stretchers.

We thought of the soda fountain, but instead of
dessert and tea, we used words more familiar, the ones
called out to us on a suburban schoolyard. FAGGOT,
FAIRY, HOMO, and COCKSUCKER poured out from
our memory onto the massive canvas in the countryside.
All the names and catcalls stood out as loudly as we
remembered them.

When Richard Marshall came to visit to consider us
for the Whitney Biennial, we hid the painting behind
another canvas. This was our first museum visit and we
wanted to make a good impression.

He spied the painting in its hiding place, and coaxed
us to reveal it. *A Friend of Dorothy* ended up in the Whitney
show.

Our ideas grew to more abstract shapes: time maps,
clocks with no hands, or china fragments in glass vitrines
labeled *San Francisco Earthquake 1906*.

That painting became a pivotal point in our partner-
ship of art. It moved us out of our parlor, leaving behind
our audience with blue-rinsed hair.

229

Robert Mangold

Red Wall 1965 oil on masonite, 96 x 96 inches (243.8 x 243.8 cm)
After completing *Red Wall*, which I painted in 1965,
I had one of those moments of clarity and purpose.
This work came out of a series of wall section
pieces. They were as much relief sculpture as they
were painting, but in *Red Wall*, the work was flatter,
more abstract, and pointed the way for the works
that followed. It reconnected my interest in the idea
of painting's inherent flatness.

b. North Tonawanda, NY, USA, 1937. Lives and works in Washingtonville, NY, USA.

Absent Image 1973 acrylic on canvas, 56 x 44 inches (142.2 x 111.8 cm) The first painting in which I included a mirror was *Absent Image*. My use of the mirror was the begining of thoughts about illusion. My intention was to expand the floor in a painting, and the result was my interest in the possibilities of illusion and space and surface.

b. New York, NY, USA, 1938. Lives and works in Washingtonville, NY, USA. 231

Sally Mann

Untitled 1969 silver gelatin print, 8 x 10 inches (20.3 x 25.4 cm) For me, a successful work of art, paradoxically, is one that is not perfect, one that leaves you hungry. It is a work that opens doors into the next piece, or has elements that challenge or are unresolved. Luckily for me, most of my pictures are that way, imperfect but containing within them some hope for improvement.

This picture was taken when I was eighteen. I married this man 6 months later and have photographed him ever since. I like the way his reaching arm leads the eye back to the menacing figure of an animal in the background and the dark, viney forest that surrounds him. Obviously Kodak would not recommend cutting off the hand but I like the ambiguity of that gesture. Much of what I have striven for as an artist in the intervening 35 years (mystery, timelessness, lush, evocative landscape, ambiguous portraiture, etc) is contained in this image.

232   b. Lexington, VA, USA, 1951. Lives and works in Lexington, VA, USA.

Untitled (Fox Trot) 1979 78 rpm record, shellac, 10 inches diameter (25.4 cm diam.) When I was an art student at the Massachusetts College of Art, I found a old wind-up gramophone in the trash with a few old 78 rpm records in its case. One day while sitting in a coffee shop on Longwood Avenue, I thought of cutting records and collaging different slices together to create a new sound-collage disc. I was so excited I had to try it right away. I ran back to school and cut a record in half, and before I could cut another one, I simply flipped one half over and taped the two together. I cranked up my old gramophone and suddenly I could hear the two sides playing at once, a fantastic hiccupy fox-trot.

Kerry James Marshall

Untitled 1971 oil on window shade, 30 x 24 inches (76.2 x 61 cm) Two prisoners in the manner of Charles White, this is the first real painting I ever made. It showed me that by copying the style and technique of artists I admired I could actually learn how to get to that level. Following Charles White's lead also had a profound impact on the subjects I would put my skills in service to.

b. Birmingham, AL, USA, 1955. Lives and works in Chicago, IL, USA.

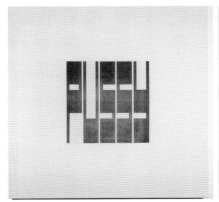  

Untitled (Pussy, Beaver, Cunt)
1990 heat transfer on canvas, three pieces, each 48 x 48 inches (121.9 x 121.9 cm) *Pussy-Beaver-Cunt* resonated beyond the claustrophobic confines of my studio into the world around me.

People who had never met me or been to my studio reacted strongly to this piece.

People who had never seen the piece registered reactions to it. Thus the piece became my first work of significance.

Suzanne McClelland

My Pleasure 1990 clay, acrylic, pigment on canvas, 42 x 42 inches (106.7 x 106.7 cm) *My Pleasure* was made with clay and clear acrylic medium. It was the first time I found a way to separate pigment and binder and still have the things hold together on the wall.

b. Jacksonville, FL, USA, 1959. Lives and works in New York, NY, USA.

From An Historical Anecdote about Fashion 2000 blown glass objects, display case, five framed digital prints; display case: 71½ x 120 x 27¼ inches (181.6 x 304.8 x 69.2 cm) framed prints: 18 x 25½ inches each (45.7 x 64.8 cm) *From An Historical Anecdote About Fashion* is one of two related works that represent the moment when a number of people's awareness of my work seemed to crystallize and become clear. The work is the result of discovering a strange label for a piece of midcentury glass at a museum exhibit. Afterwards I talked to a couple of people involved with making the object at a factory in Italy, and they told me an even more unusual story. My version (somewhat embellished and altered) forms the textual element of the installation:

"In the 1952 Venice Biennale, Venini, the famous glass design company, entered a display of vases designed not by the factory's artists and architects, but by the glassblowers themselves. The unusual shapes and cloth-like patterning were based on the haute couture fashions, which the owner's French wife wore when she visited the factory. Ginette Gignous Venini was intimately involved in running the company with her husband Paolo Venini, and could often be seen by the male workers in the furnace room as she ascended and descended the stairs to the office.

In the late 1940s, as Europe and the firm returned to life after the war, Ginette began wearing designs by Christian Dior. When his first collection debuted in 1947, it was heralded as the New Look. Dior's decadently abundant use of cloth and his regressive vision of femininity were so controversial that organized protests arose in the U.S. and Europe. However, the New Look soon became highly influential in art and design. The glass masters at Venini adopted its hourglass silhouettes and exaggerated forms. A few of these glass pieces were put into limited production and presented as designs of Paolo or Ginette Gignous Venini."

Barry McGee

San Francisco, late 1980s, early 1990s Here are some photos from the late '80s and early '90s. It is the time when I was most pleased with my work. It was underground, above ground, on tops of buildings and on delivery trucks. Best of all, it wasn't indoors or in galleries. I still hold on to this period dearly.

b. San Francisco, CA, USA, 1966. Lives and works in San Francisco, CA, USA.

Le Repos des Pensionnaires (Boarders at Rest)
(detail) 1971–72 taxidermied birds and wool, each approximately
4³/₄ x 4 x 1¹/₄ inches (12.1 x 10.2 x 3.2 cm), laid out in five rows on a folded
white sheet placed in a tabletop vitrine, 60¹/₁₀ x 36⁷/₁₀ inches (154 x 94 cm)
in total One day, during summer, I stepped on a dead
sparrow in a street in Paris. This contact with the
presence of death, both familiar and strange,
touched me profoundly.

b. Berck-sur-Mer, France, 1943. Lives and works in Malakoff, France.   239

Joel Meyerowitz

Wales, 1966 20 x 24 inches (50.8 x 61 cm) In 1966 I made my first trip abroad. I had been photographing for nearly four years and I wanted to see new things, other cultures, to open myself to new ideas and sensations. One stormy afternoon I found myself at the edge of the sea, on the coast of Wales, after making a pilgrimage to the grave of the poet Dylan Thomas.

I came upon this pool by the sea. Perhaps I was in an elegiac mood after reading Thomas's poems, but I felt the mysterious, slightly eerie power of this trapped and tamed body of water so close to the wild freedom of the sea. It spoke to me—a Pisces and a swimmer—in a way I have never forgotten, and since then, over these last forty years, pools by the sea, the tame and the savage, the known and the unknown, have called me, again and again.

Duane Michals

After Balthus 1966 silver gelatin print, 8 x 10 inches (20.3 x 25.4 cm) When I first arrived in New York in 1955, I would often visit The Museum of Modern Art and always spent time with Balthus's painting *La Rue*. It was an artificial Parisian street scene, much like a cartoon, with awkwardly posed pedestrians of peculiar demeanors. I would describe it as a stage set, and it was this quality of a fake reality that enchanted me and whose atmosphere of mystery stuck in my mind.

Maybe five years later, being frustrated with reportage and the limitations of the decisive moment, I set up my own fake street drama with choreographed actors. This photograph liberated my imagination and freed me to redefine photography, as not just a vehicle of observation, but also a way to express my imagination. At the time I thought this photograph a failure, but in fact it was a triumph.

b. McKeesport, PA, USA, 1932. Lives and works in New York, NY, USA.

Boris Mikhailov

From the series "On the Color Backgrounds" ca. 1960 photo montage, 9½ x 13¾ inches (24 x 35 cm) It was the time when the abyss between photographers and painters was enormous. This work was a probe where I, photographer—"pariah dog"—tried to invade the strange territory of Art. And even now, it is very agreeable for me to realize that this image could compete with the ideas of painters.

Russian culture is based on two visual traditions which I segregate as so important—icons and suprematism. And maybe, therefore, the old woman begging for money at the church parapet was connected, by the red square, with Malevich. I was so glad and proud of myself—I could bind real life and art.

Certainly, this composition tells neither about suprematism nor about icons . . . It tells about the old woman, standing at the great tribune, which was associated with party leaders, who usually stood there to make speeches . . . If the corner of the red paper piece were raised, you would see the outstretched appealing arm . . .

The photo is from the series, "On the Color Backgrounds," in which banal images were superimposed on children's colored paper to create an ironic feeling.

b. Charkov, Ukraine, 1938. Lives and works in Kharkov, Ukraine, and Berlin, Germany.

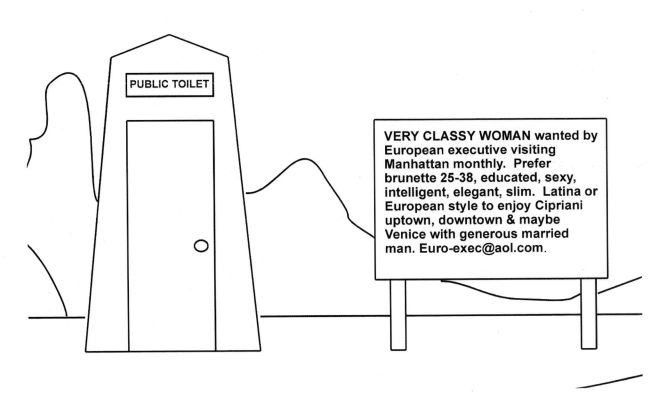

PUBLIC TOILET

VERY CLASSY WOMAN wanted by
European executive visiting
Manhattan monthly. Prefer
brunette 25-38, educated, sexy,
intelligent, elegant, slim. Latina or
European style to enjoy Cipriani
uptown, downtown & maybe
Venice with generous married
man. Euro-exec@aol.com.

Unrealized Proposal for P.S. 1's Imodium Relief Project 2003 inkjet printing on printer paper, 8½ x 11 inches (21.6 x 27.9 cm) The question of picking a first successful work immediately makes me think of Jonathan Borofsky's *Age Piece*. Borofsky presented, on wall shelves, a short chronology of his work, going back to drawings from the age of eight. Since I have always shot my own slides, I have a comprehensive record of most of the artwork I have done since junior high. This backlog of slides breaks down into two groups: ones that I usually show other people—the "official" ones, and the ones I file away and forget about. The odd times I look at the second group, it always reminds me that the official version of anything is always a straightjacket. On the other hand, if any one work were to be totally successful, it would eliminate the need to make another. So, for that reason, I have chosen to reverse the order of origin and destruction and optimistically pick a work that, so far, is only a proposal—a drawing for P.S.1's "Imodium Relief Project"—because success is an abstract idea that still keeps me working.

Richard Misrach

Trash Fire, 1969 <small>gelatin silver print, 8 x 10 inches (20.3 x 25.4 cm)</small> I grew up in Southern California in the 1950s and '60s and was often responsible for taking the family home movies. I took my first photography class in high school. But it wasn't until college, surrounded by cultural upheaval and the antiwar movement, that I became seriously interested in photography. Some of my first pictures were of the demonstrations and tear-gassings (so far I have been unable to find those).

Trash Fire, 1969 came out of the first series of pictures I made that reveal conceptual cohesiveness and technical aspiration, indicating my initiation into the world of photography as an art practice. I was a 19-year-old math major at the University of California at Berkeley, and while not particularly interested in majoring in art at that time, I began making serious work. At the ASUC Studio, a non-academic art facility on the Berkeley campus, I learned how to expose film and make fine prints in the tradition of the great West Coast school of landscape photography. Working in 35-mm format and black and white, I made a number of photographs that reflected issues I would revisit throughout my career. The '60s brought a heightened awareness of environmental challenges, and like others of my generation, I hoped to bring these issues to bear on the widely popular landscape practice of the time. These vintage prints reveal the confluence of three of my early and continuing interests: the beautiful photographic object, the remarkable light and space of the American West, and our failing stewardship of the environment. I'm not sure I would consider these early images the beginnings of a mature practice, but I am sure they represent the beginning of a life's work.

b. Los Angeles, CA, USA, 1949. Lives and works in Berkeley, CA, USA.

Tatsuo Miyajima

Sea of Time 1988 ED, IC, electric wire, 369 x 263¼ x 2 inches (937 x 670 x 5 cm). Installation view, Hara Museum, Tokyo In this, my first major work, 270 separate digital counting mechanisms (called the *Counter Gadget* and of my design) are strung together, counting "time." The *Counter Gadget* is based on the following three concepts: 1. Keep Changing, 2. Connect with Everything, 3. Continue Forever. I learned these basic concepts from Buddhist philosophy. And I believe that they can give a new dimension to human beings in the twenty-first century, which will be a borderless world.

The first *Counter Gadget* I made consists of two figures. Its repetitive display counts up from one to ninety-nine, then back to one. The point is that zero never appears. Its counting speed is revisable and you can freely change it, to make it run faster or slower.

My *Counter Gadget* symbolically represents many things, including "single time," "radiance of human life," and "single universe." The *Counter Gadget* is continuously changing and moving.

The Greek philosopher Heraclitus said, "You can never step in the same river twice." In Buddhist philosophy there is a saying, *Syogyo mujyo*: "All things are in flux and nothing is permanent," which expresses the same idea. The philosophy inherent in these two statements is that nothing remains static and that everything undergoes continuous change. I feel that the concept of "Keep Changing" represents the essential form of all creatures. I also think that "Time," "Space," and even "Art" are continuously changing. *Counter Gadget* is an exact, concrete representation of the concept "Keep Changing."

Counter Gadget, however, is not complete with only one piece. It becomes a whole work only when several are gathered together. Each *Counter Gadget* has a different rhythm which forms its "personality," so to speak. You will find a beautiful and dynamic harmony developing when the *Counter Gadgets*' personalities gather and connect with each other. It is as if you are listening to a "symphony of the universe." Goethe said, in *Faust*, "Everything we avers out of a single whole. Each has its own life and cooperates together."

Why do I create darkness instead of using "zero"? There are two reasons.

My works are usually shown in a dark place. The absence of zero produces a moment of darkness in a *Counter Gadget*. When a number flashes (like one, two, or three) it symbolizes "Life," while darkness suggests "Death." That means by creating darkness I represent the dynamic movements of "Life" and "Death."

The second reason for not using zero is because I am expressing the concept of *Ku* (nothingness) stemming from Buddhist philosophy. The number zero is a concept, dating back to sixth-century India, which originally included two controversial concepts, "increase" and "emptiness." *Ku* is thought to be a kind of "energy space" where everything comes into being. In Buddhist philosophy, *Ku* is a place which gives rise to "'Life' and 'Death' of 'the life.'" As Dr. Daisaku Ikeda, a Japanese Buddhist, said, "Northern Buddhism teaches that life and death are different time-and-space manifestations of life, which is itself a unity transcending time and space. I believe that the individual life is an actualized form of the all-embracing life force, of which death is an inactive aspect. Inactivity, however, does not imply a return to nothingness." My "zero" does not indicate "the nothingness of zero," which is a common use in a modern society, but it symbolizes the concept of

Ku, which includes the meanings of "existence" and "non-existence" at the same time as well as from where life springs.

I use Arabic numerals because, like Esperanto, they can be understood in Western countries, Japan, China, and also in African countries. I think that art is a common language of the world. By using numbers, it is possible to communicate directly with people all over the world. Also, numbers can satisfactorily represent my concept "Keep changing," by the succession of 1, 2, 3 . . . indicating a clear change in time.

I also believe materials and technique are not important as long as they are able to express my concept. Technology is appropriate for my work because through it I can achieve the concept of "eternal continuity." The conventional means of expression, represented by "materials," disappears if substance itself vanishes. However, technology continues to function almost forever; a computer can continue if damaged parts are replaced, so technology makes it possible for my concept to work eternally. However, I do not mean to praise technology itself. I think technology is neither "virtue" nor "vice." It is something completely neutral and can become both "virtue" and "vice" depending on how it is used. It can be said that the atomic bomb is one negative example. My work focuses on the spirit of the user of technology, not on technology itself. People are always important.

I am interested in art because it is born from people's spirit. Art is in your mind. I call it "Art in You." My work is equipment to look at your own self.

Tracey Moffatt

Night Cries: A Rural Tragedy 1989 35-mm color film, 17 minutes

When I was 28 years old, I made my short film *Night Cries: A Rural Tragedy* in Sydney, Australia. The film and television school allowed me to use their studio and camera, though at the time I wasn't a student.

I wanted to shoot a 35-mm color film in a studio with a stylized set of a desert. I was influenced very strongly by the formality of design in Japanese cinema of the 1960s. The exquisite ghost stories in *Kwaidan* (1964) by the director Koboyashi was in my head as was the Federico García Lorca play *The House of Bernarda Alba*. I loved this tale of women cooped up together in a house in the south of Spain in the middle of summer and all of them going mad.

With *Night Cries*, I didn't need to look for a plot; it was simple and slightly autobiographical. My story is about a resentful Australian Aboriginal woman caring for her aging white Australian mother. My film has no dialogue, just a soundtrack of harsh wind blowing, flies buzzing, and the scratching of corrugated iron. An edgy sound artist composed a throbbing industrial rumble mixed in with shrieking seagulls for the climatic sequences of flashbacks to childhood.

I am still exhausted by the emotional heaviness in *Night Cries*, so much so that I can hardly look at it.

He Kills Me 1987 offset photolithography, 24 x 36 inches (61 x 91.4 cm) Everything about this epidemic has been utterly predictable, utterly, utterly and completely predictable, from the very beginning, from the very first day. But no one would listen. There are many people who knew exactly what was happening, what would happen and has happened, but no one of importance would listen. They still won't listen. This is an epidemic that could have been contained. We definitely could have contained it.

—DR. MATHILDE KRIM,
Co-founding Chair of the American
Foundation for AIDS Research (AMFAR)

Mariko Mori

Birth of a Star 1995 3-D Duratrans print, acrylic, light box, and audio CD, 6 x 4 feet (1.8 x 1.2 m) A star radiates light worth hundreds of millions of stars at the end of its life.

Death: the absolute inescapable law of the universe.

In the vast universe, however, some stars die and yet others are brought into being through mega-explosions effected by gravity and immense pressure.

Any life, whether macroscopic or microscopic, will see its death, dissolution, and rebirth.

Portrait (van Gogh) 1985 color photograph, 47¼ x 39½ inches (120 x 100.3 cm) This photo work is my first earnest self-portrait. Since this, I have been creating artworks with a self-portrait theme. This is the work which gave me the pleasure and confidence in representing myself.

b. Osaka, Japan, 1951. Lives and works in Osaka, Japan.

Daido Moriyama

Light and Shadow 1980 C-print At the end of the 1970s, for a few years, I hardly took any pictures. Once in a blue moon I would try, but none of the images moved me. I was uncertain what I was trying to see or capture. Days went by. Eventually I put the camera down. I spent day after day in misery. The root of the problem, as I can see now, was not about the photography itself, but seems to have arisen from the mire in which my life was trapped at that time. In any case, my daily life was out of focus. I had lost touch with the passing of time.

One day, I was walking on the street in the city. A camera caught my eye. It was displayed in the corner of a secondhand camera store window. I instantly wanted this camera. Of course, I already owned many cameras, which were lying unused on shelves in a locker. My heart, however, completely fell for this used camera. Although I am a professional photographer, I usually do not have much preference for the camera I use. As long as it takes pictures, it suits me fine. Therefore, it was out of character that I wanted this old one so badly. I bought the camera without a moment of hesitation. It was an Asahi Pentax SV, with a 35-mm lens attached. The encounter with this old camera was significant. I believe my dormant desire to take pictures, and a nostalgia for those days when I constantly photographed, drew me to this camera. After that day I went back to the streets with the camera in my hand. I was there, here was this camera, and the world was filled with lights. That was enough for me. I didn't hesitate. I just needed to push the shutter. I was facing the world with this simple idea. I took this picture of a hat during that period, in that state of mind.

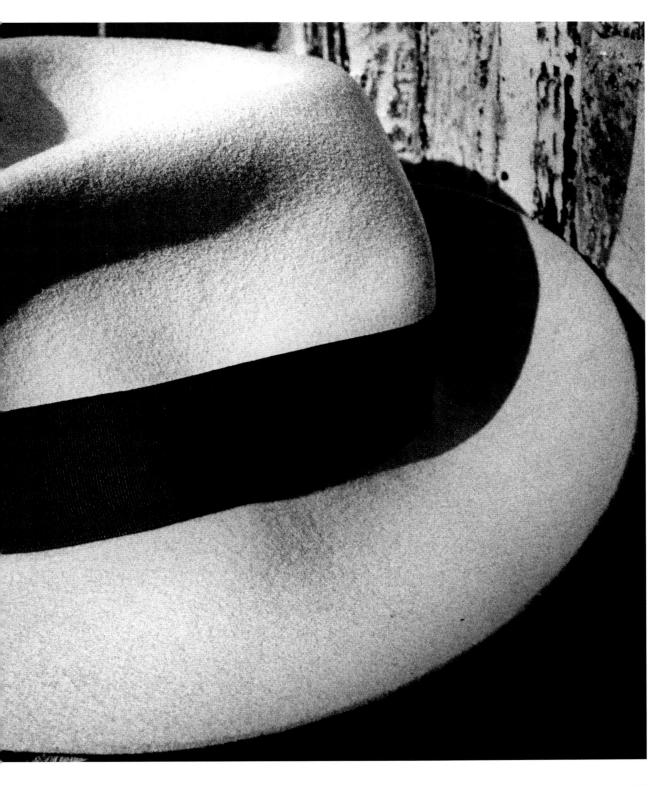

Robert Morris

Box with the Sound of Its Own Making 1961 walnut box, speaker, and 3¹/₂ hour recorded tape, 9³/₄ x 9³/₄ x 9³/₄ inches (24.8 x 24.8 x 24.8 cm) One of the first.

The first object I made when I came to New York was a box with sound, which is a cube about eight inches on a side. I recorded the sound of making this box and put a speaker in it so that it plays for three hours the sounds of its being constructed. And it wasn't conscious with me but I think this was again . . . I mean this completely split the process and the object. And yet put them both back together again. So in some way I think this was a work that allowed me then to go ahead. I mean really resolved that conflict that had occurred in painting.

Private Keep Out 1994 acrylic on canvas, 48 x 67 inches (121.9 x 170.2 cm) Art should communicate. This work was one of the first paintings that incorporated both the psychology of industrial color and of architecture, private property, and its perversity. It is pure visual ideology. My work is always about communication first.

b. London, England, 1967. Lives and works in New York, NY, USA and London, England.   255

Matthias Müller

Aus der Ferne—The Memo Book 1989 still from a 16mm film, color, sound, 27 minutes After years spent exploring my medium, carefully developing and shaping my own themes, my film *The Memo Book* presented an entirely new challenge. Stemming from a crisis situation after a former lover died of AIDS, the film follows the stages I went through in dealing with this trauma. The film was an open-ended project, spontaneous and intuitive, made with a handheld Super-8 camera and without the help of a team. During filming, there was no self-censure and very little analytical reflection on my part. Everything that seemed to be even slightly connected with this experience of death was filmed. Including interruptions and new approaches, the process lasted a period of many months. It was during the editing process that I first began to deliberately reconstruct my experiences of the past, as if it all belonged to a diary that had never been written. So the film connects the immediacy of the diary film with the analytical distance that comes from reflecting upon an autobiographical project. Originally, the project focused on remembering my dead friend, but over time it turned into a confrontation with myself. In one sequence featuring the imaginary resurrection of my dead friend, I visit myself later in the hospital—I am the patient and the visitor in one. Some of my fears that I might have been infected, too, appeared here. Ultimately, the film follows a journey: my retreat from the world and eventual return to it. Although my discomfort of acting in front of the camera is clearly visible in my performance, I felt it was important that I appear in person in this film. *The Memo Book* was created with the full participation of my entire body. A large part of the film material literally went through my hands, frame by frame, as I developed the footage myself. Even the material that I appropriated refers to my body; in a certain way, it physically places it in quotation marks, for instance, as when my legs move like a wipe in front of the TV monitor. In one shot, American actress and singer Kathryn Grayson moves across a background projection—an orgy of flaming technicolor-red evening skies. Her catchy message, "There's beauty everywhere for everyone to share," written in German subtitles across the picture, was an express invitation for me to borrow her film. The process of accumulating borrowed as well as one's own images produces alternating currents. Films oppose each other, look at each other, correspond with each other. Simply placing the appropriated images next to mine recodes them: In the context of my project, Fred Astaire and Gene Kelly dance across the sky like a pair of homosexual lovers lost to the world. In *The Memo Book*, the found footage serves to integrate introspection into a collective world of images. Creating a hybrid form allows you to recognize yourself in the stranger—and the stranger in what is supposedly yourself, as well. Drama, hysteria, pathos, sentimentality: The appropriated material forces my own images to show what lies latent in them, without casting a shadow on them. One approach might have been to contrast the opulent production values and stylistic elegance of the borrowed films with the bare bones conditions I worked with. However, I level the obvious difference between the glossy style of the appropriated material and my rough-grained, Super-8 aesthetics by embedding the citation in my own images. Although most of the found footage was produced by a film industry remote from my own reality, I was less interested in discrediting these images as fake and opposing them with my own suppos-

b. Bielefeld, Germany, 1961. Lives and works in Cologne, Germany.

Überall ist Schönheit

edly immediate, authentic experience expressed in a non-industrial but manufactured work of art. Working on this film made it clear it to me how strongly my own emotional world is affected by these kinds of media-transmitted notions, no matter how toxic the products that convey these ideas might be. The long period of time it took to produce the film, which included a process of distancing myself from the material, made it also possible to see my own creations as if they were found footage. *The Memo Book* had a lasting influence on my later films. I have often used and modified the combination of original and appropriated material in other projects. Eight years later, I worked on the theme once again, in *Pensão Globo*, this time from the perspective of a man preparing for his own death. However, the strongest, most elementary and existential experience of *The Memo Book* was that of using artistic means to work through a crisis and emerge renewed.

Matt Mullican

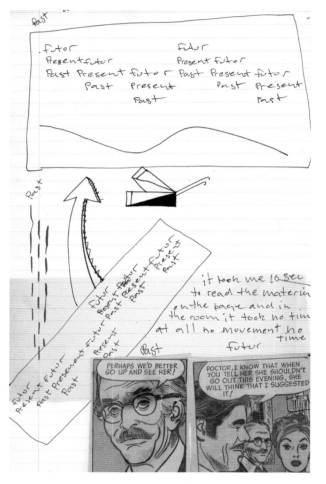

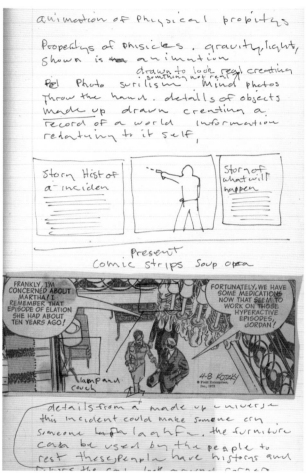

Spring 1973 notebook page with glued comics, 12 x 7.5 inches (30.5 x 19.1 cm) I jotted down an idea for a work in my notebook. It was an idea of a representation of a detail of something or some place that does not exist. In a sense it was the opening up of that place or the idea of participating in that place directly. I understood at that moment that it represented not just an idea but a body of work. I would not call it my first work, but I would call it a pivotal moment for the work I have been doing over the last thirty years.

b. Santa Monica, CA, USA, 1951. Lives and works in New York, NY, USA.

Valentina, the Fastest (from the Sugar Children series) 1996 gelatin silver print, 14 x 11 inches (35.6 x 27.9 cm) In the summer of 1995, I exchanged an art piece for a travel package to the Caribbean. Over the course of two weeks on the island of St. Kitts, I managed to befriend a group of local children who, although they lived so close to the sea, had never learned to swim. When they saw me in the water, they would venture nearby to wade. Soon, I knew each of their names and a few things about their personalities, and we all looked forward to seeing each other every afternoon. One day, they invited me for a stroll on another part of the island, to meet their parents. In contrast to the fresh, sweet demeanor of the children, their parents seemed weary and bitter, the inevitable result of an unfair exchange: long, backbreaking hours of labor at the sugarcane plantation for a meager, survival-based salary.

Back in New York, while inspecting snapshots I had taken of the children, I could not help thinking about the sad metamorphosis most of my little friends were bound to experience. I knew that some mysterious, poisonous potion would trans-

form those bright-eyed island children and give them their parents' aspect of hopelessness. At the same time, I had just read a poem by the Brazilian poet Ferreira Gullar called "The Sugar," in which Gullar questions the origins of the white substance. Where does sugar come from? he asks—is it from the store, from the warehouse? And he goes on tracing the genealogy of the substance, ending with the seminal phrase: "It is with the bitter lives of bitter people that I sweeten my coffee on this beautiful morning in Ipanema." The radiant childhood of those youngsters would almost certainly be transformed by sugar; those children would become merely the residue of the sugar we consume.

I bought some black paper and several kinds of sugar. I then tried to copy the snapshots of the children by sprinkling sugar over the paper with the help of little sifters, and I took pictures of the "drawings" with a medium-format camera. As I finished each portrait, I would put all the sugar in a little glass jar, and glue the source photograph on it as a label.

I displayed these little "urns," along with the small portraits,

in a tiny back room of a friend's gallery in SoHo. *The New York Times* wrote a nice review about it, and a few weeks later I was invited to be part of the 1997–98 "New Photography" show at the Museum of Modern Art. Today, those sugar portraits are in the collections of some major museums, as well as in the library of the little school the children attended in St. Kitts. I owe my career to those children. As I examined my efforts, for the first time ever I felt they were something to be really proud of. This work also marked the beginning of a series of collaborations with children that have increasingly nurtured my work.

Takashi Murakami

And Then, And Then And Then And Then And Then (Blue) 1996 acrylic on canvas mounted on board, 118¹/₈ x 118¹/₈ inches (300 x 300 cm) Mr. DOB has now become a kind of self-portrait for me; however, when I first created him in 1993, he was the ironic product of various ideas merged together.

First of all, the idea was that he had to be very "Pop." Andy Warhol's *Marilyn*, which frequently graced the covers of art magazines, was an icon recognizable to everyone. I felt I should make such an icon. Second, one needed a context in the world of contemporary art. I wanted to interject some sort of angle within the character that reflected the culture in contemporary Japan. Third, there was a boom of language art practiced by such artists as Jenny Holzer and Barbara Kruger in the Japanese contemporary art scene at that time. Many Japanese artists were following this boom; using unfamiliar English, French, and German words with mistakes, and quoting from Ludwig Wittgenstein and Jacques Derrida without really understanding them. So, to make a statement against that movement, I thought I would make an imitation of language art, using not a difficult text but a Romanized version of a rather silly Japanese phrase. "Dobojite" (a slang term meaning 'why?') comes from a joke in a *manga* entitled *Inakappe Taisho* (The Country General) and "oshamanbe" (a pun on the name of a town, with the sexual connotations of the syllable *man*) comes

from a joke used by the very famous nonsense comedian Toru Yuri, of postwar Japan. Making a silly phrase that perhaps was not even funny, I combined the first sounds of these two phrases, and thus Mr. DOB was born.

However, the project was initially the subject of loads of criticism from the art community. I guess I can understand why. After all, part of DOB was a backlash against that art scene. This is how my icon creation project got off to the worst possible start. Yet, faithful to my original conviction, I kept going on without changing my ideas, and gradually they began to take shape. In the end, the character that deserved birth was born, and I had my finished product. By now we have spent a lot of time together, and every day it demands more changes from me. Once a character is born and begins to move, one must willfully follow its demands. If you let it be, it will go and raise itself. With DOB as my excuse, I sometimes untie the cords of art history, touching on the school of Chuck Close–like portraiture, linking up with African or Polynesian art, sometimes letting it become optical art or even psychedelic art, sometimes staging Rinpa school or Momoyama period-like presentations, or sometimes just thinking about contemporary Japanese character culture. Now, I've got a face that can transform at will to do these things.

b. Tokyo, Japan, 1962. Lives and works in Tokyo, Japan, and New York, NY, USA.

Elisabeth Murray

‎

Painter's Progress 1980–81 oil on canvas 114³/₄ by 96¹/₂ inches (291.5 x 245.1 cm)

I started by making a bunch of little odd shapes, with no image in mind, and then put them up on my painting wall, haphazardly, trying not to have any ideas about an image, nor to have them fit together or make sense. Of course the idea of a puzzle that does not fit came to mind but the primary feeling I wanted was of a whole thing that was shattering on the wall, and this felt very satisfying psychically. When I started to paint I found myself searching for an image that would pull the shapes together, so there was always that tension in the painting. One night I was walking our dogs and happened by Pearl Paint and there it was, the neon palette with three brushes, in the window. This gave me the idea for the image I didn't want. So I understood from this painting, how the shapes could be the abstract content, and an image could make it whole. The big dream—conflict and unity, simultaneously.

‎ b. Chicago, IL, USA, 1940. Lives and works in New York, NY, USA.

The Girl with the Knife in Her Hand
1991 acrylic on canvas, 59 x 55¹/₈ x ⁷/₈ inches
(150.5 x 140 x 2.2 cm) Most of the characters and images that emerge in my work are quoted from my past experiences (also from my childhood days) and tend to be based on the dark or painful side of life.

What I want to encourage the viewer to consider through my work are not social, emotional, or generational problems, but rather possibilities for hope.

The images of animals, children, and some elements (in this case, a knife) may be misconstrued as illustrative, naive, or decorative—but this is not the case. These images stand for another possible way of living in society, one that opposes and seeks to remove the many barriers between us.

b. Hirosaki, Aomori Prefecture, Japan, 1959. Lives and works in Tokyo, Japan.

Shirin Neshat

Speechless (top right) 1996 RC print (photo taken by Larry Barns) 46³/₄ x 33⁷/₈ inches (118.7 x 86 cm), edition of 10 + 1 artist's proof

Allegiance with Wakefulness (Women of Allah series) (bottom right) 1994 pen and ink over gelatin silver print mounted on aluminum, 48¹/₄ x 40 inches (123 x 102 cm), framed, edition of three

In 1979, the Islamic Revolution had taken place in Iran, turning the country upside down, yet from a distance, in America, I found myself oblivious to the whole event, in particular to the new portrait of Iranian men and women as they rallied around a new form of "identity"—no longer as "Persians," but rather as "Islamic fundamentalists." It was not until the summer of 1990 when I finally returned to Iran and was confronted with the reality of this transformation. *Allegiance With Wakefulness* and *Speechless* are two images that reflect my humble attempt to capture the essence and complexity behind this new "identity" that at once empowered its followers with its weapon of "religion" and "violence," and simultaneously victimized them. Having lived with little or no ambition for an artistic career for over ten years, this body of work, *Women of Allah*, became pivotal as it marked the beginning of an articulation of my own personal visual vocabulary and, most importantly, my renewed faith in art as a truly transformative expression.

b. Qazvin, Iran, 1957. Lives and works in New York, NY, USA.

Colony 1989 lead pellets and stockings, dimensions variable I did this piece a long time ago; the particles are *peso* (weight), *prumo* (plumb), and *passo* (step). They are the base units of the language that can make possible the colonies, *copulas*, and *copulanias*. They are my first completely organic works, with very simple construction, using gravity as the structural power, the skin as a container of the content, and the bag as an icon of fertility. The pieces also exist as independent organs of a more complex organism, a body made up of cells built with little balls, egg cells. In addition to the conflict and contrast of the hard and soft, there is also the contrast between lead shot (male universe) and stockings (female universe). A good percentage of my work, maybe all of it, is fruit from these seeds.

Tim Noble & Sue Webster

Miss Understood & Mr. Meanor 1997
rubbish, slide projector, wood, and light sensor,
55¹/₈ x 27¹/₂ x 23⁵/₈ inches (140 x 70 x 60 cm)

Miss Understood & Mr. Meanor
—our first ever shadow work.
Its material content is worthless,
the sculpture itself is worthless,
the sculpture itself is vulgar,
which intensifies the beauty of
the shadow it casts of the two
creators. This seminal work
of art remains merely a distant
memory burnt into our subconscious, lost forever within the
embers of the Momart fire
of London in May 25, 2004.

Ex-Nihilo 1958 Magna on canvas, 67 x 63¾ inches (170.2 x 161.9 cm) *Ex-nihilo* means "out of nothing," and that is exactly what the painting represents . . . nothing. It is simply to be looked at and enjoyed, like music is to be listened to . . .

b. Asheville, NC, USA, 1924. Lives and works in Midcoast, ME, USA.   267

Daniel Oates

Happy Workers (Tom the Postman) II 1992 polyurethan and acrylic, 18 x 8 x 5 inches (45.7 x 20.3 x 12.7 cm)
This piece is based on a much smaller version which I completed about six months
earlier. At the time, I was totally sick of the art world and wanted nothing much to
do with it. I was more interested in cartoons and toys. I didn't consider these models
I was making to be art. I wasn't trying to make art. My friend Gavin Brown came
over one day and saw them. A few months later, he was curating a show and put one
of the pieces in it. It sold.

b. Lucerne, Switzerland, 1964. Lives and works in New York, NY, USA.

Tasaday 1985 acrylic, tempera, newsprint paper, and collage on canvas, 48 x 60 inches (121.9 x 152.4 cm) This was the first painting I made after I immigrated, albeit illegally, to the U.S. in 1985. Measuring approximately three by five feet long, the work was painted while tacked on a wall in the hallway of a one-bedroom flat in Los Angeles, where I was living with two families. They slept in the bedroom and living room, while I slept in the hallway next to the bathroom. I would wait for the others to fall asleep before I painted late at night. At the time, I was very much inspired by the works of George Grosz and Otto Dix.

The painting is titled *Tasaday* after the allegedly primitive tribe that was rumored to have been "discovered" by the Marcos regime in the early '70s. This remarkable group of "natives" was found to be living isolated from "civilization." Perhaps one of the greatest anthropological findings of the twentieth century, scholars are still debating the tribe's authenticity.

Marcel Odenbach

I Think I Have Lost Myself 1976 performance The performance runs concurrently with an exhibition showing my self-portraits along with hackneyed ideas of my personality. At the exhibition opening, I sit behind a window in the gallery, isolated, watching the goings-on through the glass. Only my head, over which I have pulled a black hood, is visible. I pull this black mask over my face as a symbol of my anonymity, a signal that my personality no longer exists, or exists only in the exhibition—by virtue of the notions others have of me—about me—by virtue of expectations, roles. I am like this and like that—must be so—behave wrongly in that regard—look like that. In other words, the person Marcel Odenbach, as created, as seen by others, the person I apparently am. Those clichés by which those around me think they know me! My 'real' personality is not seen objectively; this thinking in clichés can lead to a point at which I no longer know what I think I'm like as a person. And when that point comes, then I've been made by the others, I react in the expected fashion, my apparent personality runs along the prescribed lines—and that's why I have lost myself!

Albert Oehlen

Untitled 1979 collage, 4⁷/₁₀ x 4⁷/₁₀ inches (approximately 12 x 12 cm) In 1980, I made two big sculptures out of wooden planks, the ones used for rail tracks. Looking at one of them reminded me of a wheel and the other was struggling to get upstairs. When looking at this sketch/collage, which I had made for another sculpture, I realized that I wanted to get higher up and that I had to leave the material burden behind (below me). "Sculptors think they're very smart, shit on the ground and see in the darkness," said a hit song that was always playing on the radio at that time. I didn't want that. I shaved off my mustache and ever since I have only created two-dimensional works.

b. Krefeld, Germany, 1954. Lives and works in Cologne, Germany, and La Palma, Spain.   271

Catherine Opie

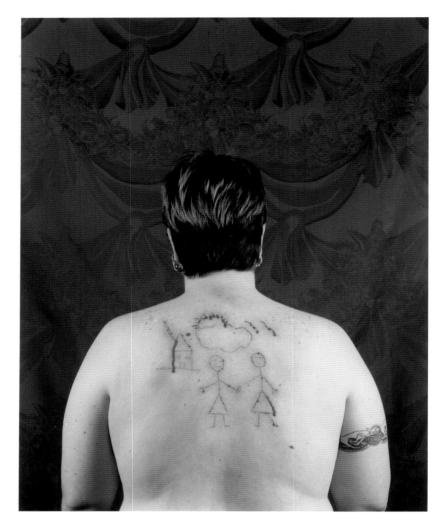

Self-Portrait 1993 chromogenic print, edition of eight, 40 x 30 inches (101.6 x 76.2 cm)
I wasn't really thinking about the art world or the impact this work would have on people. It was a photograph that I had in my head for over a year before actually making it. I had a good friend, fellow artist Judie Bamber, do the cutting. She hadn't ever done a cutting before. I wanted to be apprehensive about the style of the cutting, as opposed to the piece I did the following year *Pervert*, which was perfect. The image is about hope and being queer.

Annual Rings 1968 diagram of circles of age of trees divided by a political border, at the U.S. / Canada border in Fort Kent, Maine, and Clear, New Brunswick, 131 feet x 2⁴/₅ inches x 196 feet x 10¹/₅ inches (40 x 60 m), time: 1:30 p.m. (US) / 2:30 p.m. (Canada) *Annual Rings* was site-specific, in that it was absolutely necessary for the concept of the work that it be located between two countries. Land Art was operating way outside of the studio, not even in the street. It was operating on the land far away from urban activity. The nature of Land Art was that it was real and operating in real time, not artificial time. Land Art was made up of real physical activities which included danger, intrusions, and the consequences inherent in operating in the real world. Land Art wanted to position itself in the historical lineage of sculpture. It wanted to be considered an attempt to contrast relational, traditional forms of object-making with a kind of real-time dynamic in which the sculptural activity could be considered an activation of real time and real place.

b. Electric City, WA, USA, 1938. Lives and works in New York, NY, USA.

Gabriel Orozco

La Tierra (The Earth) 1975 pastel on paper, 17¹/₂ x 14¹/₅ inches (44.5 x 36 cm) When
I finished this painting I thought I could be an artist.

I've considered myself an artist since then. Many ideas in my work
come from that time when I was a boy.

 b. Jalapa, Vera Cruz, Mexico, 1962. Lives and works in New York, NY, USA; Paris, France; and Mexico City, Mexico.

La Última Cena (above) 11 x 14 inches (27.9 x 35.6 cm), **Retrato Salvaje** (right) 11 x 14 inches (27.9 x 35.6 cm), **Albures Mexicanos** (below) 11 x 28 inches (27.9 x 71.1 cm), C. 1984 silver gelatin prints I began showing paintings in Mexico City during the '80s. Different political and cultural notions of aesthetics clashed and struggled within the paintings to create something of their own. These works received awards and attention from critics, collectors, and galleries. Around the same time, I started taking photographs documenting my punk friends within the industrialized and polluted Aztec megalopolis. These images portrayed my experience as an alienated youth struggling to coexist with and to make sense of the contradictions of postcolonial reality. The "objective" and personal qualities of these image makes them perhaps more successful than the paintings and still of interest to me.

Tom Otterness

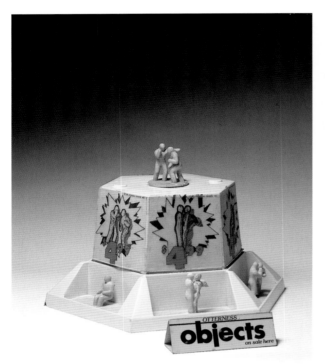

Otterness Objects 1979 sign and
display stands with four hydrocal sculptures,
24 x 32 inches (61 x 81 cm), unlimited edition
I consider these plasters my first
public sculpture. This is the
original display stand for Artists
Space, from Christmas 1979.
I also sold them in the Bronx
and on the sidewalk in front of
The Museum of Modern Art.
They sold for $4.99 each.

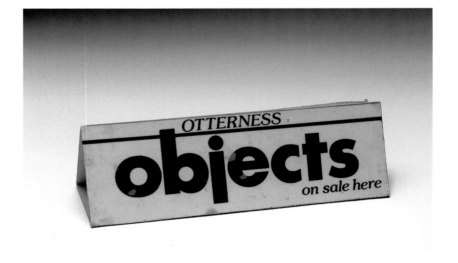

The Life of Phyllis 1976–77 videotape in five episodes, black-and-white, sound *The Life of Phyllis* is one of the first serious works that I completed in 1976 at the California Institute for the Arts. It involved hand-made sets for video and installation, as well as a temporal element: The episodes were shown daily at lunchtime. The sets for the video became a physical installation where the video was screened. This is a way of working that I used for years to come; the combination of language, sound, moving image, painting, and sculptural installation was comfortable for me. Recently, while remastering the video element for The Museum of Modern Art in New York City, where it was screened in 2003, I was struck by the parallels to and reflections of the work I have made in the twenty years since.

Also, some of the themes and resonations of the video now carry a new meaning in relation to pop culture: Michael Jackson, cloning, and reality-television snuff culture—there is an elliptical feeling to the project that deals with a neverending stream of modular tabloid narrative.

Bill Owens

Built for Edwards September 1970 gelatin silver print, 8 x 10 inches (20.3 x 25.4 cm) In 1970, I was a news photographer in Livermore, California. This gave me access to all aspects of the community, and I decided to do a documentary project on the suburbs, focusing on Livermore.

To do this project, I knew I had to do what all the great documentary photographers do: shoot with a large-format camera. The grain created in 35mm photographs sends a different message than crisp, clear documentary-style images. With the small grant that I received, I bought two cameras: a Pentax 6 x 7 and a Brooks Veriwide 6 x 9.

My grant also allowed me to work one day a week on the project. So one Saturday morning I started driving around town to make images of homes, streets, and the suburban lifestyle. I headed to where homes were under construction. I came upon a finished house with no yard. The sign in the yard said, "This home is being built expressly for Edwards." The background for the word "Edwards" was white, so when they sold the home, they painted it white again and stenciled in the next person's name. I jumped out of my Volkswagen Super Beetle, grabbed the Brooks Veriwide, and shot two or three frames of the house made specially for the Edwardses.

One year and 400 rolls later, I had 500 prints in a box and began looking for a publisher. I didn't have a title for the books, because at that time the word "suburbia" was very culturally loaded and had a negative image. We decided that *Suburbia* did fit for the project because it was an honest portrayal of the suburban lifestyle.

COURTESY OF THE ARTIST. © 1972 BILL OWENS.

b. San Jose, CA, USA, 1938. Lives and works in Hayward, CA, USA.

THIS HOME IS BEING BUILT EXPRESSLY
FOR EDWARDS

279

Roxy Paine

Displaced Sink 1993 dripping sink, stack of soap There are a lot of things in this piece that have come out in my later work or hinted at things that came later—this kind of elevating of an extremely banal occurrence like a dripping sink or leaking faucet that creates a situation where you have to focus or meditate on such a commonplace happening. You may not see it in the picture, but the water from the sink was dripping through the stack of soap and forming this system of soap scum lakes and rivers on the floor. This whole other artwork was created from this banal action or activity repeated over and over. *Displaced Sink* was a piece that was resolved in its unresolvedness. It's the first piece that I felt did that successfully.

Things I've continued to pursue after, like forcing viewers to watch paint dry and this work with the soap scum, seem to coalesce. *Displaced Sink* was done in '93 and the first dipping machine, *Paint Dipper*, was made in '96, but there were other pieces where I was playing with semi-automatic processes. There were these projects where I would drip paint and then explode the semi-dried droppings with air, forming systems of craters that became these crater paintings. *Displaced Sink* explored ideas of erosion while my later work examines the idea of accumulation. Actually, there's a project I'm working on now that's all about erosion, so I guess I'm coming back full circle.

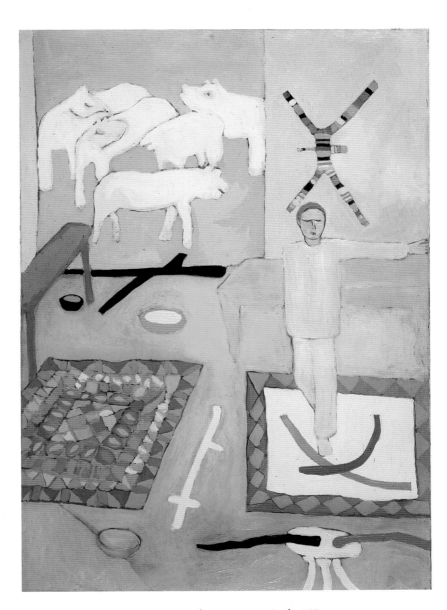

Mi ritiro a dipingere un quadro (I retire to paint) 1977 oil on canvas, 10³/₅ x 19⁷/₁₀ inches (70 x 50 cm) The meaning of this work is all in the title. Maybe it is a conceptual heritage which is based on the gesture, the time, and silence that painting requires.

b. Paduli, Italy, 1948. Lives and works in Paduli, Italy. 281

Panamarenko

Das Flugzeug 1967 aluminum tubes, steel wire, rubber driving belt, adapted bicycle wheels, leather saddle, pedals, and Styropor wings covered with canvas, 295^3/$_{10}$ x 275^3/$_5$ x 629^9/$_{10}$ inches (750 x 700 x 1600 cm)

An important early work, *Das Flugzeug* is the first of my pedal-powered flying machines.

In the functional sense, I don't consider this machine to be the least bit successful. At the time when I made it, I didn't know that in order to function it would have to be far bigger. Because I didn't know the exact calculation, I just thought that with six wings equivalent in size to those of a small aircraft, the general speed would be such that at a certain point it would achieve liftoff. But the construction was not strong enough. It couldn't be tested, because the wings would not stay up and since I first made it, they have always had to be hung from the ceiling.

But I liked the aeroplane anyway. It gave me an aesthetic effect. It was one of the first big things that I made after I left art school and was no longer forced to look at Picasso and Van Gogh and so on. Painting is such a boring thing if you are a young person. You do it ten times and if you are even a tiny bit alive you know that the rest of the world is far more fantastic than a painted imitation of it. At the same time I discovered all that stuff about art being an unconscious thing. I discovered that there was something else, an unconscious feeling: You thought that something was great but you didn't know why. I think this airplane is great but I don't know why.

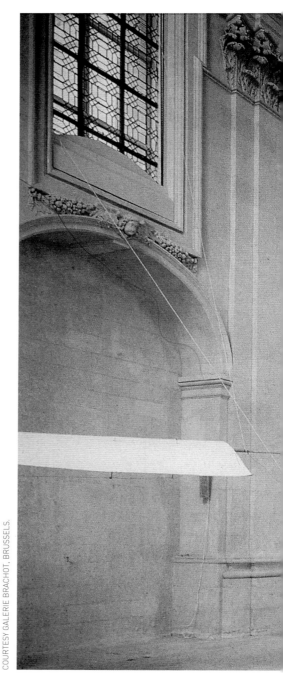

b. Antwerp, Belgium, 1940. Lives and works in Antwerp, Belgium.

Cornelia Parker

Fleeting Monument 1985 lead, wire, brass pendulums, 29⁹/₁₀ x 84³/₁₀ x 84³/₁₀ inches (76 x 214 x 214 cm) My first piece of work that I considered successful was *Fleeting Monument*, 1985, most probably because it was the first thing I sold to a public collection and therefore it was capable of holding its own out there in the big, wide world. I had made a lot of works before, which at the time I thought were good, but which in hindsight were not as resolved. *Fleeting Monument* was an attempt to take the idea of the monumental, that which is supposed to last forever, and transform it into something ephemeral like a splash of water. I bought a souvenir of Big Ben, a famous landmark instantly recognizable everywhere; it was the cheapest, crudest cipher already abstracted by mass production. By casting it many times from the same mold in lead, I eroded it even further, wearing the image away.

b. Cheshire, England, 1956. Lives and works in London, England.

Prestwich Mental Hospital Greater Manchester, 1971 black-and-white photograph I'd visited the brother of a friend from the Poly, who had been admitted to the hospital. I was so taken with the place that I decided to do some work and sort out permission to photograph there, and then was drawn in for the next three months, photographing constantly. Visually it was very striking. The whole atmosphere . . . you just knew there was scope there. When you're a 19-year-old photographer, you have aspirations, but it's difficult to know actually what to say. But suddenly I found something I wanted to articulate. That's when [my photography] really took off. I spent a lot of time there. The lecturers at the Poly tried to discourage me from spending so much time there; they thought it was taking too long. The whole idea of doing something thoroughly didn't really have currency in those days.

b. Epsom, England, 1952. Lives and works in Bristol, England.

Richard Patterson

Motocrosser 1994 oil and acrylic on canvas (three panels), 82 x 124 inches (208.3 x 315 cm)

Motocrosser was the first painting that successfully drew my interests in painting, sculpture, photography, and film into a cohesive whole. In terms of the image and the way it was made, the painting excited me enough to want to exhibit it outside of a small group of friends and I felt that it provided a fertile basis for a wide body of work.

Motocrosser was my first publicly exhibited painting, shown in 1995 at the project space at Anthony d'Offay Gallery, London.

Das grosse Weltbild 1965 oil on hard fiber, 70¾ x 102¼ inches (180 x 260 cm)

Reflections

Movements fixated/frozen on the surface—aesthetic landscape of possibilities.

Collision of figures which disclose differences so as to be model for decisions and base of continuous alienation.

The essential of a time/epoch—the Cold War and the years after—new conflicts.

The logic of those movements in their irrationality.

The romantic idea disappears through/because of the longing for abstraction.

Rational explanations disappear—the dimensions unfalter, while we are/one is working.

Transform signs to symbols and symbols to signs. Alchemy of visual information.

The "I"/Ego gets caught between the longing for completeness and the longing for abstraction.

b. Dresden, Germany, 1939. Lives and works in Düsseldorf and Cologne, Germany; Dublin, Ireland; and London, England.

Simon Periton

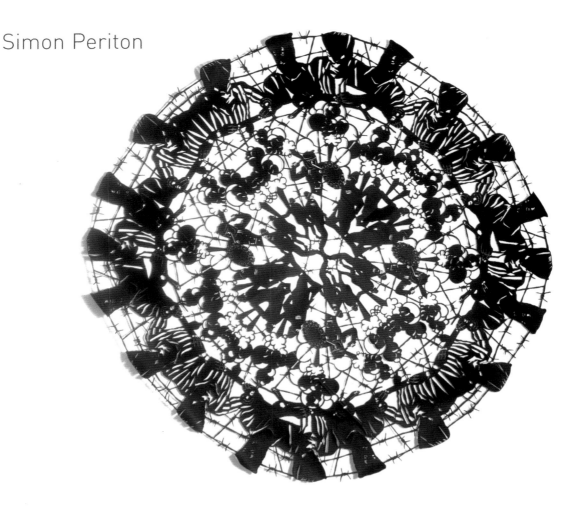

Black Riot Fart Doily 1997 cut paper, diameter: 72 inches (182.9 cm) This isn't the first piece I'd made as a doily but I think of it as one of the first important pieces for me. The image is made up of elements from a much larger piece that, while spectacular in size, lost a lot of the intimacy and pattern that I was trying to work with. In some ways that larger doily didn't work!

As a result I made *Black Riot Fart Doily* by taking the four or five key elements and producing a much more kaleidoscopic piece that still retained a lot of the properties of a doily. It's all cut from black paper and is approximately six feet in diameter. There are three main rings. The outer ring is made up of a repeat of two plane hijackers reading at a press conference in the 1970s wearing pillowcases over their heads, an image I was drawn to and have used many times. The central ring is of the London police force running into themselves during some race riots. These two rings are held apart by a band of lacy Aubrey Beardsley farts spiked with barbed wire.

It always makes me think of a Busby Berkeley dance routine. *Black Riot Fart Doily* contains the core of what I was interested in then: seduction (beauty, decoration, delicacy, intimacy) and violence all wrapped up in something essentially useless—a doily.

No Title (Don't complicate the . . .),
1987 pen and ink on paper, 24 x 18 inches (45.7 x 60.9 cm) To trace it back distinctly, I guess my first artworks were cartoons, and were a response to cartoons also. It's kind of a subtle line between that and what I do today, but in another way, it's quite a dramatic line to have crossed. From a distance, the average work of mine might resemble a cartoon. But there was a specific point where I think I crossed over into something else.

b. Tucson, AZ, USA, 1957. Lives and works in Hermosa Beach, CA, USA. 289

Richard Pettibone

Roy Lichtenstein, "Tex," 1962 1964 acrylic, oil, and rubber stamp on canvas, 4³/₄ x 4⁷/₈ inches (12 x 12.4 cm) including frame I was a young artist searching for a style, without much luck finding one, when I decided, almost as a joke, to borrow one. A style that is. So I borrowed Roy Lichtenstein's. And when I'd finished *Tex* I thought, "This is the best painting I've ever done."

Napoleon 1991 Charcoal on paper, 22 x 18 inches (55.8 x 45.7 cm) This drawing of Napoleon from 1991 isn't the first picture I ever made, but I always use it as the beginning— the beginning of lectures about my work, the beginning of books etc. For me it really is the begin-ning, the first picture I made that contained everything I believed in and everything I wanted to see. It's partly taken from a book cover of Vincent Cronin's biog-raphy of Napoleon that helped me through a very bad summer, and partly from Gros's brilliant painting of young Napoleon (I think both pictures are by Gros). Somehow I thought that when a person is in the process of becoming themselves and realizing their potential and pas-sion, there is a beauty that can be seen all over their person—in every line and shadow.

Paul Pfeiffer

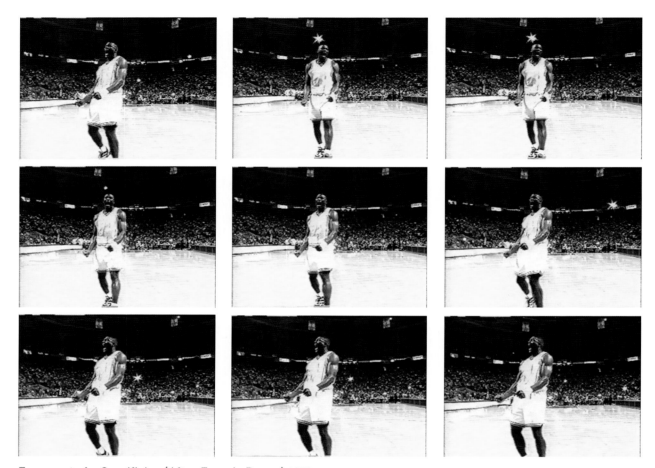

Fragment of a Crucifixion (After Francis Bacon) 1999 stills from a digital video loop *Fragment of a Crucifixion* was my first attempt to create something by digitally retouching an image from TV. I was rummaging through a stack of "Best of" NBA promo DVDs and came across this scene that suggested terrible suffering, even though the guy wasn't suffering at all but rather screaming in triumph. All the emotion is in the original footage. All I had to do was rearrange some of the pixels to bring it out more clearly. It showed me a way that I could render scenes of fantastic drama and violence without having to get too worked up myself. It's just a matter of reading between the lines of American pop culture to find the sadness, suffering, and tragi-comedy that underlies it.

b. Honolulu, HI, USA, 1966. Lives and works in New York, NY, USA.

Mask 1995 oil on canvas, 78 x 58 inches, (147.3 x 198.1 cm) *Mask* was inspired by an image in a 1970s fashion/self-help book found on the street in New York in 1994. The painting was a clear and distinctive break from previous paintings made during a stay in Tennessee that were smaller in scale and were more narrative in content and composition. The singular, iconic image of hope for renewal or what the book referred to as "what to do after the divorce" seemed a perfect start for my own renewal in painting as art. This literal depiction of a zinc-smeared face actually painted with zinc paint provided a foundation on which to build my first body of work that addressed portraiture, empty '60s & '70s fashion images, and a traditional form of oil painting in a large-pop format.

b. Marblehead, MA, USA, 1962. Lives and works in New York, NY, USA.

Pierre et Gilles

Autoportrait Sans Visage (Pierre et Gilles) 1999 two hand-painted C-prints mounted on aluminum, models: Pierre (top left), Gilles (top right), 41⁷/₁₀ x 31⁹/₁₀ inches (106 x 81 cm) each Self-portraits have marked out our work since the very beginning. It's a ritual which allows us to split, like looking at ourselves in a mirror. They are experiments, personal investigations that we can achieve only with ourselves. They allow us to go further, to be more free, to take risks, to open other doors, as we probably wouldn't do with model other than ourselves.

 Pierre Commoy—b. La Roche sur Yon, France, 1949. Gilles Blanchard—b. Le Havre, France, 1953. Live and work in Paris, France.

The Call Back 1990 Ektacolor print,
40 x 30 inches (101.6 x 76.2 cm), edition of three

The Call Back was made on my first trip to Los Angeles. I was staying with my friend, the photographer Rocky Schenk. A TV movie on the life of Lucy was being cast and a search for an "unknown" was being held and Rocky's neighbor had been "called back." It was all very Hollywood for me, and probably the first place I ever saw the word "Hollywood" was in the closing credits of *I Love Lucy*, when it said, "Filmed in Hollywood at Desilu Studios." I don't know if I can explain but there is in this picture of a an unknown actress in the '90s pretending to be a glamorous Hollywood star of the '50s who was pretending to be a wannabe actress on TV . . . a little bit of absolutely everything I care about in life and in art.

Adrian Piper

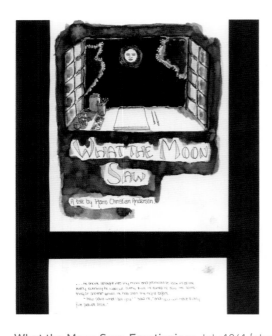

What the Moon Saw, Frontispiece July 1961 (above left)
India ink on paper, 8¹/₂ x 11 inches (21.6 x 27.9 cm) mounted on 14 x 17 inches (35.6 x 43.2 cm) board with handwritten text. #1 of 18 gouache drawings illustrating Hans Christian Andersen's "What the Moon Saw."
What the Moon Saw, Seventh Evening July 1961 (above right) India ink on paper, 8¹/₂ x 11 inches (21.6 x 27.9 cm) mounted on 14 x 17 inches (35.6 x 43.2 cm) board with handwritten text. #7 of 18 gouache drawings, illustrating Hans Christian Andersen's "What the Moon Saw."

I did this series of eighteen illustrations in the summer of 1961, when I was twelve. I already thought of myself as a serious working artist. I received a lot of approval and encouragement from my parents for this. My personal identity and virtually all of my choices were shaped around making art throughout adolescence. That I was going to continue as an adult was a foregone conclusion.

This story by Hans Christian Andersen was very important to me when I was young, because of the reflective, tranquil, detached mood the narrative itself creates. It may have been my first contact with the philosophical stance—the "bird's-eye view"—from which all transient human chaos falls into place in a meaningful order. I really liked the idea of the reflective, omniscient moon's perspective providing inspiration for the expressive, subjective artist's perspective.

However, the illustrations in the edition I had did not emphasize this, and there weren't enough of them. The narrative struck me as so very visual in its images and choice of words, and it's clear from the frontispiece text that Andersen intended this. I thought the form and content of the story deserved more visual attention than the book publisher's illustrator had given it. I felt I could do a better job.

Out of the Frost 1986 oil and acrylic on wood panel, 82 x 80 inches (208.2 x 203.2 cm) Out of the trauma of violent physical injury, I became a new person. Harder, more sentimental. A heightened existentialism conversely induced a greater love of life. Amazingly, I bloomed that following spring.

Jaume Plensa

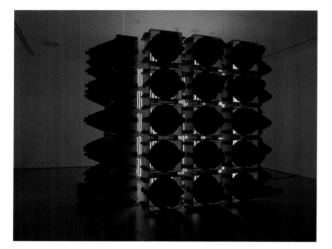

La Neige Rouge 1991 cast iron and neon, 97⁹/₁₀ x 138¹/₂ x 138¹/₂ inches (251 x 355 x 355 cm). Exhibition view, "CEL:CELLA:CELDA," Henry Moore Institute, Leeds, England At the beginning of the '90s there is a decisive turning point in the work of Jaume Plensa, one that is marked by two major works, *Désir Rêve* and *La Neige Rouge*, both from 1991. The alliance between the physical and the abstract, between idea and material, between the poles of iron and light.

With *La Neige Rouge*, Plensa develops an equally impressive image of the metamorphic power of glowing heat. Iron crucibles such as those are used in the smelting of iron, form a cell which is armored on the outside and in whose interior light shines with a red glow. The effulgence of molten iron appears in the chill brilliance of neon tubes that follow the curved lineation of heating rods. A chill dream of red snow. Coldness and heat collide. He plays with a dialectical shock of coldness, which he develops out of the confrontation of liquid and solidified matter. The heavy iron crucibles seem to be the source of the glistening light that fills the entire space with its deep red. The expansion of the light is accompanied by the sonorous tone of the transformers, whose deep bass murmur measures out the domain as a resonating space.

Light and sound, which in *Désir Rêve* and *La Neige Rouge* appear for the first time as dominant means of artistic expression, will decisively mark the sculptural work of Jaume Plensa in the following years. —CARSTEN AHRENS

b. Barcelona, Spain, 1955. Lives and works in Barcelona, Spain and Paris, France.

Orange Bump 1959 glazed ceramic, height: 14 inches (35.5 cm), deameter: 20 inches (50.8 cm) In 1954, I saw an article in *Arts & Architecture* magazine about some tall forms that were cast in clay and I thought it would be fun to try putting my drawings onto some similar objects. So, I took a clay course at Santa Monica College and there I discovered both working in clay and working in three dimensions, which I hadn't done up until then. These two things became bound together for me. I loved making objects and took lots of clay courses around Los Angeles and then did a year of grad school at Otis with Peter Voulkos. If you don't know of Voulkos, he's the hero of American ceramics, the person who is most responsible for liberating the material from craft dogma. I was very fortunate to be a student of his at that time, when he was just breaking out. He was a very powerful force, and influenced me so strongly that friends said I even walked like he did—sort of like a baritone saxophone player.

In 1958, I went to grad school at the State University of New York at Alfred to learn how to make brightly colored glazes, and also to get away from the influence of Voulkos and his approach. In those days some grad schools still operated like the guild system, where you developed your skills while working your way into your own idiom. I tried lots of different approaches at Alfred, trying to eliminate things I didn't like and things that weren't me, like the strong influence of Picasso, Miró, and Voulkos.

I got the bright colors I was after by reinventing the lead glaze. With 50-percent lead carbonate in a low fire glaze, you can get a broad range of beautiful colors, and a nice dose of lead poisoning. Then in one of the basement storerooms I found a mason jar full of uranium oxide. Legally, you were supposed to turn this stuff over to the government, but I mixed it into one of my lead glazes and used it on this piece, which was finally leading into my own direction, even though it still had some Miró in it.

Unfortunately, the photograph is a duplicate of a duplicate that I got from a friend, and it no longer shows the intensity of the orange color.

b. Los Angeles, CA, USA, 1935. Lives and works in Taos, NM and Venice Beach, CA, USA. 299

Stephen Prina

A Structural Analysis and Reconstruction of MS7098 as Determined by the Difference Between the Measurements of Duration and Displacement 1980

12-inch phonographic record

Design Program 1984 poster, merchandising display, and publicity photograph

Reconstituted Arrangement 1990 two phonograph records, framed poster, merchandising display, framed publicity photograph, integrated amplifier, turntable, headphones, table, and two chairs

This project is a relay, of sorts.

Beginning with the phonograph record in 1980, the project is focused on a preexisting recording: *Arnold Schoenberg: The Complete Music for Solo Piano*, by Glen Gould. The material of the phonograph record is foregrounded at the expense of its program and it is quantitatively "analyzed." The program, addressed as a given amount of stuff, is rerecorded and treated according to the results of its prior analysis, pressed, and coupled with a design for the jacket that incorporates the Schoenberg/Gould cover as a syntactic element, along with a poster—the "lyric sheet"—charting the process of the analysis and reconstruction. The program returns, however, when the newly fashioned recording spins, casting into high relief the incongruities of the process of "analysis and reconstruction" and the capability of it to account for all results.

In 1984, when given the opportunity to exhibit the phonograph record at Gewad, an art space in Ghent, Belgium, the record, in its entirety, is treated like the given amount of stuff it is, irrespective of its implicit or explicit aims. What was then considered a stylized version of a "conceptual art" presentation—a white laminate table, a turntable, an integrated amplifier, headphones, and two white plastic chairs—is designed for the space of exhibition.

A gold metallic poster, stapled to the wall in the hallway leading to the exhibition space, announces the availability of *A Structural Analysis and Reconstruction of MS7098 as Determined by the Difference Between the Measurements of Duration and Displacement* at the local music store, across town, adjacent to the university. In the rock 'n' roll section of the store, a six-foot tall, point-of-contact merchandising display is installed in close proximity to the product. Schoenberg is reinscribed as Rock.

In 1990, the reconstituted version of this journey is made for an exhibition at Luhring Augustine Hetzler in Santa Monica, California, but not yet in the configuration depicted in the accompanying photographic document. The poster and display are refashioned in silver metallic due to the obsolescence of the gold metallic photographic paper used in 1984. The poster, which directs viewers to a local music store within walking distance of the gallery, is stapled to the wall in the exhibition, beside the black furniture arrangement—a substitution for the white—which supports the records, posters, and audio equipment. The merchandising display takes its place in the front window of the music store, facing a pedestrian mall.

After the Santa Monica exhibition, the poster is pried from the wall, matted, and framed; the display is returned from the store and placed atop a plinth; and they both join two copies of the phonograph record with their posters, the matted and framed publicity photograph, the audio equipment, and the furniture arrangement to constitute the inevitable, reified condition of the current state of the relay.

b. Galesburg, IL, USA, 1954. Lives and works in Cambridge, MA and Los Angeles, CA, USA.

301

Richard Prince

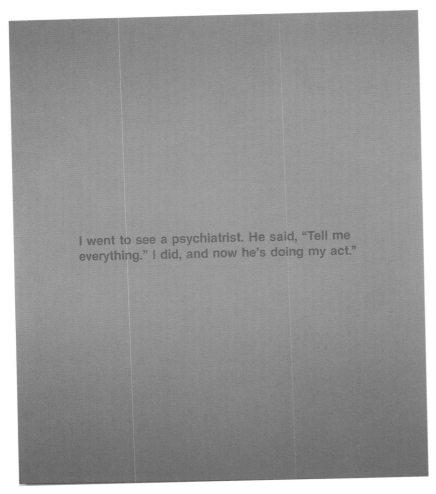

I went to see a psychiatrist. He said, "Tell me everything." I did, and now he's doing my act."

Tell Me Everything 1987 acrylic and silkscreen on canvas, 56 x 48 inches (142.2 x 121.9 cm)

Tell Me Everything was the first joke that I used in a painting. I didn't understand it at first. It had nothing to do with my own experience. When I went to the psychiatrist I didn't tell him or her anything. I always thought that my act was someone else's. After I used this joke in a painting I stopped seeing my psychiatrist.

Marc Quinn

Self 1991 blood, stainless steel, perspex and refrigeration equipment, 81⁷/₈ x 24¹³/₁₆ x 24¹³/₁₆ in. (208 x 63 x 63 cm) I wanted to make art that was real, and didn't illustrate the idea of reality. I also wanted to make a sculpture about life that was in some sense alive.

When a person dies, it seems to me all you can say is that they were alive and now they are not—you cannot say where the life went. Similarly in this frozen piece if the freezer is unplugged, the form disappears and you cannot say where it has gone—you can only say it was here and now it isn't. I was very happy with the way that freezing the blood could express that rather intangible idea in a sculptural way.

I love the way the piece is dependent; it just brings up the precariousness and poignancy of life to me. Also the incredible powers of recuperation and creation of the body—that I could over a year take out the same amount of blood from me, ten pints, as usually fills the whole human circulation system, and I'm still alive and the sculpture is still there—it is amazing to me. It is a total self-portrait: the form and the content are made by the artist and it is a moment of time forever out of time.

b. London, England, 1964. Lives and works in London, England.

Fiona Rae

Angel 2000 oil and acrylic on canvas, 97 x 80 inches (246.4 x 203.2 cm) I'd been trying all summer to include some new ideas and elements in my paintings, but nothing had worked out. Months later, this painting was the unexpected result.

I had wanted the new paintings to have a more inclusive subject matter. In *Angel*, I used letters from a contemporary font called Fufanu, which are recognizable as part of an alphabet although they have a mysterious abstract quality. I'm interested in the way paint languages can hover above any final interpretation, yet at the same time have a specific and meaningful presence.

This was the first time I used a computer to plan the start of a painting. It helped me to figure out the placing and the colors of the letters. It also meant I could visualize in Photoshop what flares and shadows might look like on each letter. Sometimes I have to scrap the plan and change things once they're on the canvas, because the computer screen is rubbish at predicting what things will look like in real life. Everything else is improvised directly onto the painting—all the drawing, marks, gestures, and painting incidents.

Using spray paint seemed thrillingly contraband—it makes for a dubious space in the painting. Something not quite fine art, something a bit outer-space. In this painting I think it suggests some terrible or beautiful alien happening. I was looking at Dürer's woodcuts, Hieronymous Bosch's paintings, and an *X-Men Classic* comic that seemed to be influenced by both of them. I felt inspired to make paintings that reflected some of their otherworldly visionary quality (dragons, heaven, and hell) as well as referenced utterly contemporary urban experiences (signs, symbols, and illuminations).

I think that *Angel* was important to me because it was a reminder that I can include and suggest whatever I feel like in a painting.

3.

305

Michael Raedecker

painting as a pastime 1991 mixed media and thread on canvas, 31⅕ x 27³/₁₀ inches (80 x 70 cm) When I left art school in the early '90s I knew I had to become a painter. Although I had just received a B.A. diploma in fashion design, I decided to move in a completely different direction.

In those first years I researched and tried to find out what 'painting' is, and could mean to me, since I felt quite intimidated by its rich history and all the masterpieces that were made by artists before me. Who was I to think that I could and should add more to that? Furthermore, I grew up in a culture with an ever-expanding, daily visual bombardment, and therefore felt even more conscious of contributing to that pile.

During my many visits to my local library I came across a book full of paintings by Winston Churchill. I never knew that this renowned statesman had been such a keen amateur painter. And he never aspired to more than that, although he took his hobby very seriously for more than fifty years. At some point he even wrote an essay titled "Painting as a Pastime." It was going on about the delights of going out there, finding a nice spot, and painting! I knew that this was exactly what I needed.

The intimidation I felt about art history and about the 1980s, which seemed to have been ruled by the legacy of Duchamp and the fashionable French philosophers, made me feel crippled. I had to stick my middle finger up to all of this, and take Churchill's advice.

The best and most anti-art form of pastime I could think of was embroidery. And I felt the way forward to go against the tidal wave of visual overkill was to go backwards and to copy Churchill's paintings. Retro was the future for me.

The color-copies of his paintings were transferred onto canvas and I decided to embroider the information I had about the original works onto the canvas, using the same colors to even downplay my "efforts." For instance, I did one of Churchill's paintings, which he called *The Twenty Minute Sketch* because that's how long it took him to paint it, whilst it took me more than a month to finish the embroideries. The first one I did was the one which is also the title of the whole series, *painting as a pastime*.

And I have been stuck with this form of pastime ever since.

Arnulf Rainer

My World at Twenty 1949 pencil on paper, 16 x 19½ inches (41 x 50 cm) Since I started drawing I was plagued by dissatisfaction with everything that I made. I wished for things without weaknesses. In 1949, I discovered what satisfied me. It was this strategy that helped me out of my dilemma, and that is an engine for all my subsequent new steps.

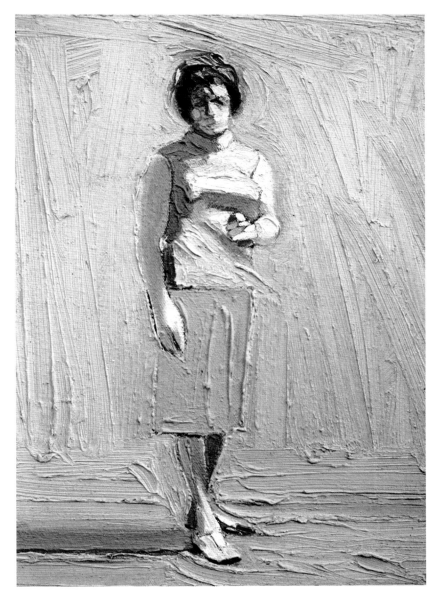

B.T. Standing 1960 oil on canvas, 11 x 9 inches (27.9 x 22.8 cm) I remember very clearly the day I painted *B.T. Standing.* It was on a fall day in Sacramento after we had returned from a summer excursion across the U.S. My wife Leta and I, along with Betty Jean and Wayne Thiebaud, drove his 1956 Mercedes to New York City to find a gallery to show our work. The New York experience must have affected me somehow but I can't quite remember what it was. I remember the euphoria that overcame me when I studied what I had just painted. I finally understood why I left the abyss (Abstract Expressionism): that I was not depressed enough to be a good Abstract Expressionist. It was the figure that aroused my passion and I wanted to paint the figure with a sense of affirmation, a celebration of positiveness. I was not interested in the dark side and did not see the figure as, for instance, Man, mired in the void and caught up in the bestial struggle against the forces of anonymity and mechanization, which was often the case in the history of art.

b. Sacramento, CA, USA, 1935. Lives and works in Oakland, CA, USA, and Horta de Sant Joan, Spain.   309

Neo Rauch

Weiche 1999 oil on paper, 84³/₅ x 74⁴/₅ inches (215 x 190 cm) Every time when I am standing in front of a blank canvas, I am at the very same time standing in front of a bank of fog. Before stepping undaunted into unknown areas, the question is what will come up and what kind of equipment I will need to master the excursion successfully. Basically a great risk should be guaranteed, and in the confrontation with the situation one discloses one's abilities.

Someone told me once that —if one did not know—one is scarcely able to assume where and when my paintings came into being. And I do not want to conceal how comfortable I felt regarding this statement. Some detect American traces in my works. Others see characteristics from the Far East. Only the nasty colleague living in the neighboring village recognizes the provincial stuff with a look at his surrounding. Somehow they all are right because my arsenal is sturdily constructed so that it is able to absorb elements of any kind and consistency. The viewer loses his way confronted with paintings, just as I would like them to be. They stop the viewer acting reasonably and suggest a possibility to leave the track of reason.

22 The Lily White c. 1950 oil and pencil on canvas, 39¹/₂ x 23³/₄ inches (100.3 x 60.3 cm) Between 1949 and 1954, Rauschenberg introduced the mediums, materials, and motifs that have continued to occupy him. During this fruitful period, he worked in photography, made his first monoprints, and became involved in performance, participating in Cage's *Theater Piece #1* in 1952. Early paintings, sculptures, and drawings already reflected what would become his long-standing commitment to extracting materials and images from his immediate environment.

Having settled in New York in 1949, Rauschenberg was introduced to the work of the Abstract Expressionists and began to incorporate free brushwork into his own paintings. Rauschenberg's first solo exhibition was held in May 1951 at the Betty Parsons Gallery, New York, which represented many of the Abstract Expressionists. *22 The Lily White* (c. 1950), one of the few extant works from this exhibition, reveals Rauschenberg's concern early on with expanding the abstract idiom to include representational subjects such as maps, diagrams, and numerals.

—JULIA BLAUT

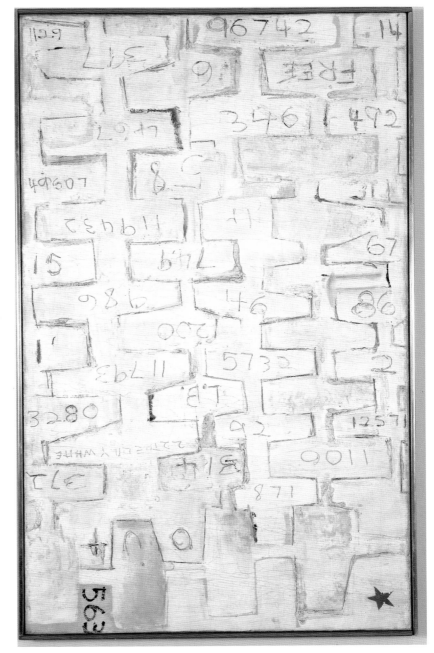

b. Port Arthur, TX, USA, 1925. Lives and works in Captiva, FL and New York, NY, USA.

David Reed

#150 1979 oil on canvas, 56 x 112 inches (142 x 284 cm), two panels, each 56 x 56 inches (142 x 142 cm) The gesture determines everything: format, size, color, and structure. This painting makes no sense unless you think of yourself standing and making the brush marks, wet paint into wet paint. The time taken to make the marks seems frozen as if by a photographic process. But, unlike the movements in a photograph, the downward pull of gravity on the paint is a reminder of weight and physicality. The boundaries of the painting, which imply extension, and the internal cut, which implies succession, together create a structure of framing similar to that of film. As it can be in these other media, drawing and color are separated and juxtaposed in the two square canvases.

Critics and painter friends had told me that I couldn't do this if I wanted to make a single painting. They said that I had to choose—make one kind of painting. But when looking at *#150*, I found that color and drawing did not remain separate. Instead, they constantly transformed one into the other. While viewing the brush marks, I found that out of the corner of my eye the external edges of the blue canvas had become drawn lines. And I found that the brush marks seemed to take on colors because of the way their warm and cool grays relate to the dark but transparent blue. After viewing *#150*, I decided that I liked the separation because of these transformations.

Dog Woman 1994 pastel on canvas, 46⁴/₅ X 62²/₅ inches (120 x 60 cm) There is a folk tale in Portugal that tells of an old woman who lived with her pets in a house by the sea. She had a goat, a dog, a cat, a pig, and a chicken. The wind from the sea would blow down her chimney and wail messages to her. One day during a storm the wind assumed the voice of a child, and instructed her to eat her pets. The animals formed a circle around the table and ran round and round to the sound of the child's voice. The old woman, crouched in the corner of the room, opened her mouth as wide as she could and the animals came running into her. She swallowed them all.

At the end of a day's work, I asked my model Lila to squat for me and open her mouth. I did the briefest sketch, which I later squared up. I transferred it squared up onto a canvas, and that became my 'dog woman.' Unlike the woman in the story, she is not old, and she wore a beautiful apron. She was a powerful domestic animal, and although cornered she could certainly bite back. When this 'dog woman' appeared, I knew she would take me to places where I had not been before. *Dog*

Woman was the first complete picture I had done with sticks of pastel, and the spontaneous and vigorous making of the image became very much part of the subject matter.

b. Lisbon, Portugal, 1935. Lives and works in London, England. 313

Tobias Rehberger

Untitled (9 Sculptures) 1992 wire, papier-mâché, wood, PU-foam, synthetic enamel, wax, poster paint. The sculptures (except two) are reproductions of large sculptures standing in front of the headquarters of major German companies and goverment central offices. *Untitled (9 Sculptures)* is somehow important for me because it was my first exhibition after I had graduated from Staedelschule and it is about a couple of things that I'm still busy with these days.

Setting an Example 2001 oil on canvas, 44 paintings of various dimensions, 98²/₅ x 196⁹/₁₀ inches (250 x 500 cm) The work is a collection of themes, ideas, and jokes that in part look back to some of the work I made in the '80s, a kind of violence and anger that haunted a lot of my work from that period. As I have become an all-around nice kind of guy over the years, my paintings have mellowed and have allowed various readings and misinterpretations to sit next to each other and work against each other, giving me the space to keep going, *Setting an Example* is an example of this process, I think.

b. Wrexham, Wales, 1956. Lives and works in Paris, France, and London, England.   315

Bridget Riley

Movement in Squares 1961 tempera on hardboard, 48 x 48 inches (122 x 122 cm)

Of my black-and-white work I made the following statement in 1965: "The basis of my paintings is this: that in each of them a particular situation is stated. Certain elements within that situation remain constant. Others precipitate the destruction of themselves by themselves. Recurrently, as a result of the cyclical movement of repose, disturbance, and repose, the original situation is re-stated."

In developing the painting *Movement in Squares*, I took a simple element—in this case, a square—and considered its four right angles, and the equal lengths of its horizontal and vertical sides. I decided to change one of its characteristics, leaving the others intact. I chose the width of the element for my exploration, and slowly but steadily reduced it.

The result is a dramatic increase in tension as the square comes under extreme pressure. A tremendous visual vibration is set up. In this critical area the contrast between blacks and whites is intensified and dazzling. Such disturbance cannot be sustained indefinitely. So I reduced the pressure on the square. It returns to more stable proportions.

QUOTE: *IN THE EYE'S MIND*, ED. ROBERT KUDIELKA (LONDON: THAMES & HUDSON, 1999), PP. 66, 68. © THE ARTIST.

b. London, England, 1931. Lives and works in London, England.

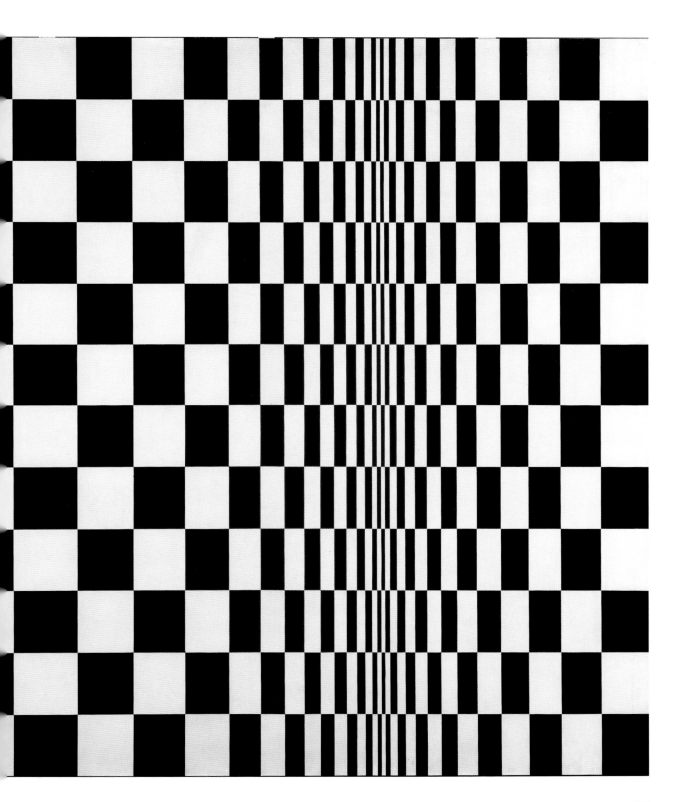

Pipilotti Rist

Mao on My Back 1979 35mm slide I stole a model
of a molecule out of the laboratory of my high
school in 1979. Ashiko Rupp drove me to the
fields, where I took pictures of the model on the
back of her Vespa. I believe this was my first work.
I brought the model back to the school. Ashiko
now lives in Sedona, Arizona, and in India, and
is a teacher of trance dance.

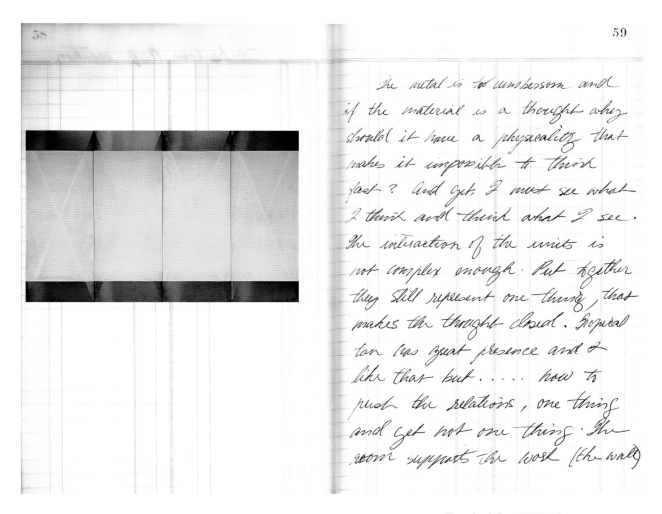

The metal is too cumbersome and if the material is a thought why should it have a physicality that makes it impossible to think fast? And yet I must see what I think and think what I see. The interaction of the units is not complex enough. Put together they still represent one thing, that makes the thought closed. Tropical Tan has great presence and I like that but ..... how to push the relations, one thing and yet not one thing. The room supports the work (the wall)

Tropical Tan 1967–69 (above left in artist's work diary) wrinkle finish paint on pig iron, 8 x 12 feet (2.4 x 3.6 m); four panels, 8 x 3 feet (2.4 x .9 m) each

b. Montreal, Canada, 1932. Lives and works in New York, NY, USA.

Alexis Rockman

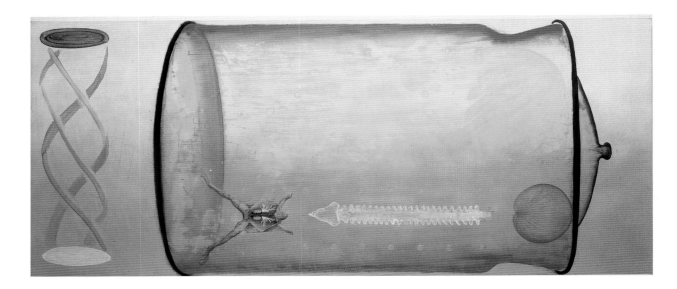

Selective Amnesia 1986 oil on canvas, 84 x 36 inches (213.3 x 91.4 cm) *Selective Amnesia* was a big breakthrough painting for me. I had been invited to participate in a group show, which I knew was going to be seen by many people, so I was feeling a lot of pressure. As a child I'd been obsessed with natural history dioramas and images that represented or articulated our relationship with nature. As a young painter, I was struggling for a way to distinguish myself from my peers. I was unaware of any contemporary artists using natural history iconography. Color-field painting, for me, was the voice of art history. This provided the context in which to put a specimen of a dissected frog. Painting the frog—the emblem of science education—and merging it with color-field painting, I felt as if I was finding my own voice. The bell jar signified a place to hide things. The paradox is that it's glass.

b. New York, NY, USA, 1962. Lives and works in New York, NY, USA.

Heyday 1995 polyester, cotton, hair, wooden floor, paint, Plexiglas, 35 x 50⁷/₁₀ x 35 inches (90 x 130 x 90 cm). Exhibition view, Galerie Walcheturm, Zurich, 1995 My little sweetheart, I say, bringing my face close enough to see the fine net of lines that carves his face. You love me, don't you, little sweetheart, little lamp? Whether or not he hears me, I always answer for him; yes, I always say, yes, I love you. He is my mother, my father, my sister, brother, cousin, lover; he is everything I think I need in the world. He is everything but real.

b. Brunnen, Switzerland, 1964. Lives and works in New York, NY, USA.

James Rosenquist

I Love You with My Ford 1961 oil on canvas, 82³/₄ x 93¹/₂ inches (210.2 cm X 237.5 cm) Many ideas came to me at once in 1959–60. I had just had a huge painting experience, painting the 58-by-395-foot-long Astor Victoria Theater sign, for ArtKraft Strauss. I wanted to invent a new kind of picture where fragments of generic things would spring forward from the picture plane instead of residing out in the aperture as in all previous paintings in art history. The largest image would be so huge that it would be recognized last, and therefore be mysterious.

Previously we were taught 'push and pull' in composition, whereas what really happens is immediate points of identification and fast associations. Simultaneously one might see a taxi driver eating a sandwich while nearly hitting you, and then the back of a girl's legs, and then a flashing sign. Also, the Beat People, who were an influence, were in another time zone where they resided in the anonymity of recent history, hence I painted a 1950 Ford in 1961. Surrealists use disparate images to set off a spark of idea. I thought of my paintings as vestigial springboards to other ideas.

b. Grand Forks, ND, USA, 1933. Lives and works in Aripeka, FL and New York, NY, USA.

Susan Rothenberg

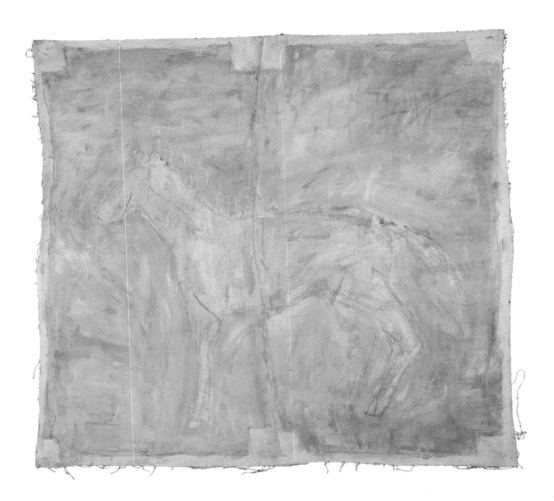

First Horse 1974 tempera, matte, flashe, graphite and gesso
on unstretched canvas, 26 x 28 inches (66 x 71 cm) I did this
small painting in the mid-'70s. I co-opted Frank
Stella's corners from his pinstripes, roughed in the
image of a horse split by a line—found it oddly
satisfying—and thus began my public art career.

 b. Buffalo, NY, USA, 1945. Lives and works in Galisteo, NM, USA.

Outside #22 1991 color coupler print, 19 x 19 inches (48.2 x 48.2 cm) *Outside #22* is part of the Outside series. I chose it because the subject matter, this house, is actually very generic, very nonspecific, basic, simple, and could be the house that every child draws, like an image of a house in a dictionary.

At the same time, in the course of working with this same house, the subject matter was no longer the house, but rather it was something else.

b. Tel Aviv, Israel, 1957. Lives and works in New York, NY, USA, and Tel Aviv, Israel. 325

Nancy Rubins

When Clay Dries Piece is Thrown Away 1974 canvas, paper cups, clay slip, 5 x 2½ feet (152.4 x 76.2 cm) In late 1973/ early 1974, while I was an art student, I made a series of sculptures consisting of wet clay slip, army surplus canvases, and used coffee cups from the coffee machine. I decided that the interest that I had for the work, and the beauty that I saw in it, only existed while the clay slip was wet. When the clay slip dried, the sculpture was over and ceased to exist. These were temporal works. I was a young artist, grappling with the boundaries of what art consisted of, both physically and temporally.

b. Naples, TX, USA, 1952. Lives and works in Topanga, CA, USA.

Interieur 1A (Düsseldorf) 1979
unique black-and-white print, 15³/₅ x 11⁷/₁₀ inches
(40 x 30 cm) This photo was taken in
1979. At that time I was studying
with Bernd Becher at the Düsseldorf Academy without really
knowing specifically where my
photography was going. I didn't
think that my photographs were
getting any better, and I didn't
know how I would continue.

Then I began photograph-
ing the chairs and corners in my
apartment, which led to this interior shot of my bathroom. This
was the first "interior" in a series
that I continued in my parents',
uncles', and aunts' apartments.

Allen Ruppersberg

Location 1969 wood, canvas, lights, glass, deer skull, rocks, leaves, approximately 15 x 20 x 12 feet (457 x 609.6 x 365.8 cm) I have selected a work that has a number of firsts already attached to it. It was a large single work, my first, that then became my first exhibition at a major gallery. It was also the opening exhibition for the Eugenia Butler Gallery in Los Angeles in January 1969, and then became the first major work that I sold. I thought then—at age 25—that I was on easy street from then on, so I guess it was also my first introduction to the realities of the art world. The show was only the one work, titled *Location*, and it was an installation built inside of an old office on Sunset Blvd. When viewers arrived at the gallery, which was on La Cienega Blvd., they were then directed to an address on Sunset a couple of miles away. When you entered the room you were forced to enter the work itself, as it filled the entire space. I see now that it was also my first installation work but at the time it was more likely to be called an environmental sculpture. This was a transitional work from the post–art school period that set the direction for many years to come and led to where I am today. Later the piece was shown at other venues where I met many of my artist friends for the first time and which also set my career in motion, another set of firsts. There were other smaller works done at this time which surround the ideas found in *Location* but it was the large scale and the use of site that pointed to the other major works for which I ultimately became known. I know that as my life and work have progressed I look back to this work and this period, and find the beginnings of the many works and ideas that have shown up ever since. I start many lectures by discussing this work. I have not seen this work for well over 30 years and I wonder now what my first reaction to this first piece would be today.

Sweetwater 1959 ink and oil on canvas, 60 x 48 inches (122 x 152.4 cm), inadvertently destroyed I hitchhiked throughout the South in the early 1950s. Coming across a town in Tennessee called Sweetwater, I remember swimming in an unattended pool by the side of the road. Later, I went to art school in Los Angeles and studied Abstract Expressionism and painted pictures of towns I had hitchhiked through, like Dublin, Georgia; Vicksburg, Mississippi; and, most memorable of all, Sweetwater, Tennessee.

b. Omaha, NE, USA, 1937. Lives and works in Venice, CA, USA.   329

Lisa Ruyter

That Obscure Object of Desire 1990 mixed media on fake fur panels, 144 x 288 inches (365.7 x 731.5 cm) *That Obscure Object of Desire* was a 12-by-24-foot piece that I made for a show at the School of Visual Arts in New York while I was a student. It was made of 72 two-foot square panels with black fake fur stretched over them. Previous to this piece I had been working on a couple of distinctly different types of work. One was very physical with a minimal edge to it: I was making paintings by starting with one material such as a patterned fabric or fake fur or found objects, and then adding another material to interact with that base, such as painting around the pattern or pouring resin onto the fake fur. The other was more traditionally drawing-oriented, with an occasional attempt at realist collage painting. I was trying to find a way to bring together images from my archives, which included photographs from magazines, medical diagrams, art reproductions, trade show brochures, and so on, in a unified manner. At the time I made this piece, I had not figured out that tracing things makes just about anything compatible.

It was the first painting that I titled after a movie—I am not sure why. I remember thinking that it had something to do with the fact that for this piece I had decided to just try to jam all of my ideas into one piece, looking for a clue as to what I should be making. There were also themes from the movie about formalized obsession and unfulfilled desire that I was interested in. I also wanted to take the reading a little past collage, and to give a tie to an implied narrative. All of my titles now come from a list of movie titles that are references to places.

It was also the first time that I did anything on a large scale. The excitement that comes with the

problem-solving in a large-scale project has become an important part of my creative life. I think this came from seeing productions coming together at the theater I worked at in high school. At school, I had to work in sections; there was no room for me to put together the entire piece at once. The performative element in this, and the fact that I would see it for the first time along with everyone else, was addictive.

It was the first piece that had for me, my specific brand of anti-painting sentiment. I hated the conflated ideas that were implied by mark-making, I thought

that art should be direct, not about exposing what you probably keep hidden for a reason. Rather than use paint to make marks, I used electric hair clippers, house paint, some kind of sculpting plaster, and spray glue to get the images from my archives in their fuzzy place. I was working around people who were so into drips, so I gathered all of the fur clippings and put them in plastic bags and dropped them on the floor underneath the piece, as if they were drips. At the time I thought that the plastic bags, along with the fur and other materials, implied some kind of sterilization of that particular idea.

The images in the piece included an astronaut on the moon, a creature made with an outline of Manhattan with a diagram of Newark airport for its eye, a silhouette of a car, a cross-cut diagram of an eye, a map of the old city of Turin, and a diagram of the path between the brain and the eye. I glued on two cartoon plastic fish with google eyes, thinking of them as a signature and also as a point of entry.

I kept the huge stack of panels for a few years, until it was destroyed by pets, at which point the materials were recycled along with the ideas.

Tom Sachs

Untitled (Nikon Camera) 1974 clay and paint, approximately 3 x 2¹/₂ x 2 inches (7.6 x 6.5 x 5 cm) My father wanted to buy a Nikon FM2 but could not afford it so he had to settle for the Olympus OM2. Dad did this by trading in one of his disapproving father's Minox spy cameras. As an eight-year-old, I wanted to solve the conflict and get for my dad what he wanted. I made a Nikon camera out of clay for him. I etched Nikon into the front of it and made little strips of film that fit in the back. As an adult, maybe I want a Glock or an HK MP-5 gun or a hand grenade or a Hermes Kelly bag—they're all symbols of status and power. But I'm not really able to spend fourteen thousand dollars for an alligator Kelly bag. The work has been a way to create satisfaction.

The Suicidist (#6) 1973 unique black-and-white gelatin silver photograph, 11 x 14 inches (28 x 35.5 cm) image *The Suicidist* is an important work for me—it is a group of pictures made at a time when I was studying psychology and art at the University of Wisconsin. It explored themes of the mythology of the self—as the yin/yang of the self's dissolution and rebirth, invention and disavowal. I built the idea on a series of short stories—which could in totality be read as a narrative in a multitude of ways: Here is a character who keeps trying to kill himself and fails. Or, here is a character who dies and is reborn each time again. Or, here is a group of actors who resemble each other, each succeeding in his own suicide.

b. Washington, DC, USA, 1963. Lives and works in New York, NY, USA, and Paris, France.

Jörg Sasse

First Photo c. 1970 instant photograph, 4³/₁₀ x 5¹/₁₀ inches
(11 x 13 cm) Along with a few technical pointers about how to use an instant-print camera, I was given two rules to take along on the way to taking my first photo:

1) If there is not a good light source indoors, then take the photos outdoors.

2) A cloudy sky provides outstanding light for taking clear pictures of subjects, because the light will illuminate all visible sides of the subject evenly.

This, along with the firm resolve to fix the distance between lens and subject with the greatest possible precision, nearly takes up all of the novice's time: It is compounded by the absence of any experience whatsoever, generating a certain agitation, to top things off. After all, in a situation like this, the objective is to keep the gap between the outcome one imagines and the actual result of one's efforts as narrow as possible.

The evaluation of lighting conditions indoors was followed by the decision to photograph the object of interest in the daylight. Situated closest to the house was the terrace, the floor surface of which had only recently been renovated with very modern, rough-textured concrete slabs. Why I decided to photograph the toy car from a diagonal angle, I can no longer recall. But I have a clear recollection of the first problem: Photographing the subject so as to fill out the format involved would have required a distance setting, which was impossible to obtain. The excitement and curiosity over the result did not, however, permit me to keep my eyes peeled for other subjects. The first compromise was accepted: The picture should be taken from the shortest distance setting possible. I recall that a measuring tape was enlisted to arrive at the precise setting

so as to better determine the camera's approximate position. There was no additional equipment available, such as a tripod or the like. The subject to be photographed was hastily aligned with the middle of the viewfinder, the breath was then held in order to squeeze the long plastic release all the way through . . . Breathe . . . The shot was in the can. The Polaroid had to be held suspended from an extra-sturdy plastic strap in order to withdraw the latent picture evenly from the film pack within the camera. Now it was necessary to allow the chemicals that had thus been discharged across the picture the time they needed. Measured in terms of a child's life up until that point, a minute is a remarkable period indeed. Finally, remove the exposure from the Polaroid carrier. This was accompanied by a pungent odor surpassed only by the additional use of the fixing stick that came with the camera. If the procedure was carried out meticulously, enlistment of this pink-colored stick treated the user to a reasonably high-gloss surface on the black-and-white photo. Yet for all the joy over the technological capability of having made a photograph all by oneself, the result remained a disappointing one. Aside from the anticipated small representation of the subject, something entirely unexpected had taken place. Despite its central position, the so highly prized toy car shown in the two-dimensional photo had lost its entire presence. The rough-textured concrete, meant to provide a neutral background, turned out to be more significant than the intended subject. In terms of the expectation involved, the photo had been a failure that for me as a child, in spite of my joy over the technological achievement, left me unsatisfied. A second attempt with the same motif did nothing to change this.

The dimension of failure and thus its potential remained hidden from me at the time.

Beyond technique and concept, amazement conceals itself in the visual.

Even in the absence of the image conceived, even when the "intention" is missed, the visual is present. Seeing the visual is the beginning of the infinite potential of images.

Jenny Saville

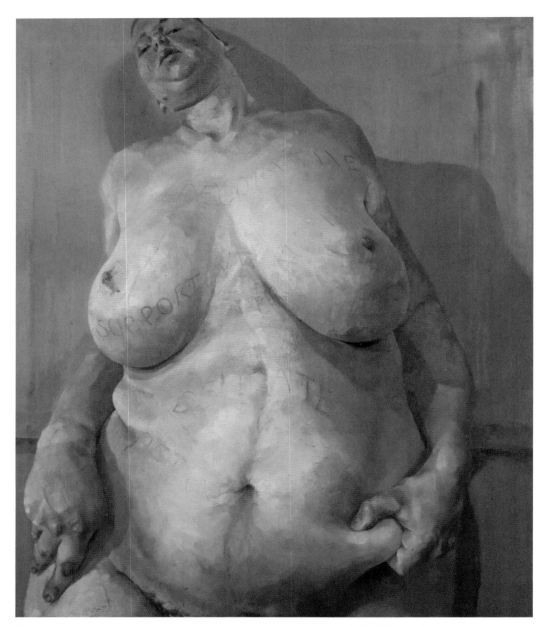

Branded 1992 oil on canvas, 84 x 72 inches (213.4 x 182.9 cm) When I made it, I knew it was my first piece.

b. Cambridge, England, 1970. Lives and works in London, England.

Barbara Simpson's New Kitchen 1978 acrylic on canvas with wood frame, 20 x 24 inches (50.8 x 60.9 cm)

I consider *Barbara Simpson's New Kitchen 1978* as my first successful work for several reasons. The excitement and giddiness I felt upon completing the piece in my dorm room at the University of California, Santa Barbara. The reaction of my roommates in the dorm was utter bewilderment. The reaction of my teachers during critique was angry and the other students were in shock. I knew I had something going on if I could get this kind of response. That painting represents my philosophy to this day. Barbara is so happy with her new gleaming kitchen she doesn't even realize a dragon has emerged from her sink. It's like being blind to the realities and consequences of our consumerist society.

b. Los Angeles, CA, USA, 1958. Lives and works in Los Angeles, CA, USA.

Sean Scully

Cactus 1964 oil on canvas, 13 x 11 inches (33 x 27.9 cm) I chose this painting partly because of its powerful frontal quality, and partly because I admire the subject. The cactus is planted against a strong regular vertical division that causes a rhythm to run across and unify the composition. This is something I do now with inset and window paintings. Secondly and perhaps even more important, I find the cactus to be an inscrutable and admirable plant. As a metaphor, it mirrors perfectly the life of a painter. It can survive drought and it flowers when ready.

338   b. Dublin, Ireland, 1945. Lives and works in New York, NY, USA; Barcelona, Spain; and London, England.

One Ton Prop: House of Cards 1969 (lead antimony, four plates, each 48 x 48 inches [122 x 122 cm]) What was interesting about *House of Cards* was that there were four plates, about 480 pounds each, leaning and overlapping each other by two and a half inches. They leaned inward to form an open, truncated pyramid. What was satisfying about the piece was that the aesthetic came from the solution of the problem and nothing extraneous was necessary. Lead with its low order of entropy is always under the strain of decaying or deflecting. So what you have is a proposed stable solution which is being undermined every minute of its existence. That piece satisfied all the problems of what an aesthetic solution could be without having to go outside the limitations and counter-limitations that it set up for itself.

b. San Francisco, CA, USA, 1939. Lives and works in New York, NY, USA, and Nova Scotia, Canada.

Andres Serrano

Milk, Blood 1986 Cibachrome, silicone, Plexiglas, wood frame, 40 x 60 inches (101.6 x 152.4 cm), edition of four Although it is not my "first work," I consider *Milk, Blood* to be my first mature work. It is the first of the bodily fluids photographs, the series that separates my early tableau work from the more abstract and conceptual pictures that followed. It is also the work that started a new trend for me that has remained to this day, that of conceiving and executing photographs as part of a large body of work rather than as singular images. Although it is not my most famous picture, I consider it to be my most important one.

b. New York, NY, USA, 1950. Lives and works in Brooklyn, NY, USA.

Untitled 1973–74 cast iron, 3⁵/₁₆ x 1¹³/₃₂ x 1¹¹/₁₆ inches (8.4 x 3.5 x 4.3 cm) I made the chair in wood in 1973 and cast it in iron in 1974. There was nothing particularly unique about the chair other than its size and placement directly on the floor. The sculpture is framed by architecture. I see the sculpture as private and the architecture that frames the sculpture as common, as public. That is the interesting discourse. The sculpture is a common, everyday object; its meaning altered by its reduced size.

The sculpture commands a disproportional amount of space in relationship to its size.

b. New York, NY, USA, 1941. Lives and works in New York, NY, USA.

Jim Shaw

The End is Here 1978 mimeographed pamphlet, 8½ x 7 inches (21.5 x 17.7 cm) Many years ago when I was a grad student at CalArts, I heard from a fellow student that my one-year review, which I'd recently passed, hadn't gone as well as I'd thought. He'd heard from another student that her boyfriend, a visiting faculty member and one half of my committee, had almost flunked me, but instead, perhaps taking pity on me, had passed on any judgment, saying he didn't understand my work.

Up until that point I'd been making a wide variety of work, making use of equipment like the video synthesizer, graphics lab, and so on, concentrating on collage-based works that imparted a schizophrenic, shattered world view in a general, impressionistic way.

Shaken by the revelation of my tenuous status at school I resolved to put together a more coherent and specific effort in my second year there. The influences I dragged into play were, on a content level, the zeitgeist of the day (late '70s pre-millenial movies like *Close Encounters* and *Earthquake* that promised some sort of extreme climax, or deus ex machina), and various quack religious and UFO groups whose literature I'd been studying. The forms taken were fake evidence (documentary-looking photos and scientific-looking samples); an altarpiece which opened up to reveal sacred celebrities; a documentary video in the style of *Chariots of the Gods* with an authoritative narrator making all sorts of ludicrous claims; and this pamphlet, which, in the form of a *Watchtower*-type periodical, lays out most of the tenets of the religion.

Since then, I always have thought of my artworks as existing primarily as books with some sort of "mass" distribution (though I only printed 125 of these initially), even if the contents are a series of art objects themselves, and I have made some effort to produce them one way or another, though the rising cost of paper has pushed me out of the business of doing it myself. This was also the first piece I made that attempted to project a direct narrative to the series as a whole, something I've tried to do ever since. It took me several years after to come up with a specific narrative I felt was up to the standards I'd set with this project (there's nothing like grad school to amplify and make useful one's self-hatred).

b. Midland, MI, USA, 1952. Lives and works in Los Angeles, CA, USA.

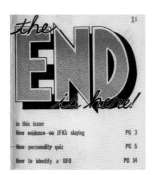

Cindy Sherman

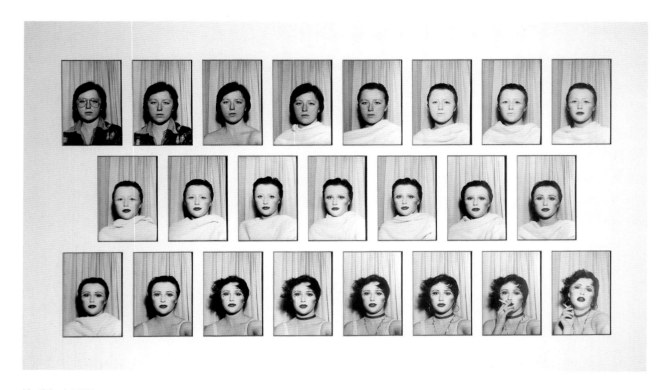

Untitled 1975 23 hand-colored, black-and-white photographs, 10½ x 33½ inches (26.7 x 85.1 cm) overall I did this transitional series—from no makeup at all to me looking like a completely different person . . . I just wanted to see how transformed I could look. It was like painting in a way: staring at my face in a mirror, trying to figure out how to do something to this part of my face, how to shade another part . . . The piece got all this feedback [and was exhibited at the Albright Knox Art Gallery]. It dawned on me that I'd hit on something.

Tarrytown, NY 1959 gelatin silver print, 6 x 9 inches (15.2 x 22.9 cm) I made this photograph when I was twelve years old in the fall of 1959. I had begun doing darkroom work about six years earlier, but at this time began to think of photography as an art and know I wanted to make it my life's work.

b. New York, NY, USA, 1947. Lives and works in Tivoli, NY, USA.

José María Sicilia

La Luz que se apaga 1997 oil and wax on wood, 99⅛ x 48 inches (252 x 122 cm) This flower is suspended in the light like a bird in its own song, an eyelid of pink velvet, when you caress it, it produces a miracle, she is still glowing, her radiance is mineral, she will soon liquefy, her eyes will fold up again, the outer world and her will just be a blurry mass of ever-changing colors, What difference does it make? It will be en exhalation, a veil through which we continue to see, but that we no longer consider.

b. Madrid, Spain, 1954. Lives and works in Mallorca, Spain, and Paris, France.

Untitled Yellow Mouth 1991 enamel on aluminum, 19³/₈ x 15¹/₈ inches (49.2 x 38.4 cm) *Untitled Yellow Mouth* is one of two paintings that were the first to be done on the type and thickness of aluminum that I use to this day. I came across the material in 1990 during a walk in the Glanz scrap-metal yard in Williamsburg, Brooklyn, after a series of walks there with the sculptor Alan Saret, who remarked to me at the time: "This is my garden." I'm forever grateful to him for those walks; before this ur-work, there were experiments on all kinds of metal: steel, honeycomb aluminum, even titanium. I was making my work more and more slowly, and on silk, just before this time, and I needed a more durable surface. I liked the modest firmness of metal, and was attracted to the workmanlike paint which is the most common available (yet very durable): One Shot sign painter's enamel. Prior to painting on metal I made my own paint: methodically, laboriously, painfully. Less time for the image. So things came together on the slab on which this picture was painted. Thick enough to need no further support (minimum thickness, maximum flatness). Dense, concentrated, heavy for its small size. And this strongly affected the imagery. What once were looser and more artfully placed situations on a tastefully spaced ground led to an unruly, warped, melted down image which emphatically strained against the limits of the support with no taste, no space, no ground (black painted first, yellow after). I wanted to make little big paintings, wrongly wrought, impossible to take in on one glance, and this was one of the first.

Santiago Sierra

4 Cubic Containers Measuring 250 x 250 x 250 cm, St. Petri's Church, Lübeck, Germany, February 1991 Santiago Sierra's engagement with Minimalist sculpture provides an important framework for his practice and it is particularly relevant to his 'first work' *4 Cubic Containers Measuring 250 x 250 x 250 cm, 1991*. The use of industrial processes and serial manufacture is vital to Sierra's examination of late capitalist culture. The sense of critique inherent in the work of artists such as Robert Morris also informs Sierra's work; the performance of seemingly useless activity as an interrogation of productivity is at the core of his work.

Whilst Sierra's aesthetic and linguistic referents are linked to the syntax of Minimalism, he subverts the autonomy of industrial seriality by injecting a political and socially conscious charge into his work. Sierra's placement of these containers in Saint Petri's Church, Lübeck is not to be seen solely within the conventional artistic context but in the broader urban and social context. The surroundings of the work are not to be neglected but emphasized as a constitutive aspect of the work. Thus these containers push forward the substance of the produced object and turn against the illusion of a moral superiority of art. Sierra fills the idealized art container with an economic, social, and political reality, removing them from the notion of an empty minimalist vessel and flooding them with real life. —TOM COLE

Drawing from India 1988 charcoal, gouache, ink, gesso, wax, 22 x 28 inches (55.8 x 71 cm)
This is from a whole bunch of drawings I did in India in 1988. It was the first time I made a bunch of work on blank paper, using the imagery in a loosely narrative and overtly emotional way on flat empty ground. I'm still doing that.

Laurie Simmons

Sink/Ivy Wallpaper 1976 black-and-white silver gelatin print, 5¼ x 8 inches (13.9 x 20.3 cm), edition of 10 In 1976 survival was my main concern. In other words, how could I make my artwork and make a living? I dreamed of being able to find the perfect job that fulfilled my needs—something creative and stimulating that paid top dollar and didn't compromise my artistic integrity. The same job every young artist was looking for. I'd never really been employed except for painting houses and giving bad haircuts. One day, a friend showed me an ad in the paper. A company on lower Fifth Avenue specializing in miniatures needed a photographer to shoot their catalogue. I was really interested in tabletop setups and thought it might be fun. I went for an interview and was given a big bag of dollhouse stuff to play around with. I'd been slowly accumulating rolls of old wallpaper, toys, and decorating books, and I started mixing my props with theirs. I put bathtubs and refrigerators in front of pictures of rooms and filled sinks with water. I was really excited by the photograph I took of a sink in front of ivy-patterned wallpaper. I loved the scale changes and the light reflecting on the water. I thought I might be on to something, but I didn't get the job.

Luncheon Meat on a Counter 1978 Cibachrome print, 22 x 28 inches (55.9 x 71.1 cm)

I stumbled upon *Luncheon Meat on a Counter* in 1978 when I was trying to make dinner and establish a bridge in my work between Minimalism and popular taste, a seeming oxymoron if there ever was one. Observing the uncanny in contradictions and similarities around us has since become one of my favorite activities as an artist.

b. Quincy, MA, USA, 1946. Lives and works in New York, NY, USA. 351

Andreas Slominski

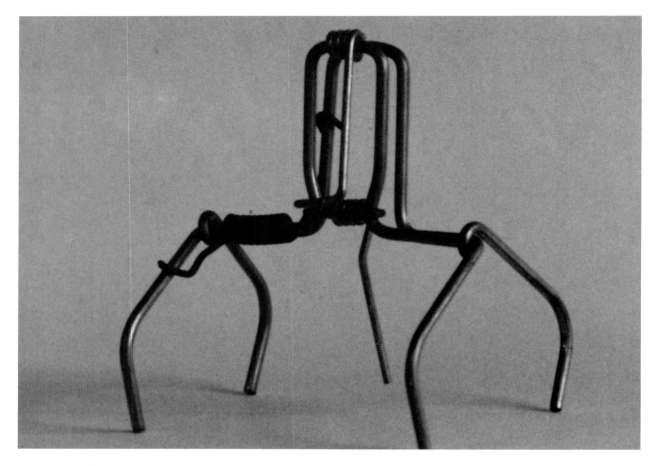

Vole Trap 1984/1985 metal, 4 x 3⁷/₁₀ x 4⁷/₁₀ inches (10.5 x 9.5 x 12 cm) The trap has a specific character that other sculptures do not have.

Kiki Smith

Untitled 1979–80 mixed media on cloth, 53 x 80 inches (134.6 x 203.2 cm) I originally made this piece as part of a group of three. This was intended as a bedsheet, another was a pillowcase, and the third, a shirt. I had been making and was interested in decorative and domestic items. This was the first time I used a body-related image in my work. From that moment on the body has been the primary vocabulary of my work. I exhibited this in the Colab-sponsored "Times Square Show" in 1980, when I was 26.

Ray Smith

Portrait of Wray Gillon 1984–85
oil on wood, 96 x 96 inches (244 x 244 cm)

In the summer of 1984, I moved from Mexico City into a loft above a movie theater on East 86th Street in New York. This loft had been a fencing studio established in the early 1900s to train actors in theater and film. The move had left me relatively broke so I used the few paints I had brought with me to paint on the plywood walls that divided the dressing rooms from the practice floor.

The subjects were portraits from memory of friends, girlfriends, family, ancestors, and people I'd meet on the streets.

Wray Gillon had been a male model who for all and no reason ended up on the streets. He carried with him a cape and an old suitcase of all sorts of clippings and photographs of himself.

Wray posed for this painting in his cape in the same manner he had for a photo-shoot 18 years earlier.

New York, the fencing studio, the subjects, and my longing for Mexico consolidated everything I had been working on since childhood.

b. Brownsville, TX, USA, 1959. Lives and works in New York, NY, USA.

Ocracoke Cartouche April 1983   reeds, 12 x 48 feet (3.6 x 14.6 m). Installation view, bay side of Ocracoke, North Carolina

While living in Paris in the '70s I carried on the Bauhaus ideas I'd learned in art school—that artists should experiment in making art. I painted with water and the contrasts between wet and dry surfaces on thin paper. I worked with arrangements of squares and orders. I moved towards lines between the squares. Then line structure only. The responses to my work were interest or silence.

In 1980, I moved to New York, where art is a well-marketed commodity and, following fashion in style, is very strongly controlled by galleries and critics. I believed the artist is the leader in art-making (not the gallery or critic) so I continued making my geometric art in my way, European or not. My refined geometry stirred little interest in the galleries and was not practiced by the new young artists.

In April 1983, I went to nature and Ocracoke, North Carolina. I had the idea to make a work out in the water, isolated and in the open so it will be seen clearly and read. I chose a site in a tidal enclosure area in shallow water. I brought my city materials, although I realized that I did not have all the right things and questioned if they worked in nature. So I gathered the dry, dead reeds that were growing along the shore instead. I broke them off and brought them out into the open area and stuck them in the sandy bottom, lining them up. That was not enough! So I wove other reeds into a horizontal band along the line of vertical reeds. I made a 12-foot square and then I extended it by adding another square. I crossed the square for visual support, and divided the second differently. I put in an axis for most of the length. I watched what happened overnight. The corners came apart.

I resolved this by putting an arch on the front and back of the work; I found that it did not come apart as easily. The sunny day turned to a fine rain when the work was completed and the tide was high. I was excited doing this. I was also fortunate to travel with a photographer (Arthur Tress) who came there to do his project. He came and photographed what I did. A few days later and after the storm passed I returned to my first site and found the work still in place, the lines not as rigid. The seed for the successive works was established. When I saw the photographs I saw that I did make a work isolated but also there was an underlining muted shadow-reflection in the slightly disturbed water.

b. Milwaukee, WI, USA, 1941. Lives and works in Milwaukee, WI, USA.   355

Doug & Mike Starn

Dark Portrait 1985–1986 toned silver print with tape, 29 x 25 inches (73.7 x 63.5 cm) When we were teenagers, in the 1970s, we learned photography, *traditional* photography—the Aaron Siskind, Minor White, Ansel Adams School of the Sacrosanct Print photography. But by the time we went to art school we felt that there needed to be a change in photography. Photography wasn't just an image, any more than a painting was just paint.

We thought that there must be a way that the photographic print could be more than simply the presentation of an image. The print is an object, and this object could be the embodiment of a concept. We felt that since in photography, physical reality was directly and perfectly captured, the real world (warts and all) should be apparent in its realization—the print. Secondly, photography captures a moment in time, but the artwork created from the photograph continues in time, the artwork is not frozen. Over the years, the work experiences changes—physically and conceptually, like the deteriorated tallow and roses in a Beuys or as with Duchamp's readymades, now rarefied (anti)heroic masterpieces of the twentieth century, which is completely antithetical to their original concept. This was our goal in art school, but didn't know how to get it out.

Our parameters were to keep the work direct, honest, and humble. We didn't like the large 30 x 40-inch lab-processed C-prints that were being used by other photographers in the art world. We saw those prints as distanced from reality. In 1985, we printed a large portrait of Mike onto a few small pieces of paper (that we could easily process in our darkroom), taped them together, hung it on the wall . . . and hated it. It seemed an abomination to photography. We rolled it up and tried to forget about our horrible failure.

In a few months, we found it in a drawer and pinned it back on the wall. Now that the experiment had fermented in our minds, we could see that we had done exactly what we intended.

b. Absecon, NJ, USA, 1961. Live and work in New York, NY, USA.

Georgina Starr

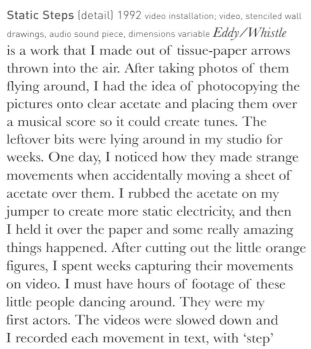

Static Steps (detail) 1992 video installation; video, stenciled wall drawings, audio sound piece, dimensions variable *Eddy/Whistle* is a work that I made out of tissue-paper arrows thrown into the air. After taking photos of them flying around, I had the idea of photocopying the pictures onto clear acetate and placing them over a musical score so it could create tunes. The leftover bits were lying around in my studio for weeks. One day, I noticed how they made strange movements when accidentally moving a sheet of acetate over them. I rubbed the acetate on my jumper to create more static electricity, and then I held it over the paper and some really amazing things happened. After cutting out the little orange figures, I spent weeks capturing their movements on video. I must have hours of footage of these little people dancing around. They were my first actors. The videos were slowed down and I recorded each movement in text, with 'step'

diagrams, as well as with special names and numbers. I asked a guy to narrate the steps in a really stiff British accent. The dance begins with both partners lying side by side in the middle of the floor. Moving individually, the man leads by kicking his left leg boldly and then returns. The lady raises her legs in a sweeping motion over her head and returns. The man's left leg kicks again, this time slightly higher, and on the second kick the lady slowly rises on tiptoes and jumps across the right shoulder to land on the left foot of the man's kick.

Apart from being the first video I have ever made, *Static Steps* was really the first work that got me totally excited about a process. It was about taking these tiny details and creating complex works around them, which is something that has continued to inspire me these last ten years.

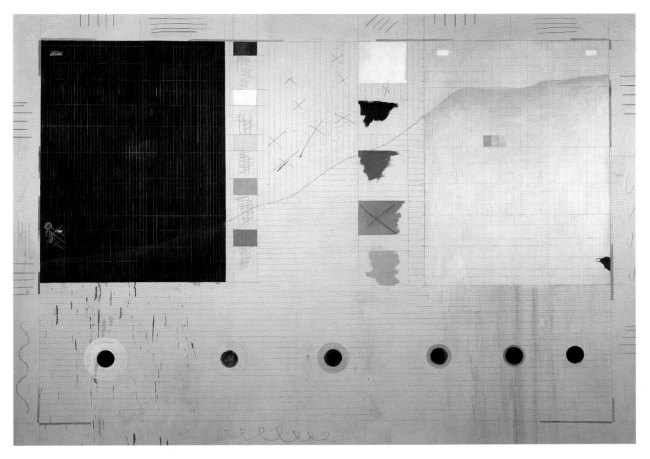

The Way to New Jersey 1971 oil on canvas, 7³/₄ x 108 inches (197.49 x 274.32 cm) *The Way to New Jersey* is one of a set of the first three paintings I made. This painting was my first step into the unfamiliar. The title is a reference to the last paragraph in the third section of T. S. Eliot's "East Coker," the second of the "Four Quartets." The part of the paragraph my title refers to begins, "In order to arrive there, To arrive where you are, to get from where you are not. You must go by a way wherein there is no ecstasy. In order to arrive at what you do not know. You must go by a way, which is the way of ignorance."

The paragraph ends with: "And what you do not know is the only thing you know. And what you own is what you do not own. And where you are is where you are not."

The Way to New Jersey is the first painting I exhibited. The first Painting I exhibited in a museum (the Whitney). The first painting I sold. The first painting I sold to a museum (the Whitney). The first painting that was reviewed (in *The New York Times* in a review of the Whitney annual of 1973.) It was my first step away from home, the way to (away from) New Jersey.

b. Newark, NJ, USA, 1940. Lives and works in New York, NY, USA, and Amsterdam, The Netherlands.

Joel Sternfeld

Washington, D.C. August 1974 digital C-print, 11 x 14 inches (27.9 x 35.6 cm) This photograph is not the flat-out first I made, but it is representative of the type of pictures I was making from 1970 to 1974 when the attempt to understand the nature of the color photograph was my central preoccupation. A few months after it was made, in October 1974, I met William Eggleston at Harvard and he graciously showed me a raft of his work. I realized that mine would have to change: He had already solved the discourse I was struggling to advance.

It's Not Over 'Til The Fat Lady Sings 1987 wood, sheetrock, paint, cardboard, paper, carpets, plaster, clothes, furniture, and papier mâché, length: 68 feet (2072.6 m)

A site specific work made at the Contemporary Art Gallery in Vancouver, Canada, in 1987.

This work is the first fully fleshed out-site-specific work that I made. It's in a Vancouver gallery, made for the people in Vancouver and for my family in the city where I grew up. My grandmother, who was at that time a fairly heavy lady, gave me the title. The title of this work could serve for all of my work.

Thomas Struth

Düsselstrasse, Düsseldorf 1979 silver gelatin print, 25⁷/₁₀ x 32⁴/₅ inches (66 x 84 cm) The character of the street as an architectonic form is one of a space that unfolds in strides, at times faster, at times slower, but never coming to a rest. Its movement demands a fitting frame, which allows the eye to pass along it, and which might draw [the eye] into its depths. Only the square, into which the street feeds, is a resting ground, granted with an architectonic frame that allows the eye to slow down and the view to widen. —ALBERT ERICH BRINKMANN

b. Geldern, Germany, 1954. Lives and works in Düsseldorf, Germany.

Allison and Erica, Marlboro, Vermont, 1970 Silver gelatin print, 8 x 10 inches (20.3 x 25.4 cm) This image represents a host of firsts for me. It is my first successful image with a 4 x 5-view camera, my first successful nude, and my first nude of children as well. And because it is a picture that just happened—what the children were doing was natural to them and in no way posed by me—it is somehow prescient because it predicted what would not truly begin to be the main focus of my work until a decade later!

Hiroshi Sugimoto

St. Mark's Cinema, New York, 1975 gelatin silver print, 16 x 20 inches (40.6 x 50.8 cm)

In 1975, I imagined what it would look like if I made an exposure for the entire length of a movie. I envisioned the screen would be overexposed, shining in the dark room of the theater. I put this idea to the test at St. Mark's Cinema, a one-dollar theater in the East Village. I set up my 8 x 10 camera with the aperture wide open. Using high-speed film, I made the long exposure. When I processed the film I found that the image I envisioned had been granted.

Metal Jacket 1992/2001 3,000 dog tags on U.S. military jacket fabric liner, 60 x 50 x 15 inches (152.4 x 127 x 38.1 cm), edition of six

The genesis of my first project took place in 1992, as a response to a problem posed by a professor of mine, Jay Coogan, asking students to "create a piece using clothing as a surrogate way to address the human figure/condition. Using clothing to speak about human concerns assumes the body as primary, but allows one to employ a larger set of associations. . . "

The realization of *Metal Jacket* was a significant personal turning point. As a serious painting student at the Rhode Island School of Design, I never considered or planned on turning to sculpture. However, Coogan's "Figures in Contemporary Art" class was where I had a sort of epiphany. It was my response to his studio assignments, and especially this one, that changed the course of my life. Destiny has its ways, because I never intended to take this particular class. A simple scheduling conflict left me with no choice—it was Coogan or nothing. It was an accident. Fortunately accidents can spawn unexpected goods.

The production of *Metal Jacket* took place within a mere six months of my arrival to the U.S.—coincidentally at the time of the LA riots. Leaving home and living in a different culture were unsettling experiences. I had an overwhelming response to the intensity of the reports and images of the events out west. It allowed me to place myself at a critical distance from who I was, and still am, in relationship to such foreign events. The LA riots also made me take a brand new perspective on myself as a Korean, who now resided within a much larger and more complex context of America.

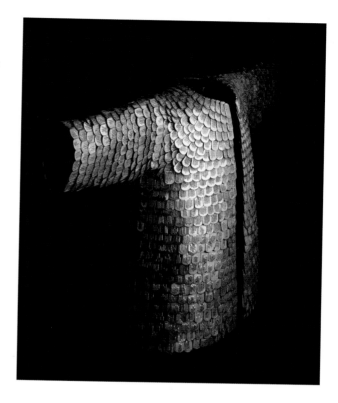

A rigorous response to this assignment allowed me to further contemplate the idea of the body, self, and gender, in relationship to space, displacement, and architecture, within the context of power, current events, history, politics, life styles, social inequities, and to define them for the individual and the collective. I continued to pursue such speculations in my work for the next ten years, and still do today. A series of change, chance, and persistence surfaced and stayed in my exploration of multiple dimensions within specific contextual situations.

Donald Sultan

Three Tables October 14, 1976 tar and tile on masonite, 12 x 12 inches (30.5 x 30.5 cm) This is my very first linoleum tile piece and the poster for my one-man show at the Willard Gallery in 1979. I made this on the kitchen stove and cut the figures with a matte knife. The lamination was black Durham tar, which later became the bases for all the large-scale tile works. It is one foot square.

b. Asheville, NC, USA, 1951. Lives and works in New York, NY, USA.

Self portrait 1971 Polaroid negative, 4 x 6 inches (10.2 x 15.2 cm)

The first photograph I ever made was with my great uncle's Polaroid camera. The occasion came at the end of a desperate search for the two *Playboy* magazines that my older brother kept in his bedroom. Out of spite he suspended my use of them—and found some unlikely place to hide them from me. The one with the pictures of Brigitte Bardot lying naked in bed was a crucial visual aid to my newly formed relationship with several household objects, the thermos and vacuum cleaner among others. Dirty pictures were difficult to come by in 1959 and this afternoon, with no one in the house except me, I really needed them.

Inspired by urgency and by an emerging sense of the ridiculous, I rifled through my father's closet and grabbed the old Polaroid camera. Standing in front of my parents' large mirror, I pulled my pants down, tucked my penis between my legs, and stilled my trembling hands long enough to squeeze the shutter button and make an exposure.

Peeling back the picture from the base was disappointing—revealing a sharp and somewhat pathetic image of my 13-year-old body without a penis. But the faint negative image that hovered on the paper backing was something else—not exactly an image of a female but with my vision clouded by desperation and desire it was close enough to be of use.

In 1971, when I was studying photography at art school, I remembered this incident and decided to re-enact it. While the resulting image (reproduced here) no longer carried the same charge as the original, it did clarify what was, and continues to be, a good part of why I make photographs. Like a ventriloquist who laughs at his dummy's jokes, I keep trying to make photographs that seduce me into believing in the image—all the time knowing better, but believing anyway.

b. Brooklyn, NY, USA, 1946. Lives and works in San Francisco, CA, USA.

Philip Taaffe

Glyphic Brain 1980–81 paper collage, 47 x 56 inches (119.3 x 142 cm) This first work involved paper collage. The lines are made from bookbinding tape, which came in various colors. I would work on a composition for the better part of three or four weeks, adding more and more sheets of paper as the image grew, taping them together and then stapling them to the wall. I would continue applying the tape, then gouge the surface while scraping parts of the tape off. I'd put more tape on, and gradually, torturously build this self-enclosed figure which resembled a walled city.

These were very focused meditations upon bringing a Constructivist approach into the realm of Expressionist gesture. They began as very searching lines and then they were concentrated into parts of an emblematic whole. This abstract "architecture" represented a primordial condition. I saw abstract painting as being talismanic.

I had taken a room in the General Theological Seminary in New York's Chelsea district. I was studying liturgy, reading philosophy and history and critical theory, listening to music, and looking at a lot of films. It was my urban monastic phase. I had a tape recorded and I would start paintings by making marks while I'd be speaking extemporaneously into the microphone. Then at a certain point when the image had been built up, I'd find myself talking less and less and getting more involved with shaping the image, until the pictorial narrative took over.

All of this work is highly ritualistic. Yet it was never enough just to make a mark: The mark had to be combined with other marks and be reflective of the total scheme of things. My thoughts were explicit, but the imagery was not. I knew the ecstasy that I was experiencing in the making of these works, and yet all the imagery and all the art that I have loved and seen and wanted to reflect upon inside this imaginary construction was concealed. I tried to make a representation of a broken point in history. It was less about constructing something than it was about rupture.

 b. Elizabeth, NJ, USA, 1955. Lives and works in New York, NY, USA.

Antoni Tàpies

Creu de paper de diari (Newsprint Cross) 1946–1947 paint, ink, and collage on paper, 16 x 12 inches (40 x 31 cm) On analyzing Tàpies's first collages, such as *Creu de paper de diari (Newsprint Cross, 1946–47)*, we cannot search for its origins either in the papiers collés of Braque or Picasso, or in Schwitters's Merz, but rather in the Symbolist movements of the end of the century.

From a Symbolist perspective, the cross represents the synthesis of everything material (horizontal) and spiritual (vertical), as well as its transcendence. The fact that in order to form the cross the artist deliberately chose the newspaper obituary section, and that together with newsprint he also used Manila paper, which looks like toilet paper, reinforces this character, since all this tells us of the transcendence of what is humble, of the spirituality of the material.
—MANUEL J. BORJA-VILLEL

Frozen dead dog Czechoslovakia 1993 C-print, 9½ x 12 inches (24.1 x 30.5 cm), edition of five After my father's death, I visited the town in the Czech Republic where he had been born, and found this frozen dead dog.

Robert Therrien

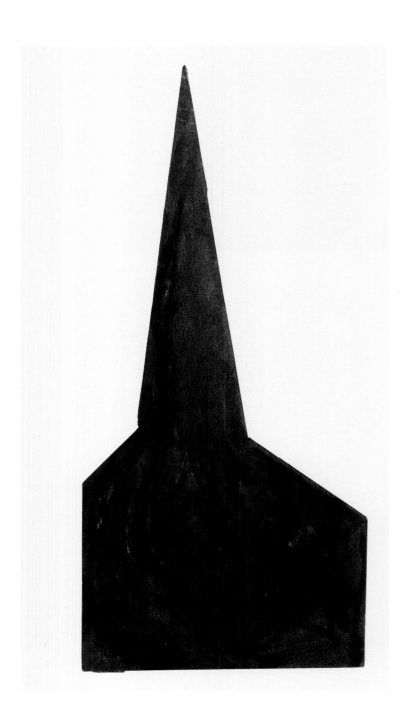

No Title 1977 ink and watercolor on paper, 9¼ x 4½ inches (23.5 x 11.4 cm) Choosing the "earliest" or the "single most significant" work is an act of reduction. This early chapel is a good symbol for the singular. It came out of a conscious gesture to represent "one"—that is, one finger out of five. It is the tracing of a pointing hand cleaned up with a ruler and filled in with black ink. This process— both figurative and reductive— ultimately produced architecture or a symbol of sorts. What an image ends up being and the idea that started it can be so different. Making this drawing also ended up producing a kind of spatial/visual game where this chapel form can be seen as either full or empty—as an object or a void on the page.

b. Chicago, IL, USA, 1947. Lives and works in Los Angeles, CA, USA.

Lacanau (self) 1986 This is a self-portrait on the beach in France, photographed down on myself. It's a pink shape, which is my T-shirt; and then a bit of black, which is my shorts; and then a bit of skin, which is my knee; and then a big space of sand. It's also my first abstract picture: You can't make out what it is, but it's actually totally concrete at the same time. And it was about this moment of reaffirmation, or self-affirmation—I am. It was like coming out to myself as an artist. It's a record of an experience I had. Once I'd experienced something, recognized something, I could take a picture of it.

b. Remscheid, Germany, 1968. Lives and works in London, England.

Fred Tomaselli

13,000 1991 pills, acrylic, resin on wood panel, 48 x 47 inches (121 x 119.3 cm) Throughout the 1980s I was an installation artist whose work investigated the mechanics of reality dislocation in the form of immersive, hybrid theme parks. In the late '80s I began to inlay pills into resin-coated paintings as a way of expanding on those ideas, and in 1991 I made *13,000* using approximately thirteen thousand aspirins. I believe this work marks the completion of my morph from an installation artist to a painter. Up until then, the works were minimalist illustrations of my conceptual concerns, but this was the first picture where the form got really physical. I was attempting to hijack the viewers' perception by seducing them into a toxic, vibratory world while simultaneously revealing the mechanics of that seduction. I was inspired by the pre-Modernist idea that painting is a window to another reality, a vehicle of transportation to the sublime. I was once paralyzed by painting's burden of history, but it turns out that making pictures has liberated me to go anywhere I want.

b. Santa Monica, CA, USA, 1956. Lives and works in Brooklyn, NY, USA.

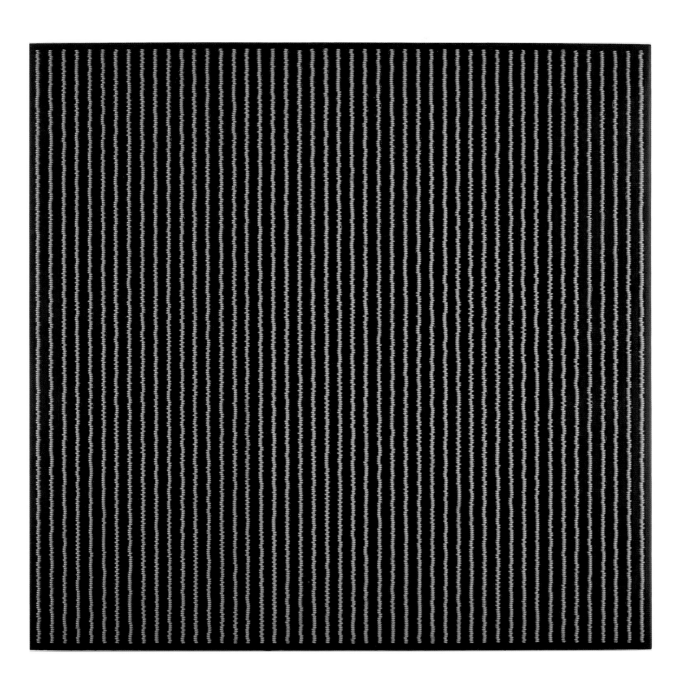

375

Arthur Tress

Hermaphrodite East Hampton, New York 1973 silver gelatin print, 20 x 24 inches (50.8 x 61 cm) In my studies of dream imagery and the collective unconscious, while reading Carl Jung's book, *Psychology and Alchemy*, I came across a strange seventeenth-century emblematic engraving with the caption, "The Hermaphrodite is born from Mercury and Venus. The Androgyne emerges from the union of the twin Principles. It dissolves and is recomposed into the One." This fusion of male and female energies seemed to mirror my own inner feelings of artistic balance and I thought to make a photograph that would have this same kind of hieroglyphic, symbolic atmosphere and archetypical resonance. Its complexity necessitated not a spontaneous fusion documentary and directed elements as in my earlier children's dream series which was mostly shot on the streets of New York, but rather the creation of a more elaborate, fully fabricated scenario and artificial theatrical staging. The *Hermaphrodite* image became the first of an extended series of male nudes dealing with the naked body as a vehicle for the materialization of both the sadistic and spiritual impulses within the exaltation of homosexual desire.

Eisberg (Iceberg) 1986 wool, linen (two-layered/hand-knitted, machine-knitted), 11⁴/₅ x 11⁴/₅ inches (30 x 30 cm) An irregular, hand-knitted mesh envelopes the tight machine-woven piece that lies beneath. The white overgrowth nearly hides from view the pure, sea-blue layer under it. This early knitted piece, titled *Iceberg* (1986) holds a key position within the series of wool works because it points in two differing directions the work has taken since. On the one hand, it inaugurated an exploration of the juxtaposition of contrasting styles and patterns that has continued to this day. On the other hand, the top, hand-made layer remained just another unexplored option until 2004, when the very concept of the tapestry was transformed in such works as *Water* and *Menopause*, large-format hand-woven wool pieces with unmistakable irregular structures and built-up surfaces.

The top layer of this small-format work from 1986 recalls the craggy exposed surface of an iceberg, and leaves us to guess at the underlying layers and the full scope of its volume.

Tunga

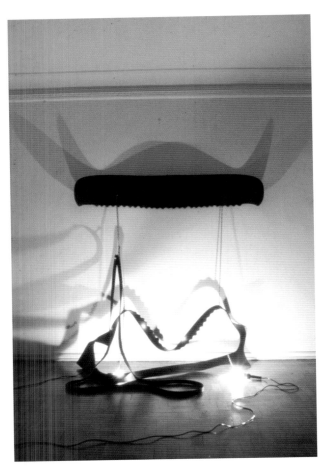

Vê-nus (See-nude) 1976 rubber sheet, rubber paste, rubber fly, lamp, approximately 97¹/₂ inches wide x 70¹/₂ inches high (approximately 250 cm wide x 180 cm high) Installation view, Núcleo de Arte Contemporánea, João Pessoa, Paraiba The classic process of conceiving this "thing" called a sculpture involves seeing what is not there, that is to say that sculpting is the same as lifting a curtain, removing the material that deprives the "thing" of its right to light. By a gesture, or a succession of gestures, the artist disencumbers the "thing" from what impedes it, bringing it to light so that the object seen is ideally what the artist had envisioned. He reveals the object that had previously been hidden.

During the 1960s I came up with an idea—"Clarity of the Nude" and, in keeping with that idea, developed this sculpture-installation, *Vê-nus*, or, "See-nude" in Portuguese.

With this piece I tried, theoretically, to reestablish the integral process of revealing a thing, its process of becoming. I wanted to create a totality where the formal process mimicked the mental one—a process of revelation whose main gesture focused on squeezing out the by-product of this new conjunction of junctions, *Vê-nus*.

In one stroke a continuous cut on a plane of soft material gave birth to *Vê-nus*. What is traditionally seen as the negative—the taken off part, the excess, the clippings—was not discarded but displaced so that it was clearly distinguishable from the positive while still being a component of the overall work.

Even though the parts had been separated they needed to be unified again—in this case that joining is emphasized by light sources that were placed where the "excess" was kept, bounded, and chained, so as to show the moment of revelation. Thus the chains, which are soldered with suckers to Vê-nus's body—a body of dense shadow that reveals its birth, its light, and its possible dissolution into the nostalgic whole.

b. Rio de Janeiro, Brazil, 1952. Lives and works in Rio de Janeiro, Brazil.

Wavy Line 1994 silver gelatin print mounted on aluminum, 60 x 49 inches (152.4 x 124.6 cm), edition of six Prior to 1994, I had worked on individual portraits in public city settings. *Wavy Line* was my first temporary, site-specific installation using more than two or three people. On a warm July morning in New York in 1994, over 25 friends and strangers helped me make this work. The resulting photographic document catapulted me into a new series that I am still working on today.

Luc Tuymans

G. Dam 1978 oil on canvas, 27¹⁄₂ x 24 inches (70 x 60 cm) *G. Dam* is for me one of my most important paintings. It is the portrait of a family member, my mother's late brother. It is based not on a photograph but on another painting showing the face in three-quarters profile. I could have no real human feelings toward this person without having a picture of him. I exaggerated this picture: His shoulders look unreal, and his head looks as though it is emerging from the canvas, like those big pictures at fairs that you can stick your head through. The head is isolated from the body, and all the intensity is concentrated in the eyes. Consequently, the picture defines its whole surroundings. It remains a confrontation. Whichever way one looks at the picture, the gaze is always present. This picture was the beginning, although unconsciously, of a painting of memory . . . How a memory should look, but how one never remembers it. It was the first step toward a picture of a picture.

b. Morstel, Belgium, 1958. Lives and works in Antwerp, Belgium.

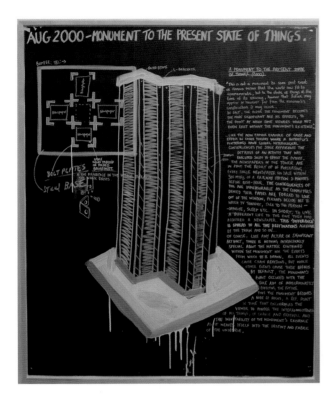

Studio Wall Drawing—Monument to the Present State of Things August 2000 mixed media on paper, 61.8 x 49.6 inches (157 x 126 cm)

Monument to the Present State of Things, from The Seven Wonders of the World series 2000 steel and newspapers bought from vendors at a railway station on a certain date, 120.1 x 44.9 x 44.9 inches (305 x 114 x 114 cm)

This piece instigates change in the future, thus it is both a starting point and a continuum.

Nicola Tyson

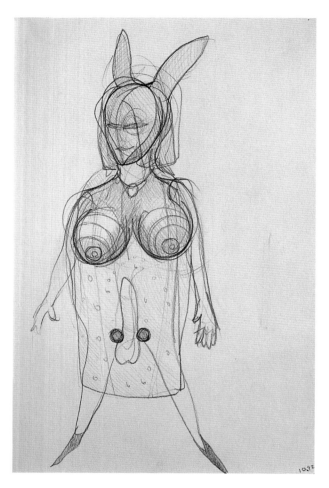

Self-portrait 1992 pencil on paper, 5¼ x 8 inches (13.9 x 20.3 cm)
Although I was trained as a painter, I initially suppressed an intuitive approach to art-making. I was more interested in consciousness-raising than in delving into my subconscious, and chose to explore through my work my urgent interest in feminist theories. This included organizing an alternative space devoted to work by women, focusing on the lesbian subculture emerging at that time (the early '90s). But as the project progressed, I increasingly felt that the rules I had adopted for my own work were too limiting; the overwhelming impulse was to turn within and work directly from the subconscious in a completely unguided manner.

Self-portrait was the first of multifarious small drawings that at first I called "diary drawings" as they were personifications of a particular fleeting mood or desire or preoccupation. This discovery quickly became a compelling game, and I rapidly filled sketchbooks with increasingly unlikely personae, registering the pure pleasure and adventure of conjuring up a presence with just the lines of a pencil. Hundreds of drawings later, the energy was spent, and I moved on to explore other means of expression, but this drawing, perhaps the least peculiar of those what were to follow, was nevertheless the first to burst forth, a pleasant surprise, and the herald of what was to come.

b. London, England, 1960. Lives and works in New Paltz, NY, USA.

Cover Girl (British Vogue) 1994 C-print mounted on aluminum, 11 x 8 ½ inches (28 x 21.5 cm) *Cover Girl*, began in 1994, an ongoing series of self-portraits in a unique magazine cover, is perhaps the first body of my work to attract a much wider audience.

b. Lagos, Nigeria, c. 1968. Lives and works in New York, NY, USA.

Juan Uslé

Boogie-Woogie 1991 painting on canvas, 78 x 44 inches (198 x 112 cm) I think that my painting *Boogie-Woogie* is a good example to begin looking back at my series, *Pinturas Celibataires*, because this particular work, along with *Mi-Mon (Miro versus Mondrian)*, *Blow-Up*, etc., points at the moment in which I began to establish a new order in my medium- and large-sized canvases. In these paintings, there is a clear awareness and the wish to differentiate them from earlier works. In them there is an evident shift from the individualized order of the celibate paintings, which are neither linked nor spring from earlier work conforming a series, to works that are born from the autonomous and independent idea of addressing the fallacies, the meanings, and the possibilities of the language of painting of the so-called stellar moments from the avant-garde to the present.

I gave the painting this title thinking of Piet Mondrian, remembering what I thought at The Museum of Modern Art in New York while looking at some of his last pieces, including *Broadway Boogie-Woogie*. I felt strongly that Mondrian contradicted himself by the fact that he continued to paint. I was also thinking what this possibility presupposed and what it could have changed with regard to the ordered discourse of twentieth-century art.

This is what I said in 1995 in an interview with another painter: "The neoplasticist utopia began to crumble when Mondrian's soul and gaze got inebriated with Broadway. His painting *Broadway Boogie-Woogie* reflects a contradiction between the purity and the rigor of a transcendent and empty space which begins to meander, to vibrate with jazz and with optical comings and goings that are hard to fasten . . ."

This comment stimulated my painting *Boogie-Woogie*. From the point of view of being now completely sunken in the twenty-first-century, Mondrian's tardy and final weaknesses, along with his awareness of the possibility of an impossible continuity, one that would shatter his previous structures, which had been so rigorously blueprinted from a different perspective, seem admirable to me.

Back in '91, when I was painting my own *Boogie-Woogie*, I was laying down the same contradiction for myself. For this reason I was pouring out organic lines, 'rivers of life,' that traversed an ideal structure that had been carefully planned. In order to achieve this, I was attempting to fasten a site for faith, which inevitably had a bitter flavor.

I was opposing the principle of non-repetition to the concept of uniqueness of style: The identity of authorship had already germinated in the family of small-scale paintings called *Nemasté*. In them, paying attention to the meaning of the word *nepalí*, I was trying to play with different syntactic identities and to broaden as much as possible my own discourse as well as the medium's specter of possibilities, which had already been brought into question. Their identity was established in advance in the choice of identical formats.

Boogie-Woogie, and other paintings from this period of differentiated syntax, extended this idea into larger formats. My *Celibataires* paintings are generally shown in the manner of parallel alignments, lines or groups of heterogeneous paintings that conform an open syntactic kaleidoscope that trigger in my work the possibility of discovery, the encounter with new identities, and the idea of non-fixity.

Jeffrey Vallance

Blinky: The Friendly Hen 1978 paperback, ¹/₂ x 5¹/₂ x 8¹/₂ inches (.6 x 14 x 21.6 cm) published by Smart Art Press, ISBN: 0964642670 (first printing 1979, second printing 1996) In 1978, when I was 23 years old, I had a job restoring antique penny arcade machines from the early 1900s to the 1950s. For the first time in my life I had money in my bank account—$5,000, to be exact. I decided to spend the entire amount on an art piece, so I self-published the story of Blinky the Friendly Hen. Blinky was a piece of meat (chicken) that I purchased at a local supermarket. (Blinky was so named due to the chicken's peculiar cockeyed gaze.) I took Blinky to the Los Angeles Pet Cemetery to see if they would bury a piece of meat— if I had the cash. They did. What followed was the entire burial ritual for a dead pet.

The *Blinky* piece was originally a prank—just to see what I could get away with. I thought it had no meaning at all. But I soon realized that Blinky was a stand-in for us. In that way, I could go through all of society's death rituals without having to produce a "real" dead body. At the time of the *Blinky* piece, I was a vegetarian, so the piece has an underlying vegetarian statement as well.

Over time, I came to believe that Blinky was an archetype of sacrifice. I saw serious correlations between Blinky's sacrifice, suffering, death, burial, exhumation, and cultification; and the story of Christ's Passion. It was as if this story (without any specific symbols) is written in our heads. Culturally we inject familiar signs into the story to give it meaning—The Meaning of Life. Take the Friendly Hen, for example: Blinky was born from an egg, the Easter symbol of birth and life; the chicken and the cock are symbols of virility and sexuality, and signify sacrifice and redemption; and ultimately the rooster is the emblem of resurrection—the cock crowing three times at the Dawn of Salvation.

Like no other work, the *Blinky* piece has caught the public's imagination. Blinky is listed in several California travel guides and there are manifold references to the Friendly Hen on the Internet. The Blinky saga has become akin to an urban legend, with even the pet cemetery workers embellishing the story of the funeral service to include "hooded, chanting mourners holding candles." On Blinky's grave, I often find strange votive offerings left by cemetery visitors. I was invited to be a guest on David Letterman to talk about Blinky. A reference to Blinky appeared on the TV show *Married with Children* in the form of "Winky the Dead Bird." On *The Simpsons* TV show, Blinky's headstone can be seen at the Springfield Pet Cemetery. Blinky is now like a cult thing. I have to be very careful in exhibiting Blinky relics as they are the pieces most frequently stolen from museums (for who knows what diabolical purpose).

b. Torrance, CA, USA, 1955. Lives and works in Los Angeles, CA, USA.

Here is Blinky in the viewing room. By this time, Blinky was starting to thaw, so she was placed on a paper towel so that the moisture would not seep into the satin. A pillow was placed where Blinky's head would have been. A subtle spot light was shining on Blinky and beads of moisture glistened in the light.

Gus Van Sant

No Title 1968 magazine transferred on to paper, 11 x 14 inches (27.9 X 35.6 cm) This is a piece I made as a sophomore in high school, with magazine cutouts and some sort of solvent on paper. I rubbed the images on to the paper like Rauschenberg was doing around that time. I don't know how many of these I was creating at the time. This was probably the only one, although I was very into selecting cutout backgrounds and cutting out people to exist in the foregrounds. In some, the slight disharmony between the foreground and background excited me a lot— this reminds me of those collages, although there is no background in this picture.

Tape I 1972 videotape, black and white, mono sound, 60 min., 50 sec.
An attempt to stare down the Self. A camera, with its live image displayed on a monitor next to it, is seen viewing its own reflection in a mirror when a man (the artist) enters the room. He sits in front of the mirror, breaking the line of sign and thus becoming both the subject and the object of a self-portrait. He stares into the lens with focused concentration, maintaining eye contact with the unseen viewer. A low howling sound is heard, the noise of the camera's microphone in low level feedback with its own speaker. The man stares at us for a long time. Suddenly, without warning, he bursts out with a loud violent scream. He then gets up and physically stops the videotape in the recorder with his hand, creating a violent disruption of picture and sound that plunges the screen into snow.

b. New York, NY, USA, 1951. Lives and works in Long Beach, CA, USA.

Charline von Heyl

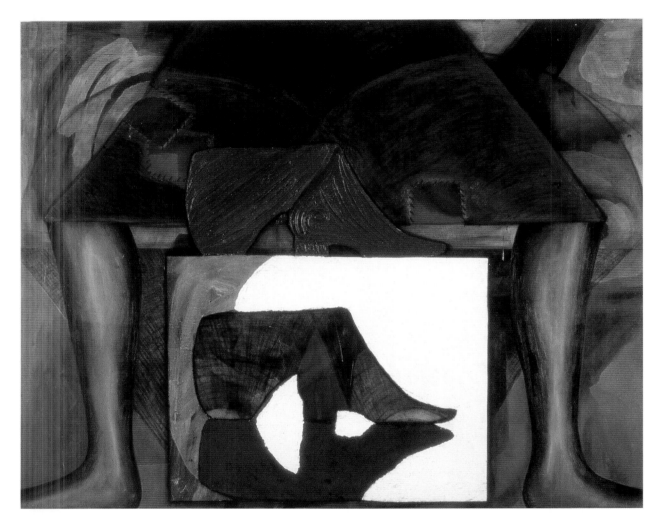

Untitled 1989 acrylic, oil, charcoal, and pigment, 48⁴/₅ X 60¹/₂ inches (125 x 155 cm) This painting was made in 1989. I had just moved into a new and much bigger studio, and in a frenzy of happy working I started to cut up older, smaller paintings and to stick parts of them on to the new work, making a formal and anecdotal statement. The resulting painting looked stubborn and at the same time light-hearted, and seemed to ask the right questions. It felt like a good beginning.

b. Mainz, Germany, 1960. Lives and works in New York, NY, USA.

Arch Construction IV Moscone Site, San Francisco 1981 gelatin silver print, 20 x 24 inches (50.8 x 60.9 cm) In the late 1970s, I began to photograph the largest construction site west of the Mississippi. The image, *Arch Construction IV*, depicts a massive rebar arch in the process of fabrication. My interest in photographing the Moscone Site was multifaceted. Conceptually, I began working with the idea of future ruins, of archaeology in reverse. Documenting the process and exploring the evidence of constant change was similar to a scientific excavation, exposing "some deeply buried remnant of the future."

b. San Francisco, CA, USA, 1953. Lives and works in San Francisco, CA, USA.

Kara Walker

Untitled Sept 1991 eight cans of shoe polish and objects, dimensions variable I was on the verge of thinking about art in a new way when this awkward "installation" of found objects made its way out of my studio and into an exhibition titled "Black Men: Image/ Reality" at the New Visions Gallery in Atlanta, Georgia.

I had only recently graduated from the Atlanta College of Art with a portfolio of nine-foot-tall paintings of mythical beasts in varying states of physical disarray. They didn't amount to much more than asserting that I was not going to succumb to being one of those "racial" artists whose aesthetics (my thought was) suffered under the weight of history and the effort towards sincerely redressing injustice. Sincerity is the thing art wreaks havoc with, thought I.

The gallery director at that time, concerned that the roster of artists was a little testosterone-heavy, called me up as a last minute addition to the show. I had nothing relevant but this little can of

Muhammad Ali shoe polish I had bought at Eckerd drugstore. Touted as "the Greatest Shine" and advertising that proceeds of its sale would go to the NAACP, it seemed obvious to me that someone somewhere was trying to pull one over on me—or someone seriously missed the irony.

When I bought seven more cans, the rest of the stock, it was my first great renegade moment—it truly felt illicit. Somehow I was both supporting a clever Klansman and unmasking his m.o. The addition of the shoeshine stand was nice, but didn't pack the same punch—other than that it belonged to the elderly black shoeshine man who worked the office complex. Oh, and the distorted mirror was truly unforgivable. But overall, making this simple action opened the door on an enormous load of suppressed material I would begin to address in my work to date.

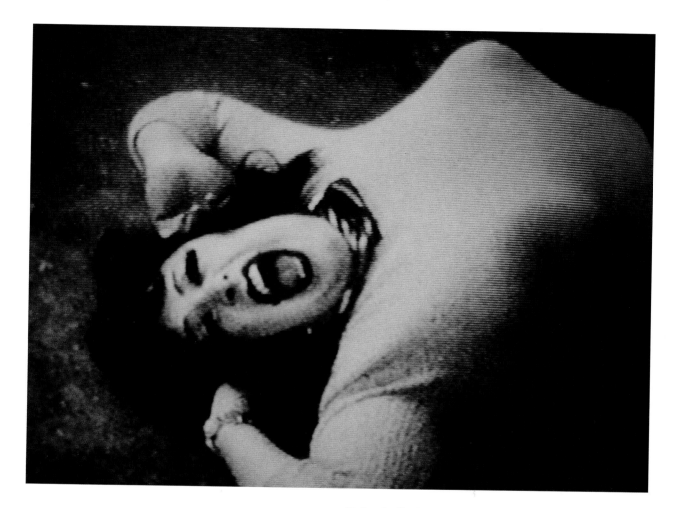

Divine in Ecstasy 1992 chromogenic color photo, 10 x 13 inches (25.4 x 33 cm) photo For my own obsessional needs, I wanted to possess a movie still from one of my earlier films that was never taken on the set. Like a crazed fan or failed press agent, I put on the video of the film, grabbed my camera and started clicking away in the dark, taking photos off the TV set. My first failed, ugly, sickeningly focused and badly framed new "little movie" suddenly was born.

b. Baltimore, MD, USA, 1946. Lives and works in Baltimore, MD, USA. 393

Gillian Wearing

Signs that say what you want them to say and not signs that say what someone else wants you to say (I really love Regents Park) 1992/93 R-type color print, 48 x 36 inches (122 x 92 cm), edition of 10 + 1 AP After floundering around when I left college, thinking, shall I try and work for the BBC as so many Goldsmiths graduates had supposedly done in the past, I started in 1990 by doing pseudo vox pop–type documentaries that were neither valid TV nor even worth showing in a gallery. There was something I definitely wanted to do with voice or language. I had tried photographing people I know, first by asking them to hold something I had written, and later by asking them to write down thoughts. The results seemed smug rather than candid because we knew each other. It's only in fit of exasperation that I decided to try asking strangers to write their own thoughts. I went to Regent's Park, knowing at least people might have more time to spare than on the streets. I took photographs of three people that day, and one I knew immediately excited me and eventually concretized the work.

The woman wrote "I really love Regents Park," and it wasn't just the fact of what she wrote that works, it is her posture, her sweet smile, the look of conviction in what she wrote, her clothes, and the way she holds the piece of paper. It's this magic combination that I could feel and see immediately—the words were filling in the blank canvas, the muteness of the photograph. I loved the fact that there was a collaboration in representing the person imaged.

b. Birmingham, England, 1963. Lives and works in London, England.

Marnie Weber

Quest for Happy 1995 video installation Happy sets out on a journey to search for a sad little bluebird who has fallen into the deep snow. She packs up her friends and drags them on snow saucers through a blinding blizzard deep into the forest. Everyone is worried, cold, and sad. The stuffed little girl doll with a rubber face cries. After much difficulty, Happy finds the bluebird by digging in the exact spot where it has been buried. The bluebird of happiness rises up and flies away. It is a miracle.

This video installation was a turning point in my work when I realized I could turn a performance piece into art that could live beyond me and without me. I had been performing in bands and solo for fifteen years, constantly hauling props, costumes, and musical equipment. I was driving home on the freeway with my second truckload of crap when the post-performance blues were really kicking in. I thought, "I can't take it anymore." I decided I would put all my characters on video and they could watch themselves on TV and I could just stay home and work.

Carrie Mae Weems

Untitled from The Africa Series

1993 silver print, edition of five, 28¼ x 28⅛ inches (71.8 x 71.4 cm) My first picture that was really a picture. Memory fails me. I can't actually recall my first picture. All I know is it was of a woman, a sexy woman, who was a friend—that much I remember, but the rest is all a blur. The image pictured here in this book represents the first photograph I'd taken that changed my understanding of the deep structures, the underlining purpose(s) and function(s) of architecture. While in this ancient city—Djenne, in northern Mali—I made many images of this building, but its power, its complicated subtext, its determined narrative was hidden in a forest of meanings; its essence revealed only after I returned home and began making the first photographic prints. And I'm crazy about it.

b. Portland, OR, USA, 1953. Lives and works in Syracuse and New York, NY, USA.

William Wegman

Cotto 1970 black-and-white silver print, 8½ x 8½ inches (21.6 x 21.6 cm) I was in my apartment in Madison, Wisconsin sitting at a table half-consciously doodling little circles with a pen on the back of my hand and index finger to go with the circular ruby settings in the ring I wore on that finger since my teens. The ring was given to me by my grandfather and has special power and meaning to me. I'm always looking at it. Later that night I went to a party where cotto salami was among the hors d'oeuvres. Reaching for a slice, I noticed how the meat of my hand sort of dissolved into the salami. The little rings of pepper in the cotto looked just like the ink circles I had drawn on my hand. I pilfered a handful of the salami, went home, and set up what was to be my first, most important photo piece. The print was graphically very strong and its striking clarity gave me the courage to go on in this direction.

b. Holyoke, MA, USA, 1943. Lives and works in New York, NY and Maine, USA.

AT LEAST THE FIRST I UNDERSTOOD. CIRCA EARLY 1960, BLEEKER STREET. COLLECTION STEDELIJK MUSEUM, AMSTERDAM

What Is Set Upon the Table Sits Upon the Table c. 1960
sculpture, size of a table, size of a stone

b. New York, NY, USA, 1942. Lives and works in New York, NY, USA and Amsterdam, The Netherlands.   399

James Welling

The Waterfall 1981 silver print, open edition, 22 x 18 inches (55.9 x 45.7 cm) While *The Waterfall* is not a first work in this series (there is a photograph of drapery I made a few weeks before *Waterfall* titled *No. 1*), it does embody most of the aims I had when I began photographing drapery in May 1981. I wanted to express a melancholy feeling as well as a sense of tragic beauty. These seem associated in my imagination with drapery and curtains; the heavy folds of nineteenth-century clothing and the terminal diagnosis William Bendix receives in *The Babe Ruth Story*, "It's curtains, Babe." Marvin Heiferman exhibited *The Waterfall* in a summer group show "Love is Blind," in June 1981. When a friend saw *The Waterfall* at the show, he said it reminded him of the Buddhist concept of noble sadness. The first print I made of the negative has a faint greenish tonality which is very special and which I've never been able to quite repeat.

b. Hartford, CT, USA, 1957. Lives and works in Los Angeles, CA, USA.

John Wesley

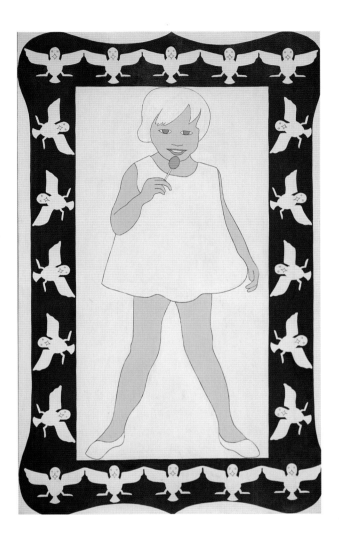

Bird Girl 1963 oil and enamel on canvas, 79 x 48 inches (200.7 x 121.9 cm) Jo and I moved to New York in 1960. I had worked for Northrop in Los Angeles, but I found a very pleasant job at the post office that allowed me plenty of time to paint. The job was demanding only on holidays, when I was asked to deliver mail in the Bronx. One of my first major works at this time was a painting of my post office badge— badge 32554. The painting was as flat as I could make it. It wasn't supposed to look like a painting, more like a banner or a poster or something. I began a series of works that resembled badges or stamps, often playing with different borders. By 1962, I was placing people within ornamental borders. I used garlands of flowers for the *Radcliffe Tennis Team, The Olympic Field Hockey Officials*, and *Faisal* a picture of King Faisal of Saudi Arabia. With the *The Aviator's Daughters* and *The Arrival of Count Baillet-Latour* I used airplanes and pointed fingers respectively. These just seemed more suitable. *Bird Girl* was defined by her legion of birds. I found a picture of the little girl in a catalogue; she was modeling clothes at children's events. Years later someone wrote that she looked like a femme fatale. I always thought she was a little less dangerous than that, though the birds appear to be very regimental, very serious.

Tom Wesselmann

PHOTO: JIM STRONG, INC. © TOM WESSELMANN / LICENSED BY VAGA, NEW YORK. TEXT: ORAL HISTORY INTERVIEW WITH TOM WESSELMANN AT HIS STUDIO ON THE BOWERY, 1984. INTERVIEWER: IRVING SANDLER.

Portrait Collage #1 1959 pencil, pastel, collage, and staples on board, 9½ x 11 inches (24.1 x 27.9 cm) I tried to work from de Kooning into something else, still abstract. Actually I went back more to Kandinsky, really. I'd do those shorthand things. This piece of collage was a bridge. And this piece of blue was a . . . lake—that's my way of making shorthand notations much more like Kandinsky than de Kooning. But always with the idea of de Kooning there. And that just wasn't quite satisfying, I felt. I was getting a little bit too frustrated by it. And this is while I'm taking education courses in the daytime; I don't have very much time here either. I was very gloomy, I guess, having to study a whole lot to get through these courses, being completely alone and lonely, and occasionally trying to paint. It was just as if I didn't have the resources to bring anything to bear at that point. So when I did try to paint, it wasn't fulfilling to the painting or to me. So I tried a few experiments. I tried to learn where I was. I did this one collage one day that was totally abstract; it was rather nice. I didn't know what I was trying to do. I didn't know why I was doing it, what I was even trying to accomplish. I didn't know anything. Now this was all determined probably from my emotional state as well, because I was going to be getting in trouble at this point, close to some kind of a serious breakdown of some sort. But literally with a flash of insight, which was important, and my reaction to it the proper one, I realized that I didn't know what I was trying to do; it was just somebody else's work I was trying to do anyway. I had to throw it all out—like I had recently denied God; I threw God out there. I had to throw it out de Kooning, because he really was after all a god to me in terms of art. I had to throw all his art out, as much as I could possibly throw out and find my own ways of doing it. Something Marsicano said, too, is, "You have to find your own way of doing everything. Matisse found his way of drawing eyes; you've got to find a way of drawing eyes. You can't do what Matisse did." It was a hell of a challenge that you had to find your own way to do it. Really! Scary as hell. But I had to find my own way of doing all that stuff. And that kind of saved my life, because for the first time I began to have something that was mine. I really felt this. The very first work that I did was that little *Portrait Collage #1*. It literally was the first; and it saved my life emotionally as well as artistically, because now I could make my own rules. I was like the king of the turf. I wasn't inhibited by de Kooning or anybody else.

Passstück (Adaptive) 1983 wood, plaster, paint, 6⁷/₁₀ x 11 x 35²/₅ inches (17 x 28 x 90 cm)
Entering the google box I was astonished, but it also looked like this.

b. Vienna, Austria, 1947. Lives and works in Vienna, Austria. 403

Pae White

Empty 7–Eleven 1982 oil on canvas, 24 x 36 inches (70 x 91.4 cm)
I made this painting as a freshman in college in my first painting class. Everyone was asked to bring in a subject, such as a flower or fruit, but I wanted to paint something that was *barely* there, such as a "feeling." The image was of an empty dance studio (not really a 7–Eleven store). I failed at ballet as a child because I was more interested in the space reflected in the mirror than in what was happening around me. I think this painting explores a little of that obsession. However, what I really like about this painting is that the ideas that I am continually pursuing in terms of space, light, architecture, and illusion are laid out as a skeleton in this early work.

Rachel Whiteread

Untitled 1987 (top) Sellotape and air
Closet 1988 (left) wood, felt, and plaster,
$62^2/_5$ x $34^3/_{10}$ x $14^2/_5$ inches (160 x 88 x 37 cm)

In 1987 as a postgraduate student at the Slade, I made a small work out of Sellotape. I suppose I was trying to create the skin of the table—an "occasional table" that had been in my family for years. The piece existed for only a few days. It was very fragile.

Almost two years on, I made what I would consider my first "sculpture," entitled *Closet*. It was cast directly from a wardrobe and covered in black felt; I was simply trying to make a childhood memory concrete. It changed my life.

b. London, England, 1963. Lives and works in London, England.

T.J. Wilcox

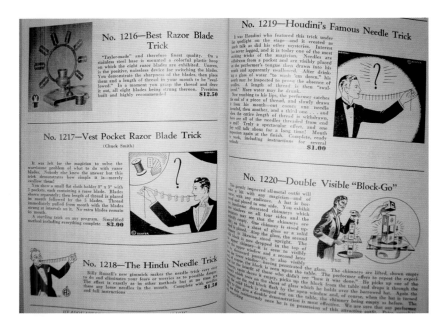

In 1976, I was enrolled in Ms. Miller's fifth-grade class at Wilson Elementary School in Spokane, Washington. One of our class art projects was a life-size self-portrait. An outline was drawn of each person's body on a large sheet of paper. We were meant to fill in "ourselves," using paints and collage, to describe the personal and professional selves we hoped to become. My dream, and hence my drawing, was to be a purple-velvet-suit-wearing magician. I think the idea that art could be something bigger (in many ways) than an 8¹/₂ x 11-inch sheet of paper occured to me via Ms. Miller's art assignment. And while my career as a professional magician didn't materialize, one of the things that attracts me to projects that employ projected film and video is those medium's ability to mesmerize and facilitate an entry into other worlds.

Sue Williams

Ow That Smarts 1989 acrylic on paper on canvas, 48 x 42 inches
(122 x 106.7 cm) I was looking for a way of working,
like a format for my words and drawings and
collected images to come together. To make a
work of art, I suppose. This was a frustrating time.
An artist friend of mine told me "just keep trying
things, and a door will open." I said, "WHAT?"
Also around this time I was impressed by a piece
by Mike Kelley. It was an installation piece about
insect eggs and seemed to go off the deep end.
I thought this was very cool; you can do whatever
you want. I didn't know that. I couldn't paint on
canvas, so I eventually found out how to glue a thin
layer of Massa paper to the canvas, and arranged
the drawings around a larger center drawing with
the words accompanying them like vignettes.
I liked it. For a while.

b. Chicago Heights, IL, USA, 1954. Lives and works in Brooklyn, NY, USA.

Fred Wilson

No Noa Noa: History of Tahiti 1987 plaster, wood, blood, mixed media, dimensions variable *No Noa Noa* was not the seminal work where I realized that conceptual art was the path I would take as an artist. That earlier work is lost, but not forgotten. *No Noa Noa* was the work through which I think I learned the most about what I was interested in and continue to be interested in as an artist. I learned that a curiosity about hidden history, culture, and race were firmly a part of me and would always be by my side like a faithful dog, occasionally nipping at my heels. I learned that I was driven to research the subjects that interest me in in order to invest my art with meaning. The gathering of information gave me the license and insiration to go beyond my research, to delve into my own thoughts, desires, and demons sparked by the chosen topic.

For the creation of *No Noa Noa*, I had to chop up a wooden mask. It was the first time I broke a cultural artifact to release meaning. I remember it distinctly. The violent act was difficult for me to do as I am perhaps impossibly nonviolent in nature. I have the utmost respect for things in the world. Yet I knew that I had to do it, and that it was an act of abandon that was completely necessary to break through received notions. I remember apologizing to the mask before destroying it, and then feeling satisfied that it heard me and gave me its blessing. After I destroyed it, I knew *No Noa Noa* was to be a milestone for me. It was as if the mask passed on to me new abilities.

I learned that the power and politics of beauty would also play a part of my art-making and thinking. While I always knew I was interested in both high art and kitsch, *No Noa Noa* was the first time I juxtaposed disparate objects to create a new thought. This thrilled me immensely. It still does.

I also learned about my interests through the viewer's response to the work when it was first shown at Artists Space in the then-prestigious "Selections" exhibition. Mostly their offhand comments or actions inadvertently made clear to me what I was not interested in, as when a couple of viewers laughed upon seeing the huge, fleshy dildo, which I intended to be a sad commentary on a moment in history. From this I realized I had to dig deeper and work harder to get my feelings to emerge and to make my art mirror my emotions. In another instance, a curator told me that he would love to exhibit the juxtaposed objects in my work, if I ever wanted to show them without the multileveled, multicolored platform. I had never thought of doing this before because it was not my intention. His offer disturbed me for a long time, because I felt strongly that the context of objects was all-important. Context was king. The "white cube" was not the right context for me, because it presumed to be a non-context. It was this nagging realization that led me to search for a context for objects that made sense to me. I eventually understood, through my life experiences, that the museum space itself, if viewed critically, could be and would be, the cogent context I was looking for.

b. Bronx, NY, USA, 1954. Lives and works in New York, NY, USA.

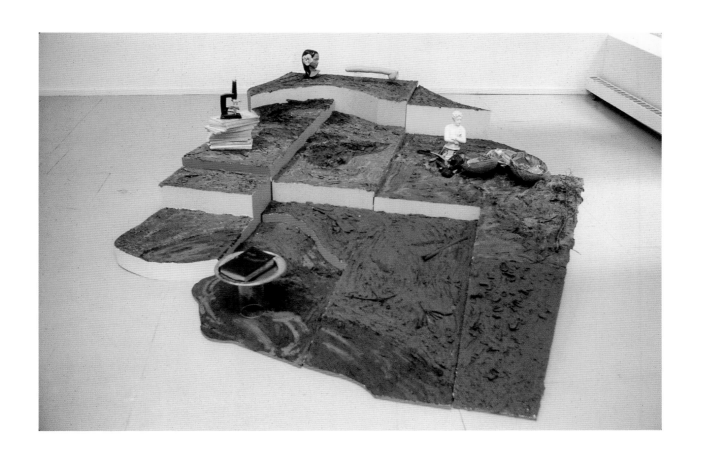

Jane & Louise Wilson

Garage 1989 two black-and-white C-prints mounted on aluminum, 59¹/₁₀ x 70⁹/₁₀ inches (150 x 180 cm) This was the first exhibited collaborative work we made and printed together in 1989. The image is called *Garage*, and it was shot in our garage at home. It depicts an activity which is caught in a cyclical loop, and it reflects just as much about the nature of collaboration as it does about our relationship as sisters. (We updated it in 1993 making it a diptych—it included a second panel with an image taken earlier that day showing the props in place before any action.)

b. Newcastle upon Tyne, England, 1967. Live and work in London, England.

Untitled 1957 graphite, chalk, and charcoal on paper, 12 x 18 inches, (30.5 x 45.7 cm) I made this drawing when I was eight. It's the earliest extant work I have and it feels completely my own.

Joel-Peter Witkin

The Kiss (Le Baiser) New Mexico, 1982 toned silver gelatin print, 28 x 28 inches (71.1 x 71.1 cm) *The Kiss* was the first image I made by providence. It was made to happen. I had the set established— that being a black velvet backdrop. The lights were set up. When I took the specimen from its wrapping and carried it to the set, its lips touched! There it was!

Simple, elegant. Mysteriously beautiful! All I had to do was stand the specimen up and arrange the more subtle details on the piece and its viscera. I adjusted the lights. I took the light reading, then composed the image in my camera. This kind of altered-state occurrence has happened many times in my career. It has made me understand that art is nonmaterial reality in the guise of its physicality.

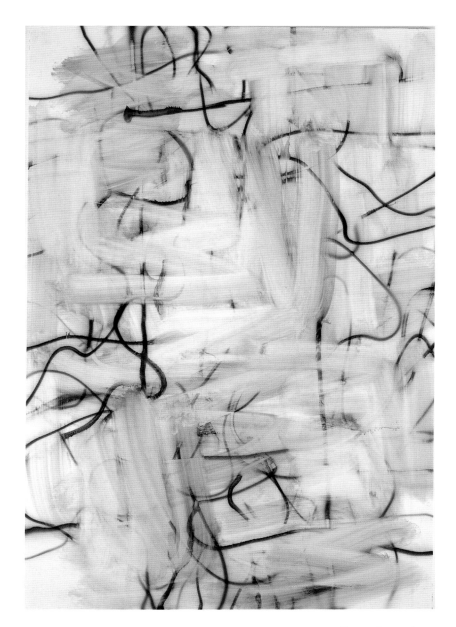

Self Portrait 2004 enamel on linen, 116 x 78 inches (294.6 x 198.1 cm) Sometimes the last feels like the first.

Richard Wright

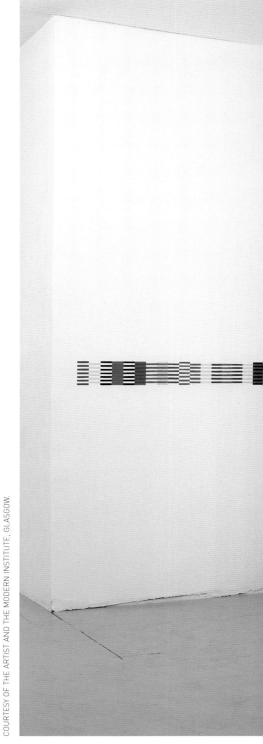

1993 gouache on wall, dimensions variable.
Installation view, Intermedia Gallery, Glasgow

This piece is from 1993. I had already made some temporary things in disused spaces (which had been seen by nobody) and it seemed obvious to take this attitude into the gallery and try to make something with what I could remember and what I was able to do—the work had no plan. It's really important to say that I did not have the feeling that this was the beginning of some kind of new trajectory; on the contrary I always had the feeling that this would be the last work that I would make.

When I look at it now I think there are too many colors (there are five), but I am still drawn to its concreteness. It is a thing made with paint rather than a painting, it exhibits no skill whatsoever.

b. London, England, 1960. Lives and works in Glasgow, Scotland.

Erwin Wurm

Untitled 1988 Neguin figure, wood, iron, 31¹/₅ x 27³/₁₀ x 16²/₅ (80 x 70 x 42 cm) For several years I was following an idea which slowly became more and more a dead end. There was a big difference between thinking about art and doing it. This piece was the first step out of my crisis, the connection of both my artistic imagination and my private passions.

Untitled 1970 plastic, rope, lock, key,
4 x 5 x 8 inches (100.2 x 12.7 x 20.3 cm)

This piece is by no means the
first artwork I ever made, but
I distinctly remember the feeling
I had when I made it. I was
connected to the "found object"
in a way I'd never experienced
until then. I'd reached a good
balance between letting the
objects be just what they were
and forcing them to become
something exclusively personal.
As a result, the whole thing
had taken on a life of its own.

b. Pasadena, CA, USA, 1948. Lives and works in New York, NY, USA. 417

Karen Yasinsky

The Liver Boys 1997 still from slide show with soundtrack by the Moho Memo When asked about the genesis of my work, I immediately thought of drawing, since it's the medium with which I've felt really good my whole life. There is a drawing that comes to mind from around 1993 which is directly linked to the animation I do now. It is an imaginary young woman's portrait done in dark pencil. She is looking at you with a small smile on her face. Painted over her face is a mint-green line drawing of a door knob that also looks like a breast—far more El Greco's Madonna than Mona Lisa. She has the awkwardness, seduction, confidence, and sad capacity for self-delusion that, for me, make her a real beauty.

In my animation, I can create these people, then bring them to life through their halting gestures and movement through time. Nothing much happens in terms of drama, but when I started animating, I began to feel successful in creating people and suggesting life in a more real, open-ended way, a way that I hadn't seen before. This is a slide from the first animation that I did, *The Liver Boys*, with a soundtrack by the Moho Memo. It's a slide show with a woman, two men, and a piece of raw liver.

The Gifts 1991 oil on linen, 30 x 26 inches (76.2 x 66 cm) In the Catholic Mass, *The Gifts* are the wine and the bread in their pre-transubstantiated state.

Andrea Zittel

A–Z Management and Maintenance Unit; Model 003 1992 steel, wood, carpet, mirror, plastic sink, stove top, glass; 86 x 94 x 68 inches (218.4 x 238.8 x 172.7 cm) In 1991 when I made my first Living Unit (titled *A–Z Management and Maintenance Unit*), I was actually breeding animals as my artwork. I lived and worked in a 200-square-foot storefront with flies, quail, and chickens, and my 80-pound pet Weimeraner named Jethro. The endeavor was to create a new breed of chicken as a designer pet. I was also designing Breeding Units for the birds to live in which resembled a cross between an apartment building and a piece of Ikea furniture. The Breeding Units were elegant and simple, and had room for everything that was needed to take care of the animal.

Even though I'm pretty well-organized, the interior of the storefront studio space was incredibly chaotic and dirty. I remember that there was a certain point when I started to look at my living conditions and thought to myself that the animals had it a lot better than I did. So around that time I started to build a unit for myself, which would reduce and compact my living functions into a 49-square-foot area. The Management and Maintenance Unit that I ultimately designed to contain all of these functions had a metal, "U-shaped" frame that reminded me of a Mondrian grid. It had cabinets and shelves to contain the necessities for things like cooking and grooming. The plastic slop sink doubled as a bathtub, and there was a loft bed that was supported by the framework.

I remember that when I first designed this Unit I actually wasn't very fond of "Modern design"—but I was interested in the way in which Modernism took qualities that had historically been associated with poverty, such as white paint, functionality, and simplicity, and by using an ethical or intellectual code translated these qualities into a design that was considered morally elite. Since I was struggling to make ends meet, and my own life was by necessity rather sparse and pared-down anyway, I thought that I could use the language of Modern design to glamorize my own situation. I often referred to this as "turning my limitations into liberations." I felt that since I couldn't afford to live the way that other people did, I would at least make them wish that they could live like me.

b. Escondido, CA, USA, 1965. Lives and works in Joshua Tree, CA, USA.

ACKNOWLEDGMENTS

This book would not have been possible without the help of many people.

First and foremost, we'd like to extend our sincere thanks to all of the contributing artists who each took the time to choose and write about a submission for the book. Also a big thanks to their studio managers and assistants who helped to make sure we received all of the submission materials on time.

So many galleries and museums helped us to contact and correspond with the artists and provided us with the images of their work and many of the accompanying statements. We'd like to thank these galleries for all of their help in putting this book together. Many thanks to everyone at 303 Gallery, Acme, Akira Ikeda Gallery, Alexander and Bonin, American Fine Arts Co., Art + Commerce, Baldwin Gallery, Marianne Boesky Gallery, Tanya Bonakdar Gallery, Mary Boone Gallery, Rena Bransten Gallery, Sikkema Jenkins & Co., Christine Burgin Gallery, Leo Castelli Gallery, Cheim & Read, Cirrus Gallery, Clementine Gallery, James Cohan Gallery, Sadie Coles, Paula Cooper Gallery, Corvi-Mora, CRG Gallery, D'Amelio Terras, Danese, DC Moore Gallery, Deitch Projects, Feature Inc., Feigen Contemporary, Ronald Feldman Fine Arts, Rosamund Felsen Gallery, Fraenkel Gallery, Stephen Friedman Gallery, Frith Street Gallery, Fredericks Freiser Gallery, Gagosian Gallery, Galeria Ramis Barquet, Galeria Soledad Lorenzo, Galeria Toni Tàpies, Galerie Paul Andriesse, Galerie Ascan Crone, Galerie Bruno Bischofberger, Galerie Gisela Capitain, Galerie Jerome de Noirmont, Galerie Eigen + Art, Galerie Lelong, Galerie Thaddeus Ropac, Galerie Michael Werner, Gallery Paule Anglim, Gallery Sprüth/Magers, Klemens Gasser & Tanja Grunert Inc., Gavin Brown's enterprise, Gemini G.E.L. at Joni Weyl, Sandra Gering Gallery, Barbara Gladstone Gallery, Marian Goodman Gallery, Gorney Bravin + Lee, Greenberg Van Doren Gallery, Griffin Contemporary, Jack Hanley Gallery, Haunch of Venison, Hauser & Wirth, Joseph Helman Gallery, Henry Urbach Architecture, Edwynn Houk Gallery, I-20 Gallery, Casey Kaplan, Paul Kasmin Gallery, Sean Kelly Gallery, Kestner-Gesellschaft, Nicole Klagsbrun, Knoedler & Company, Lehmann Maupin, Lisson Gallery, Luhring Augustine Gallery, Magnum, MAI 36, Matthew Marks Gallery, Marlborough Gallery, The Matrix, McKee Gallery, Metro Pictures, Robert Miller Gallery, Victoria Miro Gallery, Modern Art, The Modern Institute, Montclair Art Museum, Paul Morris Gallery, The Museum of Modern Art, Neugerriemschneider, New Art Centre Sculpture Park and Gallery, Nolan/Eckman, P·P·O·W, Pace/MacGill, PaceWildenstein, Maureen Paley Interim Art, Patrick Painter Inc., Friedrich Petzel Gallery, La Pocha Nostra, Max Protetch Gallery, Regen Projects, Anthony Reynolds Gallery, Ricco/Maresca Gallery, Margarete Roeder Gallery, Rose Gallery, Andrea Rosen Gallery, Saatchi Gallery, San Francisco Museum of Modern Art, Julie Saul Gallery, Tony Shafrazi Gallery, Jack Shainman Gallery, ShugoArts, Sonnabend Gallery, Sperone Westwater, Sprueth Magers Lee, Stefan Stux Gallery, Timothy Taylor Gallery, Team Gallery, Tilton/Kustera Gallery, Leslie Tonkonow Artworks + Projects, Tracy Williams Ltd, Emily Tsingou Gallery, Waddington Galleries, White Cube, Donald Young Gallery, Zeno X Gallery, and David Zwirner Gallery.

Thanks to the following people for their extra help: Joshua Abelow, Eddie Adams, Nathalie Afnan, Anthony Allen, Claudia Altman-Siegel, Stefan Andersson, Sherry Apostol, Corice Arman, Kate Austin, Jade Awdry, Malena Bach, Marianna Baer, Beth Bahls, Julie Baranes, Gemma Barnett, Jennifer Bartle, Tracy Bartley, Nejma Beard, Becky Beasley, Aniko Beitschler, Margherita Belaief, Mike Bellon, Catherine Belloy, Jennifer Belt, Erika Benincasa, Anders Bergstrom, Jane Bhoyroo, David Birkitt, Vivien Bittencourt, Katie Block, Eduardo Bobillo, Martin Bochynek, Ted Bonin, Janet Borden, Vincent Boucheron, Christine Brachot, Kurt Brondo, Missy Brown, Zoe Bruns, Andre Buchmann, Chana Budgazad, Udo Bugdahn, Nela Bunjevac, Julie Burchardi, Christine Burgin, Herbert Burkert, Chris Burnside, John Caperton, Nancy Caponi, Lisa Carlson, Walter Cassidy, Julie Castellano, Janis Cecil, Dan Cheek, Julia Chiang, Julie Chiofolo, Caldecot Chubb, Jok Church, Ken Clark, Sarah Cohen, Sadie Coles, Cristina Colomar, Romy Colonius, Clare Coombes, Carol Corey, Alice Correia, Tommaso Corvi-Mora, Felicity Coupland, Jessica Lin Cox, Cherese Crockett, Gili Crouwel, Victoria Cuthbert, Dean Daderko, Karina Daskalov, Juana de Aizpuru, Monica De Cardenas, Cordelia de Mello Mourao, Emmanuelle de Noirmont, Gianni Degryse, Eline Dehullu, Jeffrey Deitch, Celia del Diego, Bruno Delavallade, Karen Diamond, Ariel Dill, Hannelore Ditz-Rainer, Katrina Doerner, Stephanie Dorsey, Jennifer Dove, Nick Dowdeswell, Caroline Dowling, Thomas Dryll, Kirsten Dunne, Chris Durham, Winston Eggleston, Lutz Eitel, Chiara Elli, Jan Endlich, Rebecca Epstein, Sima Familiant, Henrique Faria, Regina Fiorito, Faye Fleming, Esther Flury, Monica Fornaciari, Raymond Foye, Carlo Franchetti, Alexandra Frank, Jessica Fredericks, Jose Freire, Andrew Freiser, Marina Froehling, Virgilio Garza, Victor Gisler, Frank Goldman, Ivan Golinko, Michael Goodson, Ryan Goolsby, Jay Gorney, Amy Gotzler, Wendy Grannon, Juliet Gray, Simon Greenberg, Susanna Greeves, Sophie Greig, Detlev Gretenkort, Jenny Grondin, Barbara Gross, Abigail Guay, Enrique Guerrero, Gina Guy, Lilian Haberer, Tim Hailand, Jackie Haliday, Veronica Hammett, Jack Hanley, Ben Harman, Sarah Hasted, Tim Hawkinson, Petra Heck, Kari Hensley, Sybille Herfurth, Rhona Hoffman, Katharina Hohenhoerst,

Jenni Holder, Pernilla Holmes, Cynthia Honores, Julie Hough, Stevie Howell, Hudson, Allison Hull, Katja Hupatz, Akane Ikeda, Elisabeth Ivers, Katell Jaffres, Ava Jancar, Michael Jenkins, Heinke Jenssen, Mark Jetton, Jay Jopling, Stephanie Joson, Jennifer Joy, Takuma Kanaiwa, Brad Kaye, Bronwyn Keenan, Nicole Keller, Jane Kim, Isabel King, Sabine Klaproth, Birte Kleemann, Christine Koenig, Patricia Kohl, Nina Kretzschmar, Cindy Kridle, Sarah Kurz, Anna Kustera, Luanne Kwon, Louise Kybert, Iben la Cour, Stanislas Lahaut, Carolyn Landis, Johanna Langen, Margaret Lee, Fiede Leray, Sylvan Lionni, Toni Liquori, Scott Livingstone, Victoria Long, Honey Luard, Gerd Harry Lybke, Sara MacDonald, Sara Macel, Laura Mackall, Pamela MacKellar, Maureen Mahony, Tanja Maka, Meg Malloy, Monica Manzutto, Jennifer Marra, Jessica Mastro, Timothy McCarthy, Lissa McClure, Meredith McDaniels, Dale McFarland, Anne McIlleron, Renee McKee, Trina McKeever, Jochen Meyer, Marie-Theres Michel, Vita Mikhailov, Jean Milant, Claudia Milic, Jake Miller, Zach Miner, Laura Mitterand, Claus Mittermayer, Brian Monte, Simone Montemurno, Melissa Montgomery, Lisa Mordhorst, David Morgan, Zoe Morley, Paul Morris, Hisako Motoo, Antje Ananda Mueller, Birgit Mueller, Max Mugler, Sarah Murphy, Maki Nanamori, Michael Neff, Casey Neistat, Corinne Nelson, Sarah Giller Nelson, Lucy Newton, Justyna Niewiara, Leslie Nolen, Margaret-Ann O'Connor, Hiroko Onoda, Adam Ottavi-Schiesl, Lisa Overduin, Sandra Paci, Jennifer Palmer, Sylvie Pages, Jennifer Park, Skye Parrott, Geoffrey Parton, Ian Pedigo, Laura Peterson, Friderich Petzel, Roman Pfeffer, Cheryl Pflanzer, Brenda Phelps, Rhiannon Pickles, Sophia Please, Amy Plumb, Karen Polack, Ada Polla, Barbara Polla, Anne Prenzler, Xan Price, Sophie Pulicani, Ann Do Rademaker, Julia Raml, Lindsay Ramsay, Sunil Rashel, Shaun Caley Regen, Susan Reynolds, Ember Rilleau, Markus Rischgasser, Jeremy Rizzi, Gaudericq Robiliard, Thaddaeus Ropac, Emily Rounds, Thomas Rugani, Natalia Mager Sacasa, Nobuko Sakamoto, Jay Sanders, Dianna Santillano, Samia Saouma, John Saponara, Maureen Sarro, Tanja Scartzzini, Nina Schmitz, Karsten Schubert, Elizabeth Schwartz, Teka Selman, Anja Schneider, Alissa Schoenfeld, Paul Schoenewald, Kim Schoenstadt, Ruediger Schoettle, Alexandra Schott, Jack Shainman, Prageeta Sharma, Robert Shimshak, Brian Sholis, Rose Shoshana, Michael Shulman, Andrew Silewicz, Stephane Simoens, Vincent Simonet, Clare Simpson, Susanna Singer, Ania Siwanowicz, Lyndsay Skeegan, Ethan Sklar, Megan Duncan Smith, Jodi Smith, Stephanie Smith, Milly Snell, Randy Sommer, Salome Sommer, Julia Sprinkel, Valerie Stahl, Gregg Stanger, Gail Stavitsky, Kath Steedman, Alex Steele, Rebecca Sternthal, Tiffany Stover, David Strettell, Simone Subal, Elizabeth Sullivan, Calum Sutton, Sinobu Suzuki, Carol Tachdjian, Toni Tapies, Klaus Thoman, Jill Thomas, John Thomson, Lynn Tondrick, Leslie Tonkonow, Dan Trout, Diana Turco, Jonathan Turer, Ines Turian, Lisa Ungar, Henry Urbach, Robin Vachal, Hedwig Van Impe, Jolie van Leeuwen, Kara Vander Weg, Pamela Vander Zwan, Bram Vandeveire, Sara Vilalta, Rafael Vostell, Sarah Watson, Severine Waelchli, Mary Wafer, Carole Wagemans, Waqas Wajahat, Jeffrey Walkowiak, Lindsay Walt, Uwe Walter, Ron Warren, Jessie Washburne-Harris, Helen Waters, Sarah Watson, Joni Weyl, David White, Ulla Wiegand, Rayne Wilder, Lisa Williamson, Hazel Willis, Charlotte Wilton-Steer, Audrey Ellen Wu, Sachiyo Yoshimoto, Amy Young, Doerte Zbikowski, and Bari Ziperstein.

Thanks to Robert Panzer at VAGA and Janet Hicks and Elianna Glicklich at ARS for their patience and help securing rights.

A special thanks to the folks at D.A.P./Distributed Art Publishers for their enthusiasm and expertise. Thanks to Melanie Archer, Lori Waxman, Elisa Leshowitz, Priya Bhatnagaar, Janet Parker, Sabrina Mansouri, Alex Galán, and Sharon Gallagher for their help and support.

We are grateful to Ingrid Sischy for giving us the opportunity, while we were at *Interview*, to work with artists on original pieces for the magazine, thus opening the door to projects like this one.

We underestimated the response we would get for this book, and received many more contributions than we could include. We'd like to express our gratitude to all the artists who so generously shared their work; we hope for a second volume in the future.

Big thanks to our families and friends who have offered continuous support, especially during the few years it took to put this book together; to Lesley A. Martin, Michael Famighetti, Chris McLane, Kristian Orozco, and Cary Wong for their advice; to Megumi Nagasue for lending her eye; and to Jason Harvey for his patience and support, and for living for so long surrounded by boxes of art.

Forgive us if we have forgotten anyone else who helped us along the way. There have been many, many of you.

BIOS

Francesca Richer has art-directed many magazines and award-winning art and photography books. She is the Design Director at the Aperture Foundation in New York.

Matthew Rosenzweig, a graduate of RISD, is a New York-based art and photography editor. He has produced and art-directed photo shoots and curated original art projects for *Interview*, *Out*, *Glamour*, and *Jalouse USA*. This is his first book.

No. 1
First Works by 362 Artists

Publication © 2005 D.A.P./Distributed Art Publishers, Inc.
Introduction © 2005 Francesca Richer & Matthew Rosenzweig

Editors: Francesca Richer and Matthew Rosenzweig
Design and typesetting: Francesca Richer
D.A.P. editors: Melanie Archer and Alex Galán
Typefaces: Baskerville and DIN
Printed by: Palace Press International, China
Cover concept: Francesca Richer and Matthew Rosenzweig
Cover design: Helicopter

Published by
D.A.P./Distributed Art Publishers, Inc.
155 Sixth Avenue, 2nd floor
New York, NY 10013
www.artbooks.com

ISBN 1-933045-09-4

MAGDALENA ABAKANOWICZ   MARINA ABRAMOVIĆ   VITO ACCONCI   FRANZ
ACKERMANN   ROBERT ADAMS   AMY ADLER   JOHN AHEARN   CRAIGIE AITCHISON
LAYLAH ALI   GHADA AMER   JOE ANDOE   JANINE ANTONI   POLLY APFELBAUM
ARMAN   DAVID ARMSTRONG   RICHARD ARTSCHWAGER   MICHAEL ASHKIN
KUTLUG ATAMAN   FRANK AUERBACH   DONALD BAECHLER   JOHN BALDESSARI
MIROSLAW BALKA   STEPHAN BALKENHOL   FIONA BANNER   MATTHEW BARNEY
TINA BARNEY   BURT BARR   JUDITH BARRY   ROBERT BARRY   JENNIFER BARTLETT
GEORG BASELITZ   LOTHAR BAUMGARTEN   PETER BEARD   BERND & HILLA
BECHER   ROBERT BECHTLE   ROBERT BECK   VANESSA BEECROFT   LYNDA
BENGLIS   JAKE BERTHOT   ASHLEY BICKERTON   RICHARD BILLINGHAM   NAYLAND
BLAKE   PETER BLAKE   ROSS BLECKNER   BARBARA BLOOM   CHRISTIAN
BOLTANSKI   JONATHAN BOROFSKY   LOUISE BOURGEOIS   ELLEN BROOKS   CECILY
BROWN   GRISHA BRUSKIN   CHRISTOPHER BUCKLOW   CHRIS BURDEN   VICTOR
BURGIN   RICHMOND BURTON   JEAN-MARC BUSTAMANTE   SOPHIE CALLE
PETER CAMPUS   JAMES CASEBERE   MAURIZIO CATTELAN   VIJA CELMINS   SAINT
CLAIR CEMIN   ENRIQUE CHAGOYA   JOHN CHAMBERLAIN   MICHAEL RAY CHARLES
SARAH CHARLESWORTH   SANDRO CHIA   JUDY CHICAGO   DALE CHIHULY   WILLIAM
CHRISTENBERRY   CHRISTO AND JEANNE-CLAUDE   ANNE CHU   CHUCK CLOSE
WILLIE COLE   HANNAH COLLINS   GREG COLSON   GEORGE CONDO   WILL COTTON
PETAH COYNE   TONY CRAGG   MICHAEL CRAIG-MARTIN   MARTIN CREED   GREGORY
CREWDSON   RUSSELL CROTTY   ENZO CUCCHI   JOHN CURRIN   AMY CUTLER
BRUCE DAVIDSON   NANCY DAVIDSON   KARIN DAVIE   RICHARD DEACON   TACITA
DEAN   WIM DELVOYE   THOMAS DEMAND   MARK DI SUVERO   JAN DIBBETS
PHILIP-LORCA DICORCIA   RINEKE DIJKSTRA   MARK DION   PETER DOIG
LEONARDO DREW   MARLENE DUMAS   JEANNE DUNNING   WILLIAM EGGLESTON
NICOLE EISENMAN   OLAFUR ELIASSON   MITCH EPSTEIN   INKA ESSENHIGH
RICHARD ESTES   TONY FEHER   RACHEL FEINSTEIN   HANS-PETER FELDMANN
LARRY FINK   ERIC FISCHL   PETER FISCHLI/DAVID WEISS   SYLVIE FLEURY

TOM FRIEDMAN KATHARINA FRITSCH MAUREEN GALLACE ELLEN GALLAGHE

GILLICK JIM GOLDBERG NAN GOLDIN LEON GOLUB GUILLERMO GÓMEZ-PE

GREENBAUM TIMOTHY GREENFIELD-SANDERS TOLAND GRINNELL CAI GU

CHRIS HAMMERLEIN JANE HAMMOND MONA HATOUM JOSÉ ANTONIO HEF

NICKY HOBERMAN JIM HODGES HOWARD HODGKIN CANDIDA HÖFER JENNY H

BILL JENSEN CHRIS JOHANSON JOAN JONAS BRAD KAHLHAMER CRAIG K

KELLEY MARY KELLY WILLIAM KENTRIDGE ANSELM KIEFER R.B. KITAJ IMI K

JIM LAMBIE LIZ LARNER JONATHAN LASKER ANNETTE LEMIEUX ZOE LEO

DONALD LIPSKI SHARON LOCKHART RICHARD LONG ROBERT LONGO AND

PLIMACK MANGOLD SALLY MANN CHRISTIAN MARCLAY KERRY JAMES MARS

MCGEE ANNETTE MESSAGER JOEL MEYEROWITZ DUANE MICHALS BORIS M

DONALD MOFFETT MARIKO MORI YASUMASA MORIMURA DAIDO MORIYAMA F

TAKASHI MURAKAMI ELIZABETH MURRAY YOSHITOMO NARA SHIRIN NESHAT

MANUEL OCAMPO MARCEL ODENBACH ALBERT OEHLEN CATHERINE OPIE

TONY OURSLER BILL OWENS ROXY PAINE MIMMO PALADINO PANAMARENK

PERITON RAYMOND PETTIBON RICHARD PETTIBONE ELIZABETH PEYTON

PIPER LARI PITTMAN JAUME PLENSA KEN PRICE STEPHEN PRINA RICHA

MEL RAMOS NEO RAUCH ROBERT RAUSCHENBERG DAVID REED PAULA REGO

ROCKBURNE ALEXIS ROCKMAN UGO RONDININE JAMES ROSENQUIST SU

RUPPERSBERG EDWARD RUSCHA LISA RUYTER TOM SACHS SAM SAMO

SERRA ANDRES SERRANO JOEL SHAPIRO JIM SHAW CINDY SHERMAN STEF

LAURIE SIMMONS SANDY SKOGLUND ANDREAS SLOMINSKI KIKI SMITH RA

STERNFELD JESSICA STOCKHOLDER THOMAS STRUTH JOCK STURGES HIF

ANTONI TÀPIES JUERGEN TELLER ROBERT THERRIEN WOLFGANG TILLMAN

TUNICK LUC TUYMANS KEITH TYSON NICOLA TYSON IKÉ UDÉ JUAN USLÉ

WAGNER KARA WALKER JOHN WATERS GILLIAN WEARING MARNIE WE

WELLING JOHN WESLEY TOM WESSELMANN FRANZ WEST PAE WHITE RACH

TERRY WINTERS JOEL-PETER WITKIN CHRISTOPHER WOOL RICHARD WRIGH